"..."

SUDDENLY
THEY HEARD
FOOTSTEPS

≪ STORYTELLING FOR THE TWENTY-FIRST CENTURY ≫

DAN YASHINSKY

ALFRED A. KNOPF CANADA

PUBLISHED BY ALFRED A. KNOPF CANADA

Copyright © 2004 Dan Yashinsky

All rights reserved under International and Pan-American Copyright
Conventions. Published in 2004 by Alfred A. Knopf Canada, a division of
Random House of Canada Limited, Toronto. Distributed by
Random House of Canada Limited, Toronto.

Knopf Canada and colophon are trademarks.

NATIONAL LIBRARY OF CANADA CATALOGUING IN PUBLICATION

Yashinsky, Dan, 1950–
Suddenly they heard footsteps : storytelling for the twenty-first century / Dan
Yashinsky.

Includes bibliographical references.
ISBN 0–676–97592–5

1. Tales. 2. Storytelling. I. Title.

LB1042.Y386 2004   398.2   c2003–905520–5

Page 317 constitutes an extension of this copyright page.

First Edition

www.randomhouse.ca

Text design: Leah Springate

Printed and bound in the United States of America

10 9 8 7 6 5 4 3 2 1

For my father, Jack, who liked to listen

Do we walk in legends or on the green earth
in the daylight?

J.R.R. TOLKIEN, The Lord of the Rings

Listen your way in
with your mouth

PAUL CELAN, "The Trumpet Part"

Sir, are all storytellers professional liars or just
some of them?

GRADE-TWO STUDENT, HAVENWOOD PUBLIC SCHOOL

TABLE OF CONTENTS

STORIES

≼ ACKNOWLEDGMENTS ≽

I AM GRATEFUL to the Ontario Arts Council for the grant I received to work on this book. I thank my teachers, ancestors and the Toronto storytelling community for their love and support. To Carol, Jacob, Nathaniel (and kind Bernard upstairs) I owe more thanks than even a storyteller can put into words.

≼ PREFACE ≽

I WAS ONCE TELLING STORIES at a downtown arts centre when a restless group of kids stomped in. They were ten-year-olds from a Catholic school in a new housing development, and they came in munching potato chips and blowing bubble gum. One big boy with a cast on his arm had a well-practised burp. I could tell they weren't in a listening mood. Since it was close to Halloween, I lit a candle, turned off the lights and started telling ghost stories.

It wasn't long before they were hooked. I was, after all, using the world's oldest method of crowd control: suspense. It worked for Scheherazade for a thousand and one Arabian nights and, sure enough, it worked for me. At the end I told them "The Golden Arm." You've probably heard versions of this spooky "jump" story at summer camp, or on a sleepover where the challenge was to terrify your friends out of their wits. A treacherous husband has stolen his dead wife's golden arm. He hides it under his pillow, and one night she comes looking for it. "What has become of your golden arm?" he asks shakily as she comes towards him. Then (and here the storyteller's voice becomes very quiet) the ghost . . . reached . . . out . . . and . . . said . . . *"You've got it!"* At which point my thirty cool grade-five students screamed and jumped into each other's laps. The tough kid with the cast, well, let's just say he found new respect for the oral tradition.

When the lights came on, the children lined up to leave, talking excitedly about their shocking experience. I noticed one girl standing quietly, holding something around her neck. I asked if she liked the stories and she said, "Oh, yes. But when you told the last one I didn't jump."

"I noticed," I said. "How come?"

"Because when I knew it was going to be scary, I held the Blessed Virgin Mary." She showed me the amulet she was still holding. "You should get one, too."

"I'm not sure I should," I answered. "I'm Jewish."

"That's okay," she said sagely. "Get a Jewish one."

Writing this book about storytelling as an art and a way of life, I have often remembered the girl's good counsel. When you know something scary is coming you must find and hold on to your own source of reassurance and wisdom. My young friend had an amulet. What I hold on to is the passionate belief that knowing good stories by heart and telling them to a circle of listeners makes a haven for the human spirit.

We are living through a time of unprecedented and troubling change. We have come to a crossroads where old and familiar customs break down, but the new moral frame and social structure we urgently need have not yet evolved. We step into the future with less connection to ancestral guidance than any human generation before us. Although we have invented amazing technologies for saving data, we are at risk of forgetting our personal, family and cultural stories. We broadcast our voices over vast distances, but talk less to our neighbours. Haunting these changes are the spectres of continuing violence, planetary degradation and, above all, the danger that we'll come to believe the implacable message of the powerful: that resistance is futile.

The old stories teach us that resistance is never futile. Chinua Achebe tells this African fable in his great book, *Anthills of the Savannah:*

> One time the Tortoise met the Leopard on the road. The Leopard said, "I've been looking for you for a long time. I'm going to eat you!" The little Tortoise said, "Just grant me one favour before you devour me." The Leopard agreed.
>
> "I must prepare my mind," said the Tortoise.
>
> The Leopard growled impatiently.
>
> Then the Tortoise began to jump all over the road, throwing the dust every whichaway. He scattered the sand everywhere and ran madly back and forth across the road. Then he came back and stood proudly in front of the Leopard. "I am ready," he said.
>
> "Is that how you prepare for what I'm going to do to you?" snarled the Leopard.
>
> "Yes," said the Tortoise. "Because from now on, when people walk by this spot they'll see these marks on the road and say, 'This was a great struggle between two equals.' They'll remember that even a little Tortoise once fought the mighty Leopard. Perhaps the sign of our fight will give them the courage to fight you themselves."

Tortoise leaves his marks not only in the sand but, even more subversively, in the memory of the community. If the story-traces of his struggle are remembered, he has indeed fought Leopard as an equal. We have many leopards blocking the road these days. Achebe's story suggests that, although the ephemeral spoken word seems like a frail weapon to resist these deadly opponents, it may prove to be one of our strongest tools for fixing damaged lives, opening blocked roads and fighting against mighty leopards.

In her book *The Dreamer Awakes*, the wise teacher and master storyteller Alice Kane describes how she was contemplating the state of the world one day, and wondering what she, as a storyteller, could do to make a difference. Then she remembered her own wonder tales, where the hero, often a poor and unregarded boy or girl, must earn "a talisman, a little twisted stick, a sword of power, a dead mother's blessing." Armed with this token of new power, these unlikely heroes are able to accomplish world-changing deeds. Alice Kane decided that she, too, possessed such a talisman, and it was made of all the stories she knew by heart: "The whole background of story and song poured down upon us by those who have gone before. It is reassurance and courage, a great shining that transforms dark truth into victory." Storytelling itself is, or can be, a tool for mending broken worlds.

The belief that storytelling is a necessary and beneficial art for our times has sparked a contemporary renaissance of oral literature. Achebe, describing the remarkable persistence of oral stories, has an elder remind his tribe, "The story is everlasting. . . . Like fire, when it is not blazing, it is smoldering under its own ashes or sleeping inside its flint-house." That fire has been rekindled around the world, with a variety of festivals, groups and gatherings giving storytellers new places to explore their art. There is also a strong and growing interest in the way stories frame and flow through our everyday lives, anchoring identity, preserving family heritage and building inter-cultural bridges. From the rediscovery of folk traditions to the creation of a future folklore, storytellers today are celebrating the renewal of an art many thought was an endangered species.

You may come to the art as a new teller or a devoted lis-tener. You may have a particular interest in understanding the stories of your own life and family, or use storytelling as a way to build community locally or around the world. My own path to storytelling began as a listener. Listening to told stories, by campfires, in kitchens and in concert halls, was my first love. I had to start telling because, as the saying goes, it is unfair to eat the fruit if you don't help plant the trees.

For many storytellers of my generation, Ruth Sawyer's book *The Way of the Storyteller* was a fine springboard into the art. Published in 1942, it is her account of being a story-telling pioneer. "I wish," she wrote at the time, "there might be a guild for storytellers today where master and apprentice might work together for the upholding of their art . . ." Her wish came true. An international community of storytellers has flourished since her inspiring book was written. I have felt fortunate to be part of the Canadian branch of this movement.

Suddenly They Heard Footsteps reflects my experience as a Canadian storyteller, but I hope it is true to our common dream, fired by elders like Alice Kane and Ruth Sawyer, of making storytelling a living art for our times.

The Way of the Storyteller was my literary inspiration. Becoming a storyteller fifty years after Sawyer, I have tried to show you the way of a storyteller who came of artistic age knowing his stories must have room in them for firebirds and microchips, for spirit quests and concentration camps. I offer this book as an honour-song for our storytelling ancestors and an invitation for you to join the storytellers' circle. I look forward to hearing your stories at the crossroads.

Under the touch of its words, the secret melody of
each person was awakened . . .

MARTIN BUBER, *The Legend of the Baal Shem*

I AM A STORYTELLER. If you were sitting next to me on
a train or airplane and we did the what-do-you-dos, this is
when you'd probably say: *A storyteller? What kind of job is
that?* Usually I start out with the short answer: I travel
around telling stories to people who like to listen. If you're
intrigued, and don't turn away with a polite smile to stare
at the clouds, I'll go on and say that, yes, it really is how I
make my living and, no, it's not just for children. In fact,
more and more people work as storytellers, and mostly
with adult audiences. There's a whole movement catching
fire around the world, though I'm not surprised you
haven't heard about it—yet.

Your next question is usually: *What kinds of stories do
you tell?*

I tell word-of-mouth stories, the kind people used to

know by heart and have told since the first humans sat around the fire lying about the fish they almost caught or imagining how the world was made. I've hunted and gathered about a hundred and fifty stories over the years, some by listening, most by reading, and a few I've made up myself. It's a patchwork quilt of oral literature, and includes wonder tales, myths, legends, fables, ghost stories, tall tales, original yarns, personal experiences, Chaucer's *Canterbury Tales,* the *Thousand and One Nights* stories and family lore. Also, I tell lots of stories about Hodja.

Hodja?

Hodja Nasrudin is my favourite "wise fool" from the Middle East. I grew up hearing stories about him from my Turkish grandmother. Have you heard the story about the time Hodja was on a plane when an engine caught fire? The pilot said, "Don't worry—we can fly on three engines. It just means we'll be an hour late landing in Toronto." Then a second engine broke. "Don't worry," said the pilot, "we can fly on two. But this means we'll be two hours late landing in Toronto." Third engine, same announcement: "We can still fly on one engine, but we will now be three hours late landing in Toronto." Hodja turned to his seatmate and said, "Oi! If the last engine breaks, we'll be up here all day!" You can see how dangerous it is to start talking to a storyteller. One story leads to another, and another.

Where do people tell stories nowadays?

Storytellers take their art to festivals, schools, libraries, camps, prisons, hospitals, universities, fancy places, poor places, parks, cafés, campuses, concert halls—anywhere people will gather to listen.

Why do people tell stories nowadays?

That's the hardest question of all. If we really were meeting on a plane instead of here in a book, the moment I started telling you we'd run into turbulence, start our descent, or have to watch the in-flight movie—and that would be that. How can I possibly tell you the whole story about the art and purpose of storytelling in this day and age?

Luckily, here I can give you the long answer. You can take a break if you like, set the book aside, go for a walk: the words will stay put. They'll still be there when you come home. Books are reliable that way. Mind you, the staying-put part is, for a storyteller, the doubtful thing about writing. I love storytelling because I can hear the words fresh from the speaker's mouth, not find them frozen in print or glimmering on a computer screen. It reminds me of a Hodja story. (Yes, it's true—*everything* reminds me of a Hodja story!) Once, his fellow-villagers asked Hodja Nasrudin how he'd achieved his surpassing wisdom. He answered, "When I hear that a wise person is going to speak, I go and listen to whatever they are saying. And when I find that people have been listening to me . . . *I ask them afterwards what I just said.*" As an author, unless we happen to meet—and I hope we do—I'll never know what you heard in what I wrote. To write a book about an oral art is a contradiction, and a very old one at that. When Socrates took his famous walk with Phaedrus outside the gates of Athens, he told him a story about the time in Egypt when the inventor-god Theuth came to King Thamus to show off his latest new improved time-saving invention; a veritable "recipe for memory and wisdom." He called it *writing*. Instead of praising this new technology, the king was dubious. He warned Theuth that "If men learn this, it will implant forgetfulness in their souls; they will cease to exercise memory because they rely on that which is written, calling things to remembrance no longer from within but by means of external marks." Theuth won the argument, of course, and we went on to invent ever faster and more efficient systems of external marks, up to and including our modern word processors. But Thamus was right as well. His early prophecy has come true. When words become too remote from the living voice, we risk losing a sense of our voice's value. When words become too detached from personal memory, we risk forgetting what's worth remembering in the first place.

Thamus would be pleased (but not surprised) to hear that storytelling is coming back in our time. People have a new desire to reconnect to their own voices, memories and stories. We've come to realize that we can't double-click on wisdom. You must spend time listening, and what you must listen to are stories told by word of mouth. The human race has never found a better way to convey its cumulative wisdom, dreams and sense of community than through the art and activity of storytelling.

Perhaps storytelling is our oldest art, the first that marked our difference from the other species. "So why do I say that the story is chief among his fellows?" Chinua Achebe has an elder ask in *Anthills of the Savannah*.

The same reason I think that our people sometimes will give the name Nkolika to their daughters—Recalling-Is-Greatest. Why? Because it is only the story that can continue beyond the war and the warrior. It is the story that outlives the sound of war-drums and the exploits of brave fighters. It is the story, not the others, that saves our progeny from blundering like blind beggars into the spikes of the cactus fence. The story is our escort; without it, we are blind. Does the blind man own his escort? No, neither do we the story; rather it is the story that owns us and directs us. It is the thing that makes us different from cattle; it is the mark on the face that sets one people apart from their neighbours.

To provide their communities with this escort made of oral stories, Native elders around the world have been telling creation myths for many millennia. Stone-age storytellers sat in the entrances of their caves, looked at the Milky Way and told stories about the spirits of their ancestors travelling to their resting-grounds. The troubadours in medieval Europe sang their romances in the castles of Provence. Homer chanted the *Iliad* and the *Odyssey* in Greece and Ionia three thousand years ago. The elements of this art haven't changed significantly over the centuries. In some traditions storytellers use music, in others their voices are unaccompanied. In some traditions the storytelling experience is very participatory, with the audience involved throughout. In other places, people are happy to listen quietly for many hours and let the storyteller transport them. But the fundamental experience of storytelling hasn't changed since the beginning of human history. One person speaks to a circle of listeners, who give their attention; if the story is told well, its words have the power to spark across the gap and take root in the listeners' souls.

Many countries now have their own storytelling movements. In Canada most major cities have a storytelling festival, as do cities in the United States, France, Brazil, England, Ireland, Scotland, Germany, Sweden, Holland, Israel, Austria, Singapore, Australia, Senegal and New Zealand—to name a few. But it is still a renaissance at its very beginning, and anybody who sets out on the storyteller's way today is still a pioneer. There are far more questions than answers at this early stage of the story-telling movement. What kinds of stories should we tell today? Where will we find our audiences? How can we learn from our master storytellers? What new approaches can we bring to the storyteller's art?

Since contemporary storytellers haven't inherited a liv-ing body of oral literature, we've had to improvise both the customs and content of the art form, reinventing story-telling as a new artistic vocation.

Each storyteller finds his or her own repertoire, and the voice to convey it. I have heard the French troubadour Bruno de la Salle tell the Arthurian epic of the Grail all night long on the steps of Chartres Cathedral. I have lis-tened to Alice Kane tell Irish wonder tales to five hundred listeners in a tent at the National Storytelling Festival in Jonesborough, Tennessee. I have watched African-American teller Brother Blue dance his stories barefoot on the sidewalk, burning with a passion to change the world through his bebop narratives. I have listened to the Metis storyteller Ron Evans recounting the true story of Marie d'Orleans, a Native woman who escaped with her young sons from the devastation of an enemy attack, and taught these little boys to survive in the snow-covered mountains while she, starving and frost-bitten, trekked out of the Rockies to find help. The storyteller wept as he told of her extraordinary courage and love, and I wept with him. I have heard Tagish mythteller Angela Sidney tell how Crow made the world, as a crow hopped past us on the grass beside the Yukon River.

I've also delighted in the story my youngest child tells about catching his first bass, and the stories my father-in-law tells about his adventures as a Canadian Mountie, and the anecdotes that get traded back and forth by travellers on long flights. I love to hear about how your grandfather survived the war, or how your parents met on a blind date, or how you once had a dream that came true. Storytelling is an art that lies close to everyday life. We practise it every time we gather at the coffee machine at work, or put our kids to bed with a made-up yarn. You can hear the art in every schoolyard when a kid retells last night's television show or runs a verbal replay of a winning overtime goal. We refold time and space through our stories, keeping a personal oral heritage alive through daily reimagining and conversation.

But what is it that holds us so rapt when stories are told? What are we listening for in the storyteller's words?

My partner was once putting our first-born child to bed. He was about three years old, and he liked to postpone sleep for as long as possible (this hasn't changed much now that he's a teenager). In a monotonous murmur she began to tell him the most soporific yarn she could make up. It was a very, very, very, very repetitive story about how all the animals in the barnyard were going to sleep: "Once upon a time it was bedtime in the barnyard and the piggies were getting sleepy . . . and the ducklings were getting sleepy . . . and the ponies were getting sleepy . . . and the little chicks were getting sleepy. . . ." Our son had almost succumbed to its sleep-inducing spell when he managed to rouse himself from his pillow and interject: "*Then suddenly they heard footsteps!*" The story picked up from there, and he sat up to listen.

Even at three he knew that something was missing from his mother's stream of words. The story-part wasn't there, that moment of transformation that leaves everything different in the imaginary world of the tale.

My Romanian grandmother used to begin her fairy tales with a traditional opening: "Once something happened. If it hadn't happened, how I could tell you about it?" Our son sensed that there didn't seem to be a "something" about to happen at the heart of the story. Without this moment of change and revelation, the words remain only a dull sequence of talk.

An Armenian saying distinguishes between listening to a story's language and understanding what it has to say: *Three apples fell from heaven—one for the storyteller, one for the listener, and one for the one who heard.* I once heard the American storyteller Donald Davis explain to an audience in Montreal, "As a storyteller, I only give you the words. It's how you hear those words that turns them into a story." This is listening with a mind to remember, where listeners know that one day they may pass the tale on in their turn. The story speaks to you, in other words, only when you are willing to lend it your own voice. Our three-year-old was ready to both listen and hear; it was just that the teller's apple hadn't dropped all the way.

My favourite literary example of the power of spoken-aloud stories comes from J. D. Salinger's short story "The

Laughing Man." Every afternoon, a gifted camp counsellor tells his tribe of high-spirited nine-year-old New York boys—the "Comanches"—a new chapter in the continuing saga of a hideously deformed, miraculously good-hearted criminal mastermind known as "the Laughing Man." The story infiltrates and guides the lives of these boys. It becomes their escort. The Comanches hear the Laughing Man's brilliantly heroic footsteps on the streets of New York, and it changes their lives are changed forever.

The storyteller's mission is to remind his listeners, young or old, that those footsteps aren't just coming towards a fictional barnful of somnolent animals. They may also be stepping towards us. Stories reflect our own possibilities for transformation. In J. R. R. Tolkien's *Lord of the Rings*, a skeptical rider doubts the existence of hobbits—"'Halflings,'" laughed the rider . . . 'Halflings! But they are only a little people in old songs and children's tales out of the North. Do we walk in legends or on the green earth in the daylight?'" and Aragorn replies, "'A man may do both . . . for not we but those who come after will make the legends of our time. The green earth, say you? That is a mighty matter of legend, though you tread it under the light of day.'" The purpose of oral stories is to help us remember that life on our green earth is lived by daylight *and* by story-light. That is why even the most skeptical listen with open hearts when the storyteller begins. Storytropic, we're drawn to narrative as naturally as sunflowers opening to the light.

On a recent visit to Toronto's exquisite Textile Museum of Canada, I found myself playing with a heddle. I read that this simple device was one of the greatest innovations in the history of weaving. By passing the warp threads through heddles and fixing a series of heddles to a single bar, the weaver was able to create far more complex patterns than if each thread was individually pulled through the weft. It occurred to me that oral stories work in much the same way. In a told story, the weft of life-experience is entwined with the warp thread of imagination. Like a heddle, stories allow us to bring warp and weft together in a way that creates variation, colour, texture and design. Thus the woven material, whether of words or yarn, becomes a pattern complex enough to reflect life itself.

I was once walking with my boys along the esplanade at Niagara Falls. I'd promised that we'd have lunch out. We'd been walking for an hour when I realized I'd left my wallet back at the hotel. We were a mile and a half along the promenade by the river, it was hot and dusty, there were ten thousand tourists around us, and it was definitely time for lunch. Three-year-old Jacob had slowed from a fitful trudge to a reluctant scuffle, seven-year-old Nathaniel was frantic with hunger and recrimination. Truth to tell, I wasn't feeling all that inspired myself. I broke the news: no, we couldn't have lunch because I didn't have any money; yes, I know I'd promised; yes, of course I knew it was lunchtime; no, we couldn't take a cab or bus or subway back to the hotel; yes, I knew it was too far to walk; yes; no; whatever. We were a grim little band as we turned around and started slouching back the way we'd come.

"You guys want to play Twenty Questions? Come on, come *on,* keep walking!"

"No."

"Do you want to look for cars from Ohio?"

"Ohio's dumb."

"Do you want to hear a story?"

"Okay," from the little one, the older abstaining, though circling within earshot.

"A long story or a short story?"

"Long."

Mindful of the Gaelic saying that "storytelling is the shortening of the road," and knowing there was a god-awful amount of road to shorten, I started telling them one of the longest stories I know: "Once upon a time there was a poor woodcutter, and his name was Ali Baba . . ."

Three things happened at that moment.

My younger son took my right hand in his left hand, where it stayed for the entire walk.

Our pace picked up considerably.

Niagara Falls disappeared.

Tourists, traffic, heat, hunger, sore feet, dust, kvetching: gone. One of the wonders of the natural world: gone. Instead, we were standing in front of a mighty rock. Forty robbers had been and gone, leaving their loot inside the hill, and galloping off again. Perching in a tree, we overheard the magic spell they used: two ordinary words that could open a mountain.

Now we're standing here alone, about to unlock our destiny with those same two words of power. We murmur them to the hillside: "Open Sesame." A passageway appears. We enter, step carefully into the darkness. A cool, dimly lit cave, illumined by the cracks in the vaulted roof. We behold what Allah has granted into our possession. Gold gleams in countless sacks that fill the cave. Diamonds shine on the floor, emerald bracelets crunch underfoot as we enter the cave, going where no woodcutter has ever gone before. This hoard of riches, accumulated by what must have been generations of thieves, belongs to us now. Knowing the secret of the cave, we have become the masters of the treasure—that is, if the robbers don't find us and cut our throats first.

We were no longer a bedraggled trio but a band of intrepid heroes setting forth with newfound spirit to the cadence of a seven-hundred-year-old wonder tale. It was an irresistible world that called to us, a world of gold and danger, where treasure could be both hidden and found, where everyday words could be charged with rock-splitting power, where great courage was needed to conquer great evil. In this story-world made only of words, you certainly don't drag your feet, even if you're only three years old and tireder than you've ever been. Pride, alertness, bravery, high spirits—these are the qualities you live by in such a world. "Listen your way in / with your mouth," wrote the great Jewish poet Paul Celan. Or with your feet, I thought as we marched towards the hotel restaurant, and your hands, as I found I was still holding my little boy's hand. You have to bring all of yourself to the story if that story is going to carry you in turn.

The hour-long walk sped by and we ended the tale at the table. Marjanah did her famous Dagger Dance. The men—Ali Baba, his son, and the robber chief disguised as a family friend—were entranced by her grace and beauty. Then she took her emerald-hilted dagger and stabbed the false Hassan straight through the heart. He fell, as the story says, dead "among the carpets." Marjanah and Ali Baba and the son (whom she married, of course) lived in great wealth and peace for many years until they, too, were visited by the one who cuts down mighty kings and humble peasants, the one who waits at the end of all our journeys. Only when the story was over did we order lunch.

So why are storytellers returning to twenty-first century life? That reminds me of a story passed on by the theologian Martin Buber in his *Tales of the Hasidim*. This one is told about Moshe Leib, a student of the student of the great Jewish rabbi, the Baal Shem Tov:

> The rabbi of Rizhyn related:
>
> "Once when the holy Baal Shem Tov wanted to save the life of a sick boy he was very much attached to, he ordered a candle made of pure wax, carried it to the woods, fastened it to a tree, and lit it. Then he pronounced a long prayer. The candle burned all night. When morning came, the boy was well.
>
> "When my grandfather, the Great Maggid, who was the holy Baal Shem's disciple, wanted to work a like cure, he no longer knew the secret meaning of the words on which he had to concentrate. He did as his master had done and called on his name. And his efforts met with success.
>
> "When Rabbi Moshe Leib, the disciple of the disciple of the Great Maggid, wanted to work a cure of this kind,

he said, 'We have no longer the power even to do what was done. But I shall relate the story of how it was done, and God will help.' And his efforts met with success."

But what do we do if we hear the cry of the sick child— that eternal human need for intimacy, community, a connection with the sacred—in an age when the story-fire is almost extinguished, when news replaces narrative, and broadcast voices jam the living tongue's frequency; when screenglow replaces hearth-fire, and data replace wisdom? At such a time, which is our time, it isn't enough to remember the story of the Baal Shem Tov's prayer. We must rediscover the very form of storytelling, and through that begin to find the stories that will mend the world. The story, for me, continues:

Time passed, and generation followed generation. The world entered a time of forgetfulness, a time when the link to the past was broken and the future seemed unreal. The child's cry for help was almost impossible to hear in that violent, amnesiac world. Yet some people heard it, and wanted more than anything to offer succour to that sick and frightened soul. But they did not know what to do. They hadn't heard of the Baal Shem's prayer, or the forest, the tree, the trail, the candle of purest wax. They didn't even remember how to pray. Everything had been lost. The only thing that remained was a distant memory of a good man who had once upon a time told stories to comfort a lonely child. And so they tried to become storytellers.

We do not yet know if this will be enough. I do know that, fired with the age-old desire to heal a world beset by loneliness, the storytellers are on the move again. They have come back to serve as the earth's storytellers in residence. They have heard the footsteps of a new story coming over the horizon, and want more than anything to give it voice.

⋞ FRANKIE AND THE FIREBIRD ⋟

> I think the mood of a story that is told to children
> should be one of kindliness.
>> PADRAIC COLUM, "Storytelling New and Old"

FRANKIE WAS NOT A GOOD LISTENER. In fact, he may
have been the worst listener in the world, a dragon in the
shape of an eight-year-old boy. I'm glad that I met him in
1972, the summer that I entered the Muse's service.
Frankie taught me the most important secret of storytelling. Here's how it happened.

I was working as a counsellor at Bolton Camp, a camp
for kids from the poorest neighbourhoods in Toronto.
That spring, I'd finally graduated from university. I tried
a few jobs, but nothing stuck. I noticed Bolton Camp was
looking for a replacement counsellor after the summer
season had already started. When I drove up to camp to
report for duty, I found out the other counsellor had run
away. A particularly rambunctious cabinful of eight
eight-year-old boys had driven him crazy. I was his
replacement.

As I did a walkabout with the camp director we passed a boy sitting on a hillock chucking rocks at the passersby. "Frankie!" shouted the director, "Stop that right now—you might hurt somebody!" He whispered to me, "Frankie's got some problems with anger management. He's in your cabin." Further along we encountered young Mario. He was weeping at operatic pitch as he sat on the ground nursing a bruised knee. "Mario, this is Dan. He'll be your new counsellor." More tears. Later I met my two Davids. One was an Ojibway boy, a great naturalist who liked to spend his time down by the creek or off in the woods. He liked to find things and bring them back to show his counsellor, often at mealtime. "Where've you been?" I'd ask, as he sat next to me at the table.

"Creek." He never said more than necessary.

"Find anything?"

"Yep."

"Want to show me after lunch?"

"Nope."

"I'll bet you want to show me now?"

"Yep." Then he'd dig deep into his grubby pocket and haul out half a frog, explaining that the snake in the water was busy digesting the other half.

The other David was a sad, strange child. He'd had his birthday just before I came to camp, but apparently something had happened, something unnameable and bad, which involved his trunk and which nobody was prepared to tell me about. He never opened his trunk, and there was an odd smell at his end of the cabin. This melancholy boy seemed haunted by his own private ghost.

Bolton Camp, of course, had a resident ghost. I've since learned that all summer camps are haunted. The ghosts go by different names: Sulphur Man, Bloody Mary, Three-fingered Willy (you don't really want to know how he got that name). Ours was known, simply, as Old Man Bolton. I heard the whole story the day after I arrived, when we had a campfire a couple of hundred metres up the hill from the last cabin. The campfire began with songs. The kids, who'd come from pretty rough backgrounds, loved to sing about the *Titanic*, that great ship of doom:

> Oh, they built the ship *Titanic*
> To sail the ocean blue
> And they thought they had a ship
> The water couldn't go through,
> But the good Lord raised his hand
> Said, 'This ship will never land,'
> It was sad when the great ship went down.
> It was sad
> —So sad!
> It was sad
> —Too bad!
> It was sad when the great ship went down
> —To the bottom of the
> Husbands and wives, little children lost their lives
> It was sad when the great ship went down
> Kerplunk
> —It sunk
> What a lousy piece of junk
> —'Cause the captain was drunk
> Glug, glug, glug . . .

When I looked around at my boys singing merrily about the drowning children, women, men and crew of the mighty and indestructible *Titanic*, it occurred to me they'd spent most of their young lives staring helplessly at the various icebergs approaching their own frail vessels.

After the songs were done, the counsellor took a long moment to fix the fire, placing a branch here, a log there. Then he stood quietly and gazed out over our heads to the trees that circled the clearing. Finally, he looked around the boys and said, "Ever heard of Old Man Bolton?"

Nervous laughter from these first-time campers.

"Well, they say he used to live around here. All of this land once belonged to him."

The boys peered out into the dark forest.

"His cabin was just up the hill, not far from where we're sitting right now. It burned down a long time ago— after it happened. . . ."

"What happened?" asked Mario.

"He went crazy one day. Yes, Old Man Bolton took an axe and chopped everybody up into little, tiny pieces. The cabin burned down and just the foundations are left. Tomorrow I can take you on a hike up the hill and show you where the cabin once stood . . . Anyway, they say he cut his own foot with that axe, and when he limped off into the woods he left a trail of blood. The police showed up after a while, and found what he'd done, but they never did find him. Old Man Bolton had simply vanished."

A long, thoughtful silence ensued.

Campers shifted on their logs, edging closer to the fire.

The forest beyond our circle of light seemed very, very dark.

Mario shakily put his hand up. "If they never found Old Man Bolton, where is he now?"

"Well," said the storyteller, "that's the strange thing about my story. You see, some people say he's still out there, wandering the hills with his hurt foot—and his axe."

"Hey," Frankie piped up, intrepid and skeptical, "is that story true?"

"Probably not," the counsellor said, "Nah, I don't think it's true. But there's just one thing . . ." The Bolton Camp yarnspinner took his time getting to the startling conclusion of his tale; sparks cracked up into the dark air as the circle of boys waited patiently. "Boy, if you're ever out in the woods at night, and you get lost, and it's very dark, and you're way out past the last cabins . . . and you hear a sound coming towards you, something like this," and he clumped back and forth in front of the fire, demonstrating exactly how an axe murderer might limp around in the forest, "even though it's probably not Old Man Bolton . . . my . . . one . . . piece . . . of . . . advice . . . is . . . *run like hell!!!*"

He screamed and leapt towards the children, who tumbled off their logs and lay gasping in the dirt.

We picked them up, dusted them off, sat them back down, put new marshmallows on their sticks, and tried to sing "Cumbayah" to close the campfire. Then they marched single file down the trail, listening more intently than they ever had in their young lives for the telltale echo of approaching footsteps. A few years later, the administration decided that the children, coming as they did from troubled homes, shouldn't be exposed to stories about this terrifying ogre of the forest, and so the counsellors were forbidden to tell the tales.

My feeling is that they were wrong to ban the story. Many of these boys had already met Old Man Bolton in their homes, neighbourhoods, schools. He was the drunk who beat up their mama, or the bureaucrat who decided they couldn't get welfare that month, or the ongoing horror of a life lived in the shadow of hunger. Hearing a story about Old Man Bolton meant they were no longer alone. When you name evil you begin to conquer it. Besides, the ghost came to them in the form of a story and in the voice of a counsellor who could also make them laugh, sing and talk. Old Man Bolton may be strong and wild, but the circle of listeners and storytellers is even stronger.

This was the heaviest real-life magic I'd ever seen. These boys sitting so rapt around the campfire were the same bunch who liked to run through the camp, playing pranks, bashing each other (rarely—I was strict about that), farting as noisily and often as possible, and generally earning their reputation for being the camp's most extravagant lords of misrule. Yet when the storytelling began they became utterly quiet and well behaved. Even after marching in trepidation back to their cabin, they kept their mood of awe and even reverence. By some mysterious power the storyteller was able to transform my wild pack of boys into a community of listeners Homer himself would have been proud to play for. Every one of them had been labelled by teachers and social workers as having "severe attention deficits" and "unmanageable behaviour." Yet when the stories began, I watched them relax and breathe more deeply, their eyes shining with joyful—and sometimes fearful—anticipation. What was the secret of this astonishing art?

Even before coming to camp I had travelled via books to the storyteller's shire. I had had a great Chaucer teacher in college. Professor Marvin Mudrick read the Middle

English of the *Canterbury Tales* aloud in his Philadelphia Jewish accent, and led us into a world where everybody—or at least pilgrims sharing the road to Canterbury—could be counted on to have a remarkable story to relate. Falling in love with Chaucer, I then read the other great medieval story collections, Boccaccio's *Decameron* and the *Thousand and One Nights*. Each collection reflected its own culture, but shared a common vision of stories being rooted in oral communication. In Boccaccio, the stories are told by young survivors of the Black Death. In the *Thousand and One Nights,* the stories are told by Scheherazade. In a cross-cultural leap, I also found myself reading my way through the Icelandic sagas. Then I discovered epic. During my last year at the College of Creative Studies at the University of California at Santa Barbara, I lived in the world of the *Iliad* and the *Odyssey*. In all of these studies, the storyteller seemed like a wonderfully romantic figure from bygone days. The idea that bards like Homer once travelled the countryside, finding a welcome in every royal court (and probably every roadside wineshop, too), carrying epics they knew entirely by heart—it all seemed tremendously noble and compelling and impossibly remote for a suburban kid who grew up in the 1950s as a member of the first television generation. I spent my childhood watching *Batman*, not hearing bards chant epic or troubadours recite courtly romances. I never dreamed that the storytelling tradition might be alive and well in my own society. Yet here at a summer camp for kids from Toronto's poorest neighbour-hoods the art of storytelling burned as richly and brightly as the fire we encircled.

Everything about that fire pleased and thrilled me: the clearing in the woods, the children's intent faces, the teller's

voice carrying clearly over the simmer and spark of the
fire. This was the same fire around which the human race
had gathered since our earliest days, listening for wisdom
and entertainment. By such fires Native elders conjured
the creation of the world, hunters told spear stories, Irish
shanachies spun long wonder tales, African *griots* chanted
ancestral history, Homer sang of the king of Ithaca's long
journey, caravan travellers shared desert yarns, grannies
told folk tales. This was the oldest fire in the world. As I
sat by the fire I remembered a moment from the *Odyssey*.
At a feast in King Alkinoos's hall on the island of *Phaiakia*,
Odysseus praises the art of the royal bard Demodokos:

> Alkinoos, King and admiration of men,
> how beautiful this is, to hear a minstrel
> gifted as yours; a god he might be, singing!
> There is no boon in life more sweet, I say,
> than when a summer joy holds all the realm,
> and banqueters sit listening to a harper
> in a great hall, by rows of tables heaped
> with bread and roast meat, while a steward goes
> to dip up wine and brim your cups again.
> Here is the flower of life, it seems to me!

We were eating toasted marshmallows instead of royal
wine and meat, and our bottoms were falling asleep on
hard logs instead of the queen's soft cushions. Still, the
same summer joy held our realm, although its borders
covered only a few hills fifty kilometres northwest of
Toronto, and its citizens were a couple of dozen scruffy
boys from the inner city and their teenage counsellors.
This was as close to the "flower of life" as I had ever come.

I decided that despite being shy, tongue-tied, stage-frightened and forgetful, I had to master this art.

I started by reading stories aloud to my boys. On my days off I'd drive back to Toronto and head for Boys' and Girls' House Library, which used to be at St. George and College (it's gone now; like Old Man Bolton's cabin and the camp itself, only the foundations remain). The Folk and Fairy Tales section of the library—398.2—was my stomping-ground. I plunged into the stacks with indiscriminate delight, hunting and gathering stories because I liked the colour of the book cover, or the country the tales came from, or the name of the writer. I feasted on folk tales. Every week I'd bring back a stack of books, and read them to the guys after their night-time snacks.

The time finally came for my debut performance, the night I was going to *tell* a story instead of read it aloud. I'd picked a Russian wonder tale about Prince Ivan and the Firebird, learned it by heart, and now I was ready to give storytelling a try. I settled the boys in their bunks, lit a candle and began:

"Once upon a time there was a king and a queen and they had three sons."

So far so good, I thought—I can do this! Just then, Frankie blew a mouth-fart. The boys cracked up, and my story was derailed. I was pretty cross but I tried to stay calm. There's a school of child psychology that suggests when a kid misbehaves you should ignore the misbehaviour and it will go away. So I decided to carry on despite Frankie's rude interruption.

"The king and queen had three sons. The first two were very proud and clever, but the third son was lazy and good-for-nothing and his name was Prince—"

Frankie's fart was even louder the second time.

I felt cold fury. To hell with books about child psychology. This was a showdown. I stopped telling the story, walked over to his bunk (an upper bunk), and looked at Frankie who lay grinning impudently at me. I spoke to him very slowly and very clearly and never stopped staring at him while I spoke: "If—you—do—that—one—more—time—I—am—going—to—kick—your—little—butt—out—of—this—cabin." I wish I'd remembered that children, especially ones like Frankie, are filled with a great natural curiosity. They'd rather suffer the consequences than never know whether you're serious or not.

I walked back to my chair and continued: "The prince's name was Ivan, and he was always getting into trouble around the palace. Instead of working, he liked to lie around under an apple tree in the royal garden. One day their father the king went blind and called his three sons. 'My boys,' he said, 'it is up to you to find a cure for my blindness. Go far away to a land I've never seen and bring back something you find there. You'll know what it is when you find it. That will be my medicine.' The two elder brothers rode off, proudly and cleverly, but Ivan just went out to the garden to have a nap under his favourite fruit tree. And when he fell asleep he had a dream, and in the dream he heard a voice, and the voice told him—"

"PPPHHHAAAFFFFFTTTTT!" Frankie struck a third time.

What do you do at a moment like that? I know now, thirty years later, that the best thing is to continue telling your story, and trust that the audience will eventually settle down. I could have told the story sitting close to his bunk, and probably quelled the rebellion before it started.

I could have joined the boys in laughing at the mouth-fart instead of taking offence, perhaps even made it part of the story: "Prince Ivan liked to sit under an apple tree in the royal garden daydreaming and practising irritating and unpleasant sounds that drove everybody crazy . . ." There are many things experienced yarnspinners would have in their toolbag for just this kind of situation. At the time, I knew none of them.

What I did know was that this was my world story-telling premiere, and a little punkass camper had just sabotaged my beautiful fairy tale. I was royally pissed off. I jumped up, turned on the light and went straight to his bunk. I yanked him out of bed in his pyjamas, opened the cabin door and deposited him on the step outside. Then I locked the door, turned off the light and continued telling the story of Prince Ivan and the Firebird to my now very attentive audience. There were many incredible adventures as Prince Ivan, with the help of a magic horse, found the golden feather of a firebird, battled dragons, married the firebird maiden and cured his dad's blindness. (The version I tell now comes from Charles Downing's *Armenian Folktales and Fables*.) I told every detail to the very end, accompanied by Frankie's frantic banging on the door as he shouted, "Let me in! Old Man Bolton's gonna get me!"

When the story ended, there was a long silence. Some of the boys had fallen asleep during my telling. (I've learned since that this can be a tribute to a storyteller's soothing voice, if not to his or her ability to create breathless suspense.) David, the sad boy with the sealed trunk, got out of bed and unlocked the door. I didn't stop him. Frankie trudged in quietly, climbed up to his bunk, and soon the whole cabin was peacefully quiet—my eight young boys breathing gently in the summer night.

A few days before the period ended, I sat with David, my quiet child. I thanked him for being kind to Frankie, and asked him if he was happy to be going home.

"When my mother opens my trunk," he whispered hopelessly, "I'm dead."

I knew I couldn't ask him directly what the problem was, so I made a wild promise. I told him that I was going to Toronto for my half-day off, and that I would take his trunk with me. I told him that since I was a camp counsellor I could fix anything. I tied David's trunk on the roof rack of my 1959 Volkswagen and drove to my parents' house. I put the trunk on the front lawn and opened it. Inside, neatly folded, were David's camp clothes, mostly unworn. On top of them, fully loaded, was a pair of underpants. On his birthday, just before I'd arrived as their replacement counsellor, this child had pooped his pants. Mortified with shame, he'd stuffed them in a bag and hidden the evidence in his trunk. Those undies had been in there a long time.

I gingerly picked out the poopy underpants and buried them in my father's rose garden behind the house. I'm not sure why I didn't just throw them out in the garbage. Somehow it seemed they deserved a more formal interment. I washed David's clothes at the local laundromat, cleaned out the trunk, refolded everything and drove back to camp later that day. When I slid the trunk back into place at the end of his bunk I told him, "Your trunk's clean now. Go have some fun."

His eyes opened wide and he nodded. Then a very small smile opened, and he ran off to play. Two days later, the buses came to take the children back to Toronto. By the end of that summer, I had decided to become a storyteller.

Why did the Muse send Frankie, my boy-shaped dragon, to block my path on my very first attempt to become her apprentice? I think she was trying to initiate a newcomer into the deepest secret of the teller's art: *the listener is the hero of the story.* A tale about Prince Ivan or Jack or Cinderella must have room in it for the real Jacks and ash-girls in the audience. Ever since that summer, whenever I meet an audience I try to remember that the hero of my story may be sitting right in front of me. He or she is the one who is labelled a slow learner, the goofy kid, the child at risk of dropping out. For these listeners, the story is much more than an entertaining stream of words. They are listening because they desperately want a story of their own, one that can include even their wild passions, terrors, frantic misbehaviours and possibilities of change. My trouble-making camper had no polite and civil way to let the story-teller know of his ferocious need—farts were the best he could do as he sought admittance to a world where apple trees can speak, and good-for-nothings can discover golden feathers. I always look for the Frankie in every group where I'm telling stories. I still owe the greatest of all listeners his fairy tale.

≼ THE STORM FOOL'S TALE ≽

The world is gone
I must carry you.

PAUL CELAN, "Vast, glowing vault"

I FIRST HEARD THE TERM "STORM FOOL" from Ron Evans, a Metis storyteller from northern Saskatchewan. He remembers how he and his family would be camped out on a trapline in the middle of a blizzard. They would settle in for a long stay, knowing it would be days before they could get back to the village. Then, through the blowing snow, an unexpected visitor would show up. "You could be sitting in your lodge in a winter camp in a storm, snow blowing, and all of a sudden—'cause we didn't knock on doors—all of a sudden the door flap parts and in crawls this guy with snow all over his hair and coat, shaking the snow off, and it would be a storm fool who'd just come out of the storm. . . . They wandered about from camp to camp telling stories, bringing news. They were definitely regarded as medicine people, elders. They were seen as just a little mad—that's why they were called 'storm fools.'" These intrepid northern narrators told myths, legends, news of the tribe, tall tales, jokes; their purpose was to keep people connected to the community. Then they would travel on to the next group of storm-stayed listeners.

Storm fools are one of the oldest artists' alliances in the world. They include all the storytellers who have ever left their own house and village and set out to bring their stories to new listeners in other places. Homer was a storm fool, and so was Peire Vidal, the Provençal troubadour who travelled from court to court in late medieval France. The Irish Traveller described by Ruth Sawyer in *The Way of the Storyteller* was a storm fool. He went from village to village mending tin pots, and drew his customers by telling wonderful folk tales by the side of the road: "He gathered a crowd in no time. Words became living substance for all who listened. . . . For the duration of the story nothing lived but the story, neither listeners nor storyteller."

Martin Buber evokes another, more spiritual kind of travelling storyteller. The great Jewish rabbi known as the Baal Shem Tov has come to a village marketplace and begun telling stories. First one man begins to listen, then "a second man came up, soon after a third, then ever more and more, mostly servants and poor people who begin the day early. They all remained standing, listened eagerly and called over still others from the houses. As the hour advanced, the maids came with their water-jugs on the way to the fountain and stopped, the children came running out of the rooms, and the family heads themselves left their businesses and their pursuits to hear the strange man." The strange thing about the Baal Shem Tov's tale was that whenever a new listener arrived, he or she found its "red thread" (a wonderful German phrase for the inner life of a story). "His narration . . . was so delightfully intertwined that whenever some one came up it seemed to that person to be at the beginning, and those who earlier had not been curious were now entirely concentrated on what would happen next and awaited it as if it were the fulfillment of their most precious hopes. Thus they all had one great story, and within it each had his own small and all-important story." And what did these spellbound villagers hear in the storyteller's intricately woven narrative? Buber answers somewhat mystically: "[I]t was no report of distant times and places that the story told; under the touch of its words, the secret melody of each person was awakened. . . ." In other words, each listener heard the story he or she most needed to live.

I include myself in this alliance of storm fools, and this tradition continues, except that today's storm fools don't get around by dog team. We go by subway, car and plane. Our audiences may not be separated by weather and desolate terrain, but other forces can be equally isolating and soul-chilling. I've been to countless North American suburbs where the nearest sign of life was the mall three kilometres away. The highways are packed every morning and evening with parents commuting to work. What family time they can poach from the global economy is usually spent staring at screens. The names of the streets in these raw subdivisions echo with lost history: "Wildflower Way" and "Apple Grove Circle"—these are the developers' epitaphs for the flowers and trees they uprooted or paved over. In Mississauga, Toronto's westernmost bedroom community, there's a street called "Folkway Avenue." Ironically, you'll never see a human being walking there.

Real folkways are kept alive through direct human contact, through daily conversation, through a shared sense of purpose and identity—things that are hard to find in a world of non-stop rush hours and distant shopping malls. Mississauga itself is named after a tribe of the Anishnabe First Nation that once lived in these lands. They've since moved on, taking many thousands of years of folkways and stories with them. When I go tell stories to the children in these farflung communities I feel like an ambassador either from the distant past or, on cheerful days, from a possible future.

The marvel is that the same children who spend so many hours in front of screens and so few hours conversing with parents and grandparents are still such avid listeners. They have never lost their deeply human hunger for wonder, and they are ready to listen to every story their teachers, librarians, parents, grandparents and occasional storm fools can tell them. It always amazes me how quickly they are able to step from the fluorescent-lit gym into the reverie of storytelling, to move from clock-time to story-time. After a storytelling session, the teachers will often tell me afterwards that they've never seen the children sit still for so long. They tell me about the students—the one who has zero attention span, the 50 percent who speak English as their second language, the one who interrupts all the time— and say how amazed they were that they all listened to a forty-five-minute fairy tale without wiggling once.

I think I know why they listen so well. I take little credit for their miraculous transformation. It is the experience of hearing good stories told by word of mouth, spoken by a storyteller who is there *in person* that turns them from distracted, unsettled children into dedicated listeners. The stories are being given to them directly. At a gut level they know that if they can remember them, the stories are theirs. Alice Kane once wrote in a letter to me: "I love storytelling because it is so intensely individual. The story-teller chooses her own story and tells it as she sees it and feels it. The listener brings his own different background and experience to the story and interprets it in his own way. To both the story becomes their own and grows and is enriched as they themselves grow."

I always make sure to tell the children traditional folk and fairy tales. I know that after I leave, these stories will travel out into the schoolyards, down the streets, back to their kitchens. The stories will be retold in Tamil, Russian, Chinese, Spanish, Greek, Arabic, Hindi. A new oral tradition is being kindled, which will eventually be a new way of connecting to each other, to the land, even to the mall-centred world around them. Through their shared and multilingual stories, the future "folkways" of the outer suburbs are being born.

Storm fools not only bring stories to these isolated areas, they also remind their listeners that they, too, have stories worth telling. In 1993 I developed a curriculum project I call a Telling Bee. It begins by having each class create their own talking stick. My talking stick is a sawed-off broomstick that an artist decorated with ribbons and rattles. Along the way it has picked up new ornaments: New Orleans carnival beads, a medallion of the Deer Clan (which includes poets and storytellers), a twist of hide, a bear's tooth, an image of Ganesh. Wherever I tell stories I like to offer it to anybody who will exchange stories with me. In every class there are those who like to talk and those who would rather swallow fire than open their mouths in public. I was one of the shy ones myself, and I understand how paralyzing this can be. Instead of asking who would like to tell stories (thus terrifying the quiet kids), I can ask, "Who would like to hold the talking stick?" Invariably, even the shyest children are eager and willing to hold it and proud to tell their stories.

Some groups get very creative and make something that includes artifacts and images from all of the students' stories. I've even seen a talking hockey stick. The object itself doesn't matter, but the values it represents are the essence of the Telling Bee project: listening with respect, passing on family heritage, honouring the community through your storytelling, being open to all the stories in the class. Talking sticks are a lot less expensive than computers, and I think they add quite a bit more to the children's lives.

The motto for the Telling Bee comes from a Portuguese proverb: *First you listen, then you talk.* Everybody in the school—children, teachers, caretakers, principals—collects a story that they've heard by word of mouth. The children ask their parents and grandparents questions like

- Have you ever known a true-life hero?
- Did you ever get in trouble as a kid?
- Did you ever move to a new home? What surprised you there? What did you miss from your old home?
- Did you ever know an unusual animal?
- Did our family survive war or other disasters? How?
- Have you ever had a supernatural experience?
- What was I famous for as a baby?
- Were you (or I) ever lost? How were you found?
- Which of our ancestors do you think of the most?
- Is there a story behind the names in our family?

They bring the stories to class and retell them, with the permission of the person who gave them the story.

After the storytelling, the stories are written and published. One of the marvels of desktop publishing is that any school-size community can produce a wonderfully designed book of stories. Often, when the book is published, schools will have a celebration and book launch. I'll never forget a Greek grandmother coming up to me at the McMurrich Public School book launch and saying, with great pride, "Did you read the story about the Greek girl in the civil war who rode the truck with the soldiers? That was *me!*" She was very moved that her granddaughter had listened, remembered and retold her own memory of war.

Sometimes within a classroom, one story will spark another. Edward Bavington, a grade-six teacher at McMurrich, heard one of his students tell a story about surviving the Gulf War. He in turn contributed a story about a landlord he'd had who had lost his entire family in Auschwitz. He ended his story by writing, "If I appear hard when I hear a degrading remark, it is with the memory that slurs, unchecked, rise to mountains of dead."

Often the stories people bring in for the Telling Bee have traditional motifs. The principal at McMurrich, Mel Beyea, told "The Blanket," which you may recognize as a fable:

> The house was very crowded. Grandpa was getting on his son's nerves. Grandpa did nothing but eat, sleep and complain. To his son he was a nuisance. The son decided that his father must move away and live somewhere else. Soon the day came. The son decided to give his father half a blanket. The son's wife pleaded that grandpa should be

given a whole blanket. The son insisted that it be half a blanket. They quarrelled. Finally, the son agreed to give his father a whole blanket. "No," said the grandson. "Give grandpa half a blanket. I will need the other half, father, to give you on the day that I decide that you must move away and live somewhere else." Grandpa stayed.

Beyea heard this story, appropriately enough, from his own grandmother.

In another Telling Bee, this one in Gogama, Ontario, a young Ojibway boy took the talking stick and told another story about grandparents and grandchildren. "I know how my town got its name," he said shyly. "I heard it from my grandma."

A long time ago the people who lived here wanted to do something really special. They decided to have a race. But instead of having the strong young warriors race, they wanted to do something unusual. So they had a race of old women. All the old women got ready for the race. They practised and practised by running up and down the main street. There was one old woman who had a grandson. He was very little. He used to call her his "Gama." He was very excited about the race. "Gama going to win?" he asked her.

"I hope so, grandson," she said. "But I don't know. I'm eighty-two years old, and there are some racers who are a lot younger than me. There are seventy-year-olds, and even a sixty-year-old. But I'll do the best I can."

The day of the race came. All of the old women tied on their racing moccasins and lined up at the starting line. The signal went and they started running.

The little boy was sitting on his dad's shoulders so he could watch the race. He looked for his Gama at the front of the runners, but she wasn't there. Then he looked at the back. She was running as fast as she could, but she was way behind everyone else. The boy started bouncing up and down shouting, "Go, Gama! Go, Gama!" She looked up and saw him, and it made her run faster. She really took off! In fact, she won the race. And everyone was so proud of that little boy who helped his "gama" that they named my town "Gogama, Ontario."

After telling his story, he said, "I live with my grandmother. She's raising me."

As the Telling Bee goes on, the schoolyard begins to fill up with stories. At one school, the gym teacher told a remarkable story about a wartime romance. Children talked about it during recess. At another school, the caretaker turned out to have been a classically trained actor in the Philippines. After people heard his story, he was no longer just the guy with the mop cleaning the floor. One boy told the story about how his face had been burned, and from then on nobody stared at him. Among the parents, too, there's a buzz as they compare notes, and talk about their family stories. Soon not only the school, but the whole neighbourhood is filled with the sound of storytelling.

Whenever I animate a Telling Bee, I also tell a number of traditional folk and fairy tales. I want them to hear the connections between their family stories and the great themes of oral literature: heroism, tragedy, hilarious comedy, romance, triumph over catastrophe—all of which can be found in the stories every family keeps alive. I was on the Web the other day and noticed a site devoted to something called (and trademarked!) the "Digital Storytelling Bee." It struck me as a dreary and disheartening occupation, trading stories through screens and keyboards. Stories, from folk tales to family lore, are meant to be told live and direct. The Romany people have a saying: *A millionaire is someone who has spent a million dollars.* So it should be in the world of stories and Telling Bees. If you'd like to run your own Telling Bee, you're welcome to visit (yes, digitally!) www.tellery.com. The guidelines are free for the borrowing.

In the summer of 1999, I had the chance to take my talking stick around Canada. I co-created (with David Carroll, the producer) a national radio show called, appropriately enough, *Talking Stick*. (Our motto was Have Talking Stick, Will Travel.) We taped storytellers at kitchen tables, downtown cafés, festivals, concert halls, and all the other natural habitats of the oral tradition in today's society.

One afternoon we dropped in to visit Louise Bennet-Coverley, known to West Indians everywhere as "Miss Lou," one of Jamaica's national treasures, who is now living in Canada. She told story after story about the great trickster Anansi, who is sometimes a man and sometimes a spider. She told us about the Jamaican ghosts known as *duppies*, which are dangerous if you show them disrespect, but kindly if you honour them. Throughout her stories, marvelling at Anansi's hilarious misadventures, she would burst out with the wildest, most infectious laugh, as if she knew Anansi personally and had witnessed his tricks herself. I've often found with traditional storytellers that they seem to inhabit the same world as the people in their stories. In my book *Tales for an Unknown City* I included this recollection from Jim Strickland, a Canadian who had heard a great traditional Scottish storyteller named Jeanie Robertson: "I had never heard a traditional storyteller. I was absolutely and totally spellbound. . . . I can't say that I heard her story. I *saw* the story. That's the extent of her power as a storyteller. You saw it all happening. I wasn't aware that I had listened to her language." When we finished taping Miss Lou, I felt that Anansi had moved with her from Kingston, Jamaica, to Canada. He was no doubt riding the subways, selling fruit in Kensington Market, playing his shape-shifting tricks as much in Toronto as he did back home. When we left Miss Lou's apartment she called out her jubilant blessing: "Walk good, and good duppy walk wit' you!" Three weeks later, a hundred thousand radio listeners heard the irresistible cadence of Miss Lou's voice as we broadcast her Anansi stories across the country.

On our travels we caught up to Charly Chiarelli and over a glass or two of grappa we heard about how he grew up in Hamilton, Ontario, in a neighbourhood that had more people from Racalmuto, Sicily, than still lived in Racalmuto. He told us about the time the welfare officer came and he was pulled from his grade-five class so he could translate for his mother. The welfare lady asked questions his Sicilian mother found humiliating: "Do you own other property? Do you own precious works of art?" Finally, Chiarelli's mother exploded with injured pride and operatic anger. "Tell her we own many villas in Milan, Florida and Paris! We only live here because we love cockroaches! And she can find the *Mona Lisa* in the closet, behind those rags we call clothes!" The little boy, caught between his mother and English-Canadian bureaucracy, turned to the welfare officer after this three-minute outburst and said, simply, "My mother said no. We need a lot of words to say no in Sicilian."

We met Itah Sadu in her bookstore and heard her recount the story of how Thornton and Lucille Blackburn escaped slavery via the Underground Railroad. They wound up prosperous citizens in early Toronto, and created the city's first horse-drawn cab service. One long afternoon, we listened to Dennis Mann in his kitchen north of the suburb of Pickering. This is probably the last rural area left within thirty kilometres of Toronto. As he told story after story of the local characters and history, we could hear the sound of the heavy machinery clearing a path for highway 407. Soon, all of that prime farmland would be yet another featureless subdivision, and all of Mann's wonderful yarns would be the only trace of his deeply rooted community. The people driving in on their hour-long commute will never pull off the highway long enough to hear, as we did that day over endless cups of coffee, a thousand and one Pickering stories.

The radio show helped launch its own mini-oral tradition. Marc Kuly, a young man working as a blacksmith at a national historic site wrote in to describe how his friends listened to the show: "It all started with one of my co-workers hearing the first episode of the program. Before long his report led to a few of us listening and swapping tales . . . Slowly but surely we began to adapt the stories for telling to tourists visiting the workplace. By the end of the summer a library of borrowed books of folk tales and legends . . . had accumulated in our lunchroom. From the original three or four of us who listened to the early episodes, a group of nearly fifteen staff members were avidly listening to the show."

Throughout our quest, I kept thinking of one of the first tellers we taped, a remarkable raconteur named James Zavitz. He told us about an experiment his grandfather, an agricultural scientist called Charles Zavitz, had run on a field of barley. After a vicious hailstorm devasted the plot, wiping out years of careful work, he went out and examined every plant. He found one still standing, and from that stiff-stalked specimen he cultivated the hardy Ontario Agricultural College Number 21 Barley, a grain that helped Canada survive the Great Depression. This piece of Canadian and family history (Jim is my father-in-law, and of course when he told me that story it was the one time the tape recorder didn't work) is an apt image for what storytellers do. Every family, neighbourhood and community has someone who distills our experiences, histories and dreams into stories. They teach us to value the things that are most likely to withstand the hailstorms of time and forgetfulness. Like the special barley, these durable, storm-resistant narratives can nourish the imaginations of a whole country.

That summer we discovered that radio is a great medium for the art of storytelling. In a much-divided country like Canada, with its many regions, two languages, three founding peoples (English, French, aboriginal) and numerous immigrant groups, the storytelling voices that were broadcast every Friday night carried an extra message. Our listeners heard the beginning of a new story, a rich and polyphonic epic of national identity, expressed not through one official story but through many individual voices. Taken all together, they made a Canadian story far greater than the sum of its parts.

*

One of the greatest joys of a storm fool is to visit distant lands and make storytelling connections with new listeners. I've had the opportunity to travel to Israel, Ireland, Germany, France, the U.S., Singapore, and throughout Canada as a storyteller. One of the most challenging and exhilarating storytelling celebrations I've performed at is the Graz Tells International Storytelling Festival in Austria. One afternoon near the end of the festival, I went wandering through the streets of the city; I was saturated with stories and needed a break. Graz is a beautiful European city, full of cafés and galleries and nice cars and well-dressed people. The Graz audiences are warm and knowledgeable. They laugh at all the right places, even if a story is told in English, not German. I love the place— and at the same time (like some of its native sons and daughters), I am haunted by it. As a Jew who performs in Austria and Germany, I can't help feeling like an ambassador from a shared and tragic past. On an earlier trip I had visited the Jewish cemetery at the edge of town; the gravestones told a chilling story. Most of the Jewish community of this charming town was transported to the camps during the war. Few returned. Their neighbours watched them go. A German friend once explained that post-war culture practised a kind of willful forgetfulness, a deliberate silencing of painful truths.

Folke Tegetthoff, an Austrian writer and teller, wanted to stop this silence, and his method was to found and host an international festival of storytelling. As he came to know the storytelling movement around the world, he was like a man who tastes a rare and exquisitely delicious fruit. Instead of hoarding the flavour, he set about cultivating an orchard for his fellow Austrians to savour. His hosting is itself a brave and unexpected deed in a land where the old have kept too many secrets, and the young are only now learning to tell ghost stories. I thought of this as I strolled through the superb arcades, along the river, and past the perfect façades.

On this particular afternoon, I was basking in the sounds and vistas of the town when I heard something I hadn't heard before: the sound of children laughing. I continued around a corner and found myself in a little park not far from the river. The park was filled with Turkish children, running, playing, laughing with glee. The scene was more like my multicultural Toronto than the decorous and homogeneous town of Graz. The kids played while their mothers sat on benches nearby wearing what my Jewish grandmothers would have called babushkas. These kids would not have the chance to come to the festival. They probably hadn't heard such a thing was happening in town that week, and even if they had they wouldn't have been able to afford it. All of a sudden I had a great storm fool's desire to tell my stories, not as "Herr Yashinsky," an honoured guest at one of the world's greatest storytelling festivals, but just as myself under a tree with these raucous, lovely children.

We dragged milk crates into a semi-circle, I gave a taxi-stopping whistle, and they started to gather from their games. A woman volunteered to translate into German, although the park supervisor pointed out many of them didn't even speak German, let alone English. When they'd all tumbled into place, I began to tell. The listeners, with dark, intent eyes, shifted between both streams of language, English and German, catching at the suspense of the stories. I told them the classic English folk tale about Lazy Jack, featuring a noodlehead hero who does exactly what his mother tells him. "Jack," she tells him after he's dropped his first day's pay into the river by accident, "you should have carried it in your pocket." The next day, when he's paid with a jug of milk, he remembers what his mother told him. The story goes on from there. He does end up marrying the daughter of the richest man in the land, so maybe the moral is "Do what your mother tells you." I also told "The Gunniwolf." This story for the very young can be found in many versions in most children's libraries. A little girl goes out to pick flowers and, despite her mother's warnings, wanders into the forest. There she encounters the Gunniwolf. Luckily, she knows a beautiful flower-picking song, which she sings, putting the Gunniwolf to sleep. Then she runs, he wakes up and chases her, she sings again, he sleeps, she runs, he chases and so on. She barely escapes with her life. The moral? If you do find yourself in the forest, it's a good idea to have a powerful song (the Native people would call it her "medicine song") in case you run into any gunniwolves. I sang my Turkish children a song or two. I promised to come back the next day with other festival tellers (which I did), and that was it.

They listened well, all the rowdiness and wildness gone while we spun our bilingual yarns. Underneath the unfamiliar languages, they caught the drift of the stories. "Lazy Jack," a story about a lazy, unregarded lad who finds success in the end—well, aren't immigrants often considered lazy welfare bums by the fine people driving by in their BMWs? That prejudice unfortunately exists in Canada and I suspect it's present in Graz as well. And "The Gunniwolf," which features a little girl who enters the forbidden territory of the forest—what is that but the experience of immigrant children making their way in a strange new culture? The girl in the "Gunniwolf" survives because she sings a good song. These Turkish children, too, needed a strong inner song to protect themselves from the disapproving stares of white burghers. The stories were about them and for them and, at some gut level beneath the words themselves, the children knew it.

That night, onstage in front of a thousand human listeners and a couple of dozen birds, I had another storm-fool moment. We were at the Kasematten, an open-air theatre carved into the side of the mountain in the middle of town. The humans were on seats and the birds perched on the parapets.

I didn't know there were birds in the audience until I started my story. It's called "The Bird Colour-of-Time" (you can find the full version on page 266 of this book). In the story a sick princess dreams of the fastest bird in the world, a bird called Colour-of-Time. When she asks her father, the king, to find this dream-bird, he stages a flying contest. The eagle, king of birds, is about to win the race when all of a sudden a little bird who had stowed away in the eagle's neck-feathers darts ahead and wins the race by the beat of a wing. It is the princess's bird, of course, the one from her dream. The king her father is outraged that the little bird stole the race, but the princess is delighted.

I came to the line "the birds rose up and raced across the sky in a vast cloud of every colour and hue, each one straining to fly faster and higher than the rest, passing overhead with a great beating of wings and piping of bird-cry"—and at that very moment the birds began to sing. All around the theatre the birds warbled and squawked, an avian chorus coming in right on cue. Perhaps I shouldn't have been so surprised by the birds' response. Ten years earlier, something similar had happened. I was on the very first "Long Night of the Storytellers" tour (the precursor to "Graz Tells"), and we were at the University of Salzburg before our show. I was sitting by a pond on campus playing my "puny tune" (it looks like a sawed-off soprano recorder and has a sweet, clear sound). I closed my eyes while I played, and when I finally looked around, a circle of bull-frogs had gathered, listening silently on their lilypads. When I stopped playing, they began croaking. Rainer Maria Rilke's famous poem about Orpheus seemed to come true at Tegetthoff's festival. All of this storytelling had begun to make for frogs and birds (and Turkish children, too) not (in Rilke's image) a rough *Hutte* for their listening but rather "a temple deep inside their hearing."

After the birds' grand finale the entertainment drew to a close. As tellers and listeners walked down the hillside and decompressed over glasses of good Austrian beer, the birds stayed up on the theatre walls, no doubt talking late into the night about the pleasures of hearing a story in which they were the heroes.

I think one thing that pulls storm fools away from their own hearths and out into the world is the conviction that stories can make a difference in the ongoing struggle for social justice, freedom and equality. They are tools for bringing about social change. In 2002–03, as UNICEF Canada's first storyteller-in-residence, I had the opportunity to travel through Canada. To prepare for this role, I collected a number of stories that illustrated themes that UNICEF advocates: social justice, children's rights, the ability to make change (these stories are available at www.unicef.ca). Many traditional fables address these themes, as do a number of folk tales. My aim was to train UNICEF volunteer speakers in storytelling skills, and provide them with a repertoire they could draw on. Here is one traditional riddle about a man who learns the difference between heaven and hell, which was a perfect UNICEF story:

There was once a man who wanted to know the difference between heaven and hell. One night he had a dream. In his dream he visited hell. Hell looked like a big Chinese restaurant, full of round tables and crowded with customers. The tables were piled high with delicious Chinese food: moo shu pork, Shanghai noodles, spring rolls, the works. But the people in hell were starving. They were holding very, very long chopsticks that reached to the middle of the table, and they couldn't reach the food in front of them. They were screaming with hunger and disappointment.

Then he went to heaven. Heaven looked just like a big Chinese restaurant: round tables covered with wonderful food. Strangely enough, the people in heaven also had very, very long chopsticks, reaching to the middle of the tables. But unlike the people in hell, those in heaven were eating happily and laughing together.

The man woke up. He tried to remember his dream. What was the difference between heaven and hell?

When I tell this story I never provide the answer. The group must figure it out. Interestingly, over the years I've noticed that groups that are friendly, warm and trusting will always guess the answer right away. Groups that feel unsettled and suspicious take a long time to understand.

As you may know, the answer to the riddle is this: the people in heaven used their long chopsticks to feed their neighbours. The people in hell thought only of feeding themselves.

One day, while telling it, I said to the children, "This story is about you. You raise money here in Canada to help children in Bangladesh or Ghana. Your chopsticks are so long that you can feed children on the other side of the world." Another time, I was working with a group of UNICEF volunteers in Winnipeg, and I asked the question that ends the story: what is the difference between heaven and hell? To my surprise, a man from Sierra Leone said, with great conviction, "I know the difference. Living here is heaven. Back home is hell." He explained that the civil war in Sierra Leone had torn apart his family. He had barely escaped being attacked and mutilated. He and his wife had somehow managed to be reunited and they came to Canada. To him, this new land was heaven.

Another story we used was a traditional fable from Cameroon.*

A king was going to throw a feast. He invited everyone from miles around. Everything would be free: the food, the music, the dancing. But he asked that everyone bring a calabash of palm wine. The king had a great earthen jar in the middle of his compound, and after everyone had

---

* Adapted from *The King's Drum and Other African Stories* by Harold Courlander, copyright © 1962, 1990 by Harold Courlander. Used by permission of The Emma Courlander Trust.

filled up the jar, the palm wine would be served out to every guest.

One man wanted to go to the king's feast, but he had no palm wine. His wife suggested he purchase some from a neighbour, but he thought that was a silly idea. "I'll save my money," he said. "I'll fill my calabash with water. Nobody will ever notice one small calabash of water in a big jar full of palm wine." And so, with his calabash of water, he went to the feast. Hundreds of people were coming down the road towards the king's great feast. The man took his place in line, emptied his calabash into the king's jar, and sat down, waiting for the feast to begin. The servants began to dip out the palm wine and bring it around to the guests. When the king appeared, they lifted their bowls in honour. This man was so much looking forward to drinking the refreshing palm wine! He sipped from the bowl. It didn't taste right. He sipped again. This was not palm wine. It was water. Everyone had thought as he had: someone else will bring the palm wine. Ever since then, they say in Cameroon, "If water is all you bring to the feast, then water is all you'll have to drink."

In Canada, children collect coins for UNICEF on Halloween. The connection between this kind of fundraising and the work of UNICEF in distant countries can be hard for the children to understand. The story of the king's feast lets them feel that the coins are their version of the palm wine calabash. If everyone brings their share, then the feast will be good.

If you'd like to become a storm fool, you need three things: a headful of stories, a willingness to hit the road and the belief that storytelling can change the world. I *don't* recommend following the storm fool's way if you are looking for fortune, glory and fame. That lesson is one I learned early in my career. After just a few gigs, I was invited to the High Park Public Library, in Toronto's west end. The ambitious children's librarian had postered Roncesvalles Boulevard with a sign that said, "Come and hear Famous Storyteller!" Unfortunately, despite this enticing ad, nobody came. The undaunted librarian quickly press-ganged several children who were hanging around the library that day. She sent them downstairs to where I was waiting to tell my stories. One eight-year-old girl took a long and dubious look at me, and said, "Hey, mister—what's so famous about you?"

Grete chiere made oure Hoost us everichon . . .
CHAUCER, Prologue to *The Canterbury Tales*

IF THE ARMENIAN APPLES fell for the teller, the listener and the one who heard, a fourth apple (or better, all three together) should fall from heaven for the one who hosts: the master of ceremonies who comes early, sets out the chairs, makes the coffee, lights the candles, welcomes the tellers, makes the audience feel at ease and generally helps weave the stories into a memorable tapestry. The host is the one who creates a shelter for stories, tellers and listeners. He or she must have patience, a sense of community, curiosity and above all a love of listening. I'll describe some of my own experiences, both good and bad, as a storytelling host, and hope that you can use these ideas to kindle your own storyfires.

There have been several great storytelling hosts in literature, and we can learn much from our literary ancestors. Chaucer gave us Harry Bailly, the redoubtable Keeper of the Tabard Inn, a popular spot for wayfarers and pilgrims on their way to Canterbury. Besides being "boold of his speche, and wys, and wel ytaught," this spontaneous, irresistible hotelier was also "a myrie man." When a likely-looking company of pilgrims stopped at his inn, he cajoled and persuaded them to tell each other "tales of best sentence and moost solaas"—of wisdom and solace—on their way to Canterbury, and soon decided, for love of a good story, to go with them:

> Ye goon to Caunterbury—God yow speede!
> The blisful martir quite yow youre meede!
> And wel I woot, as ye goon by the weye,
> Ye shapen yow to talen and to pleye;
> For trewely, confort ne myrthe is noon
> To ride by the weye doumb as a stoon . . .

In Italy, a little before Chaucer's time, Boccaccio also wrote of a host who had amazing power to inspire a group of strangers to tell each other stories. His setting was considerably more dangerous than the Canterbury pilgrimage. In the frame-story of *The Decameron,* Boccaccio describes the ravages of the Black Death in Florence. In the middle of the devastation (at least a third of the population died), a young survivor named Pampinea persuades nine other young people, six women and three men, to accompany her to a villa outside the city. There they tell each other stories with themes like "the tricks which, either in the cause of love or for motives of self-preservation, women have played upon their husbands" or "those who after suffering a series of misfortunes are brought to a state of unexpected happiness." The plague has devastated their city, broken every bond of civil order, left most of their families dead or dying; yet Pampinea insists that the company tell each other stories, not about death, but about *amore*. Chaos rages just beyond the gates of the villa, but she knows that stories are more than just entertainment. They carry the seeds of whatever future these young Florentines, if they live, will build together.

But it is King Alkinoos who is perhaps the greatest host in world literature. When a sailor is shipwrecked on the island of Phaiakia, Princess Nausicaa finds him and brings him to the king and queen. They offer him their hospitality, but strangely enough, he doesn't tell them his true name; just makes up a yarn about a storm, a distant war, a bewitched island, a god-cursed effort to reach his home. When Demodokos, the royal bard, begins to sing of a warrior-king named Odysseus, the guest weeps secretly behind his cloak. Only King Alkinoos, great host that he is, notices those secret tears. After the banquet, there is track and field, then circle-dancing, then back for more barbecue; and now the bard takes requests, and the stranger asks for another tale about that selfsame hero:

> Sing only this for me, sing me this well,
> and I shall say at once before the world
> the grace of heaven has given us a song.

Knowing how hungry freelance storytellers can get, he sends a plate of choice meat to sweeten his request. The bard tunes his lyre and begins to sing; and this time the castaway can no longer hide his tears. Finally Alkinoos demands to know the truth: "You must not be secretive any longer! Come, in fairness, tell me the name you bore in that far country. . . ." To complete his hospitality,

Alkinoos promises his mysterious guest safe passage home on one of his magic ships, vessels that move as swiftly as their navigators' dreams. The stranger replies, "I am Laertes' son, Odysseus."

Halfway through his epic tale—for Odysseus takes over the telling from Demodokos and goes on to tell his own adventures—he stops, afraid his audience may be getting bored. Here Alkinoos, most noble of hosts, shows his true greatness. He reassures the storyteller with words that still encourage all tellers and listeners nearly three thousand years later:

> Here's a long night—an endless night—before us,
> and no time yet for sleep, not in this hall.
> Recall the past deeds and the strange adventures,
> I could stay up until the sacred Dawn
> as long as you might wish to tell your story.

When the story has come to an end, King Alkinoos completes his hospitality by giving the wanderer a dream-guided ship to carry him home: "Clear sailing shall you have now, homeward now, however painful all the past." In the shelter of Alkinoos's generous listening, Odysseus can finally land on the shore of his own story, and from there find his way home to Ithaka.

One of the host's primary roles is to ensure that stories aren't used inappropriately. Stories are not ads, sermons, lectures or doctrines. They do not increase productivity, move merchandise or convert the heathen. In *The Canterbury Tales,* Harry deals with a potential disaster when the Pardoner tries to hijack the storytelling by using his tale to solicit donations from his listeners. He is as drunk as a skunk—not an auspicious way to win anyone's trust. As if that weren't bad enough, he begins by boasting to them about how he makes his living using storytelling to persuade stupid peasants to pay for the privilege of seeing his phony holy relics. "I preche nothyng but for coveitise" (I preach only for covetousness) is his foul and cynical confession. Then he tells the pilgrims his story, a famous medieval legend about three drunken, boastful youths who scoff at the power of death, only to bring fatal calamity upon themselves through their greed, sacrilege and violence. At the end of the story, the Pardoner gets caught up in his own con. He starts in on Harry Bailly, of all people, as if he were just another ignorant paisano ready for the gulling: "'Come forth, sire Hoost, and offre first anon / And thow shall kisse the relikes everychone, / Ye, for a grote! Unbokele anon thy purs!'" Wrong move. The innkeeper's righteous indignation still echoes six centuries later. "'Nay, nay,'" he fumes, "'thanne have I Cristes curs! . . . Thou woldest make me kisse thyn olde breech (undies) / And swere it were relyk of a seint, / Though it were with thy fundament [shit] depeint!'" In his rage at this flagrant abuse of a sacred trust, Harry tells the Pardoner to get stuffed: "'I wolde I hadde thy coillons in myn hand / In stide of relikes or seintuaries / Lat kutte hem of, I wol thee help hem carie; / They shul be shryned in an hogges toord!'" Yes, enshrined in a hog's turd. So much for storytellers who use the art for fraudulent ends.

As the contemporary storytelling movement has evolved, many of the customs of oral culture have been rediscovered and put to new use. Diane Wolkstein, in her great collection of Haitian folk tales *The Magic Orange Tree,* reports that in Haiti the storyteller calls out "Cric? . . . when she or he has a story to tell. 'Crac!' the audience responds if they want that storyteller to begin. If they do not respond with *Crac!* the storyteller cannot begin." Wolkstein's book has had its effect: at storytelling events around the world today, you can call out "Cric?" and sure enough you will hear an answering "Crac!" In my work, I carry a talking stick and pass it to the storytellers. In northern Canada, native tellers often pass an eagle feather from speaker to speaker. In our houses of Parliament, the Speaker of the House holds a Speaker's Mace. Such rituals recognize the authority of the speaker, and remind the community of the importance of listening.

Reaffirming this intimate bond between teller and audience is often the essence of the host's job. I was once hosting a storytelling evening and a group from Sierra Leone dropped in. We invited them to tell stories and, before the first man took the talking stick, he walked three times around the candles in front of the teller's stool. We asked him why, and he said that in his tradition the story-teller must circle the tribal fire to thank the community for letting him speak. Other cultures take a somewhat slyer approach. In Tuscany, Alessandro Falassi noticed that the *nonna,* the grandmother who was the best storyteller in the district, made sure her listeners were wild with antic-ipation before she opened her mouth. Refusing to tell her stories on demand, she made her audience wait for it. Wait?—she made them beg. "The children had been mur-muring since dinner was over. 'Come on, grandma, tell us a story,' and they kept it up while the table was being cleared and as the dishes were being washed. The old woman procrastinated . . . She scoffed and joked, being careful, however, not to give a flat refusal . . . 'No, now there is work to be done . . . But, sweeties, I am dead tired . . . Who can remember stories! Ah, if I could only remember them.'" Only when she was comfortably ensconced by the fire with a warmer in her lap and a glass of sweet wine in her hand did this master-teller deign to begin. Falassi observes that at these Tuscan gatherings, "almost never have I heard storytellers start out with the story most requested." My favourite depiction of a story-teller's need for her listeners' maximum attention is in Rafik Schami's book *Damascus Nights,* a contemporary take on the *Thousand and One Nights*: "'I'm going to drink my tea and go,' said Fatma. 'You must forgive me for saying that your reception is not worthy of my story. You can't tell anything to people with faces as twisted as yours.' Fatma closed her eyes. 'No!' she said very quietly, 'By the soul of my mother, if you can't come right out and beg me for the story then I am going to leave.'"

Whether you circle the fire, hold the talking stick, yell *Cric!,* play the *nonna*'s game of hard to get or simply say, as Fatma does, that you expect more enthusiasm, the under-lying principle is the same. To tell a story well, the listeners must be involved. This is an art of conversation more than monologue. The host, teller and listeners are all complicit in the mission of keeping the stories alive.

A good host must be willing, as Alkinoos said, to stay up until the sacred dawn. The storyteller's shire lies in its own time-zone. When stories are told, we leave behind the world of instant noodles, high-speed downloads, split seconds and rush hours. Here people say "Come sit down," instead of "Hurry up! Hurry up!" In a well-hosted story-telling event, nobody looks at their watch, but everyone always has enough time. Once you step away the clock-ruled world, there's no need to keep stories short. In fact, the opposite is true. The late Joe Neil MacNeil, writing about his Cape Breton childhood, remembers that when the neighbours gathered in the evening, "The long tales were the ones that most pleased people. . . ." Pennishish, a great Omushkigo storyteller and oral historian from the west coast of James Bay, Canada, has collected traditional myth-cycles that take ten weeks to tell. I've heard him tell many of these, and once he starts, there are no shortcuts in recounting the creation of the world. This kind of marathon storytelling works best in the winter, when the nights up north are very long.

Most of my own experiences as a host have been at 1,001 Friday Nights of Storytelling and the Toronto Festival of Storytelling. When I decided to follow the way of the story-teller, I wanted to tell to adults as much as to children. In 1978 I approached some friends who ran a small café in the Kensington Market area of Toronto. Markets have always been congenial places for storytelling. Kensington Market—the old Jewish Market—was and still is one of the liveliest *quartiers* in the city, full of Chinese and Korean greengrocers, Portuguese fishmongers, cheese shops, bakeries, cafés, second-hand clothing stores, West Indian record stores, Middle Eastern and Latin American food stalls and one Jewish department store. The name of my friends' café was, appropriately enough, Gaffers. They were happy to let me tell stories on Friday nights, between the sets of an unremarkable folksinger.

Eventually more people started coming for the stories than the music, and the singer left. One night, a friend of mine mentioned that he knew some stories by heart, and might be willing to tell one. I was overjoyed. I had never intended this to be a solo performance, and anyway I was quickly running out of repertoire. So a week later, we had our first open session. After a while it became known as 1,001 Friday Nights of Storytelling and twenty-five years later it is still happening, though it takes place in a church now.

Here's how the evening works. The host comes early, sets the chairs around the teller's stool, lights the candles and prepares the talking stick. The crowd gathers, always a mix of old-timers and newcomers. The host dims the lights, stands by the stool and says, "Welcome to a Thousand and One Friday Nights of Storytelling. Who is here for the first time?" The host explains the custom of the talking stick: whoever holds it carries the attention of the group. Then the host asks, "Who has the first story?" and the stories begin. Sometimes there are long pauses between stories, and the host simply waits, knowing people are making connections in their minds and trying to choose the right story for the moment. If it weren't for the buzz of a light plane banking towards the Toronto Island Airport, or the echo of cheers from the ballpark a kilometre away, we could be back in Harry Bailly's inn.

I usually like to stay behind after the evening has wound to a close. Before joining folks at the café across the street I sit in the cloisters outside the church hall. A caretaker once told me that ever since the fire destroyed the original church, he's heard voices murmuring in the belfry of the old tower—the only thing that didn't burn down in the fire. "And I hear, from your voice," says Kublai Khan to his master raconteur Marco Polo in Italo Calvino's *Invisible Cities*, "the invisible reasons which make cities live, through which perhaps, once dead, they will come to life again." As I sit in the garden after a long night of stories, I find it heartening that a haunted tower stands sentinel over this tribe of downtown yarnspinners. It reminds me that calamities can be survived, whether of fire or forgetfulness, and that the voices of its storytellers may indeed be the reason a city has a centre, a past, a dream, a story. As for the midnight sounds in the tower, perhaps they're the whispered echoes of a thousand and one Friday nights of storytelling.

I used to open the Friday Nights by saying, in my youthful ignorance and enthusiasm, "Welcome to Gaffers Café, home of the world renaissance of storytelling!" In 1978 the storytelling movement was just beginning, but our café was not the only place where this art was reawakening. A group called the National Association for the Preservation and Perpetuation of Storytelling (now called National Storytelling Network) had, under the leadership of Jimmy Neil Smith, launched a national storytelling festival in Jonesborough, Tennessee, a few years earlier. Bruno de la Salle had founded the Centre de la Littérature Orale, just down the street from Chartres Cathedral. In England, Ben Haggarty was busy lighting fires for the English storytelling movement. Diane Wolkstein ran a storytelling series at the Hans Christian Andersen statue in Central Park. Dr. Hugh Morgan Hill, a.k.a. Brother Blue, had started telling stories in Harvard Square in Cambridge, Massachusetts; Liz Weir, in Northern Ireland, went through the land like a narrative Johnny Appleseed, planting seeds of storytelling events that brought people together across religious and cultural divides. Chava Lieber was building an Israeli storytelling movement through the

Beit Ariela library in Tel Aviv; and Folke Tegetthoff, was beginning to pull together his "Long Night of the Story-tellers," an international ensemble that toured Austria and eventually grew into the major international festival in Graz.

Through these people and others the idea was catching fire in many countries. In Canada, a group of seven tellers co-founded the Storytellers' School of Toronto, in 1979. A few years later, tellers from across the whole country created Storytellers of Canada/Conteurs du Canada. If my own experience is typical, the story-hosts of this generation were often catalysts who came at the right moment to make things happen. Often it seems like a whole community had simply been waiting for the right place and opportunity to gather.

As new venues sprang up, traditional storytellers found new audiences for their art. In Cape Breton, Nova Scotia, a wonderful traditional storyteller named Joe Neil MacNeil was "discovered" by the folklorist John Shaw. Shaw had gone looking for Gaelic speakers and his keen interest in MacNeil's stories encouraged this master teller to remember tales that, as he later told an audience in Toronto, he thought he had forgotten. Shaw's gentle persistence was the magic force that brought his vast repertoire of stories back. Angela Sidney, a Tagish elder in Yukon Territory, returned home from a storytelling festival in Toronto and inspired her friends and family to found an international storytelling festival in Whitehorse that would feature northern elders and tellers. Camille Perron, a Franco-Ontarian with a rich tradition of Ti-Jean stories, began to appear at festivals throughout Canada.

Many of the events and gatherings that were founded in the 1970s are still going strong. Even better, new hosts are emerging, with new ideas and audiences. After I did a residency at the Faculty of Education at Queen's University, some of the students started hosting a storytelling jam at the Sleepless Goat, a café in downtown Kingston, Ontario. After doing a storytelling unit at Woburn Collegiate in Toronto, the students began meeting at a doughnut shop down the street to swap their stories. A wind of creativity is carrying new storytelling seeds around the world.

Sometimes the simple fact of hosting a storytelling evening is a courageous act of social challenge. Liz Weir, a storyteller from Northern Ireland, launched a number of gatherings and festivals where tellers came from both sides of the religious divide. Storytelling was her way to heal a much-fractured history. Here in Canada, there was a referendum held in 1996 in Quebec on the possibility of separating from the federation. In the days leading up to this historic event, Canadian politicians became more and more hysterical in both of our official languages. Thinking that storytellers could build the bridges that the politicians were destroying, we hosted a bilingual storytelling evening in Toronto. Three French tellers joined four English speakers for a show in a downtown cabaret.

So it was that two days before the referendum, instead of watching the television news, I was listening to Jocelyn Bérubé play a lightning fiddle and whinny like a horse. He was telling the story of Alexis "le Trotteur," an extraordinary runner from the Gaspé region of Quebec. Jocelyn had heard the legend from his father, who'd heard it from his father, whose best friend had been there on the fateful day back at the turn of the century when Alexis had run the world's first—and perhaps only—three-minute mile. Fuelled by nothing more anabolic than poutine (an indescribable delicacy eaten in Quebec made of French fries covered with melted cheese curds and gravy) and perhaps maple syrup, this greatest of all Québécois marathoners broke every record held by human or beast. He had already beaten all the local racehorses when a new challenger came to the Gaspé: a locomotive. His race against the "iron horse" was, alas, the last he ever ran. Trying to outsprint the train, the mighty heart of Alexis "le Trotteur" burst. He died by the side of the tracks, the locomotive steamed past oblivious of its mechanical victory, and his glorious career fell to the storytellers to celebrate.

Bérubé came to Toronto with Michel Faubert and Marc Laberge. They told in French, we—Itah Sadu, Bob Barton, Lynda Howes *et moi*—told in English, and for one brief and bittersweet evening I understood what Canada could be. The storytellers were doing what our politicians had been unable to accomplish. We weren't trading lists of grievances, arguing over constitutional amendments, effusing over or shunning our neighbours. We were simply listening to each other's stories. A wise writer, stating her philosophy of teaching, said: "Put your play into formal narratives, and it will help you and your classmates listen to one another. In this way you will build a literature of images and themes, of beginnings and endings, of references and allusions. You must invent your own literature if you are to connect your ideas to the ideas of others." Vivian Gussin Paley was describing how storytelling helps her class act like a community in *The Boy Who Would Be a Helicopter*. She was talking about three-year-olds.

If this works for her preschool class, why not for the citizens of Canada or any other troubled land?

"Invent your own literature," as Paley says. Seven stories in two languages isn't much, but it is surely a beginning. The stories were told by word of mouth, in living voices, and, as Joe Neil used to say in Gaelic and English, "What the ear does not hear cannot move the heart." Because these stories were told and heard, I know that hearts were moved. Over a beer late one night we wound up talking politics and the future of Canada and Quebec. My French friends were astonished to find so many eager listeners in Toronto willing to receive and trade stories. They went back up the highway to Montreal vowing to build stronger connections between our two cultures.

Bérubé made up this French proverb: *Life is a pair of trousers held up by the suspenders of hope*. Canada, like many parts of the world, is still in a state of uncertainty, still trying to know and claim its proper destiny. Perhaps the greatest value storytellers bring to this public realm is the idea that stories can make a difference in the real world. Change begins when we listen to one another's stories.

When a host offers a talking stick to an audience, we must be ready for whatever kind of story the Muse sends. Once when I was hosting an open session at the Toronto Festival of Storytelling, a little boy took the talking stick, perched on the stool and proceeded to tell, in a shrill, unstoppable voice, an absolutely appalling story:

> Once there was a little boy
> and he was running away
> and he came to a big dark forest

and there was a big hole in the forest
and then he fell in and he couldn't get out
And then his Mommy was looking for him
but she couldn't find him
But then she did and he heard her footsteps coming
and then she looked in the hole
and the little boy looked up at her and said:
"Get me out you fucking bitch!"

The audience was shellshocked. The boy, in the aftermath, swung his legs back and forth on the stool, knocking my talking stick against his shoes, oblivious of the havoc he'd just wrought.

People looked at me, waiting for some hostly word or gesture that could repair the damage. At first I was just as speechless and horrified as my audience. The boy's blast of harsh language threw me for a loop. I felt as helpless as the mother in his story, too late noticing her son's absence, too late to the rescue. I noticed the young storyteller's mommy wasn't looking too pleased herself just at the moment. The silence was excruciating.

My Romanian grandmother used to ask a riddle. *How does the recipe for Romanian cake begin?* The answer is: *Steal two eggs.* That is, improvise. At a moment when you're not sure what to do, it's a useful thing to remember. Fake it. Go through the motions. Pretend you know what you're doing and sometimes it turns out that you really do. I got up, took back the talking stick and escorted the boy over to his mother; then I went back to the stool and stood there clutching the talking stick. And as I held it, I finally realized its deep ancient purpose: it stands for protection, a kind of guarantee that the host will keep life at a certain distance while the stories are being told. My grandmother's saying: *Once something happened. If it hadn't happened, how I could tell you about it?* flashed through my mind. Stories mark the "happened somethings" that are the most memorable and valuable in our lives. A woman gives birth, and it's the most astounding story in the world; but we don't expect her to tell it while it's happening. The story's for afterwards, when she draws a frame of memory and language around the miraculous event. The little boy's ending broke that frame; it was a *cri de coeur* that came too directly from the heart of a five-year-old's worst nightmare. As listeners, we didn't feel embarrassed. We felt betrayed.

Remembering my grandmother, I thought about where such terrible stories come from and why we tell them. In her family just about everyone and everything disappeared, thanks to fascists and fate, down the coldest, darkest, most lost hole humanity ever fell into. Stories were almost all she brought over from Europe—and a pair of silver candlesticks that now sit on our dining-room table. I grew up feeling responsible for keeping alive the stories of people I never had a chance to meet.

At that point I knew what had to be done. Holding the talking stick, a host's antenna for the world's hardest-to-tell stories, I said to my tribe: "We've just heard the essence of all fairy tales: *I'm lost! Find me!* It is the oldest story ever told, and our young friend gave it to us straight from the source. I thank him for telling it. Now, who has the next story?" My own family history had reminded me that, even if the stories are almost impossible to tell or hear, we must keep listening. Only if we listen can the sanctuary be rebuilt, and the stories continue.

"Well," she concluded one afternoon, "I have no
money to leave to my grandchildren. My stories are
my wealth."

YUKON ELDER ANGELA SIDNEY,
Life Lived Like a Story

PEOPLE OFTEN TELL ME they didn't hear any stories
when they were young, because, they say, their families
were too busy or too shy, or simply didn't remember
much. But when I, ever curious, ask a few questions, they
invariably think of a story, then another and another.
Everybody grows up surrounded by a web of narrative.
These include the little pieces of story that spice up everyday conversation, and the more "official" anecdotes and
special sayings that make up each family's body of oral
lore. It is true that these are rarely thought of or even
referred to as formal "stories." Mostly, they float, barely
noticed, through our daily talk and only long afterwards
do we realize we've been hearing and unconsciously collecting them all along.

Some families are better than others at keeping their stories alive. My friend Grace Nostbakken grew up in rural Saskatchewan with five brothers and sisters, sharing a room on the second floor of a farmhouse that got so cold in the winter that they could keep a side of beef frozen in the room next to theirs. Now living all over Canada, they share a common e-mail mailbox; when one of them posts a family memory, the others chime in with their own versions. Thus electronics help a farflung family re-collect their precious history. My cousin Mark, a bridge engineer living in Sacramento, California, publishes a four-page weekly family magazine. It is a remarkable chronicle of the lives of the subscribers, of which there are about ten. To keep getting the magazine (which comes by post, not e-mail) we have to send in articles about our lives. Deaths, bar mitzvahs, weddings, adventures at work, children's mishaps and triumphs—all of this is faithfully and lovingly reported within our own small network of readers and writers.

Our stories and sayings make a frame within which children make sense of their place in the world. Through often-repeated stories a family remembers its history, moral stance, ability to laugh at itself, moments of heroism and triumphs of survival. Growing up, we hear these little stories and fragments of memory all the time and don't especially value them; later, we treasure them. They are how we know our passage through life has been seen, remembered and valued.

I grew up in a crossroads family, the only child of an American father and Romanian mother. If I still spoke the languages my grandparents knew, I'd be able to tell stories in French, Romanian, Turkish, Greek, Hebrew, Latin,

German, Polish, Swedish, Yiddish and Japanese. Unfortunately, except for French and English, this rich heritage didn't survive in the New World.

Our house was haunted by the deaths and dispersals of my mother's Romanian-Jewish family during the war. Her father had been kicked out of Romania by the fascists, and he spent the war years in Detroit, Michigan, separated from his wife and only child. Her extended family wound up scattered around the globe in São Paulo, Tel Aviv, Paris, Bucharest, St. Louis and Detroit. On my father's side, little was known or told about our ancestry. He knew his mother had escaped pogroms in Russia, grown up in Sweden, and wound up in the United States. His father had come from Poland.

As a child, I grew up with big ears and a closed mouth, doing more listening than talking. Some of my parents' closest friends had been in the concentration camps, but they said almost nothing about their experiences—at least when a child was in the room. I became adept at listening to clues and hints and story-fragments of lost lives and vanished families. I grew up as a war-haunted American kid in the fifties, tuned to a story frequency and feeling that if I lost the signal in the static entire Jewish villages would suffer a second disappearance. The boy Mowgli, in Kipling's *Jungle Book*, was raised by wolves and humans, and his words could have been mine: "My heart is heavy with the things that I do not understand." Growing up as a war-haunted American kid in the fifties, I knew the feeling.

We are born into houses made of brick and wood. We are also born into houses made of stories, memories and sayings. The stories kept alive in families mark the crossroads of past, present and future. They are how ancestors encounter their descendants, they transform the memory of past terrors and triumphs into sources of courage for following generations, they confirm one's place in the intimate network of one's relatives and in the wider realm of the community.

My mother's father, Nathan Louis Paves, was my chief storyteller. I could always count on him for a good anecdote. He'd led an adventurous life and he liked to talk about it. One story I liked to hear over and over again concerned an incident with a bully. It happened when my grandfather was about five years old. A big, mean kid named Vasily accosted him on the sidewalk. Vasily said, "Hey, Nick, wanna learn a new word?" My grandpa did, but the word he heard was one he didn't know. Turns out, it was one of the worst words in the Romanian language. When he told Vasily he didn't know what it meant, the bully sneered, "Why don't you go and ask your mommy?" He did, and was promptly referred to his father. When he said the bad word aloud, his father slapped him. He told me it wasn't a hard slap, but he wasn't used to getting slapped at all, so it felt pretty bad. He cried; then asked his father, "Why did you slap me?"

"Because you said a very naughty word. Anybody who uses language like that in this house gets slapped."

"But, Daddy, I didn't know it was a bad word," he said, "Vasily told it to me and said I should ask Mommy what it meant."

"Ah," said his father, who was, despite the slap, an intelligent and kindly man, "in that case, the slap is not for you. I gave it to you so you can give it back to Vasily. That slap belongs to him!"

My grandfather felt better. He went outside, found Vasily, and gave the slap back as hard as he could. He told me the bully never bothered him again. (Strangely enough, there is a Hodja story with a similar plot. As a child, I was rather pleased to discover that my grandfather and Hodja Nasrudin had some things in common.)

When he was a young man, my grandfather left Romania to study engineering in Paris. While there, to my amazement, he belonged to a club called the Society for the Prevention of Seasickness, which believed that strenuous exercise with Indian barbells was one of the best preventative methods available. He used to demonstrate these exercises with a pair of barbells he kept in his room at the Jewish Home for the Aged, in Detroit. As he swung them wildly around his head, I'd duck and pray nobody got hurt, and I'd listen as my barbell-waving grandfather told me stories of his life.

From Paris he went to Japan, where he helped build the first skyscrapers. He added Japanese to the languages he already spoke: French, Romanian, Latin, Yiddish, Hebrew. Once, when he'd turned his ankle on the street-car tracks, they brought a blind bone-setter to help him. In Japan, they explained, the blind were considered to have the gift of healing. My grandfather was impressed by the way the Japanese saw a disability as a gift. (Another Japanese custom he appreciated was mixed bathhouses— my grandfather liked women).

From Japan, he moved to San Francisco and got a job laying out power lines in the high Sierra. I, a skinny, bespectacled, middle-class kid in the suburbs of 1950s Detroit, loved to hear about how my irascible, fiery Romanian grandpa rode a mule in the mountains of California.

When he was ready to get married, he wrote to his mother back in the old country asking her to find him a suitable wife. The candidate should meet three conditions. He requested that she be beautiful, have a good singing voice, and come from a port city. The reason for this last, rather unusual stipulation was that he expected a woman raised in a port city to have a certain worldly wisdom, and not be merely a sheltered, over-refined Eastern European *bourgeoise*.

Such a miracle woman was found. My grandmother Fanny was beautiful, gracious, unaffected, cultured, a marvellous singer, an amateur painter and an inveterate journal-keeper; and she happened to come from the greatest port in the history of the world—Constantinople (once Byzantium, now Istanbul). He went home to Romania, married, had an only child, and did fairly well trading with Palestine. Then the fascists came to power; on the eve of the war, they kicked him out of the country. He had to leave his wife and ten-year-old daughter behind. He didn't see them again for seven years.

Even though he was an engineer specializing in concrete, he was open to the possibility of supernatural experiences. When he was living in San Francisco, he felt very lonely and missed his family in Romania. One night in a dream he saw his grandfather walking towards him, his body filled with light. His radiant grandfather spoke to him, and said, "I've come to say goodbye. I love you very much. Don't be sad now—your life will get much better." So saying, he disappeared. In the morning my grandfather remembered his dream. He knew his grandfather had emigrated to the United States several years before and was living in St. Louis, Missouri, but he didn't have his address. He wanted very much to get in touch with him after his dream, but he didn't know how. He wrote a letter to Romania asking how his grandfather was, and where he could reach him. It was several weeks before he had a reply. The letter from home contained sad news. His grandfather had died a few weeks before. My grandfather remembered his dream and checked in his diary. To his amazement, his grandfather had died on the same day he'd had his dream.

My grandpa was a man of science, an engineer and an amateur mathematician. Yet after this experience he also understood that life had mysteries that science couldn't fathom. There was a life of the spirit as undeniably real as the facts, figures and equations he used in his work. When he wanted to teach me his belief, he drew the mathematical sign for infinity—a horizontal figure eight—and explained that every creature possessed something infinite within them, something that could never die.

He's gone now, and the grandfather he dreamed of died more than a hundred years ago. Only the stories remain.

My parents both have written brief memoirs. Reading them, I'm struck by how the stories I heard as a child have stayed with me. The themes of memory, survival, risk-taking and abandonment run through my family lore. When I think about the stories I choose to tell, they often explore similar themes.

Here is a story from the memoir written by my mother, Palomba Paves-Yashinsky:

Winter 1945: It is 2:00 A.M. and a sudden sharp noise wakes us. A Jeep drives into our courtyard, its headlights flooding with a sinister white light our bedroom window;

the Jeep drives up and stops right at our front door. We jump out of bed terrified. My mother lifts a corner of the curtain, very carefully. She turns pale, she whispers: "It's a Russian army vehicle! What do they want here, in the middle of the night? God help us! Quick," she tells me, "go hide in the kitchen!"

The doorbell rings; I run in the dark and hide. My mother hesitates; a loud knocking on the door, then a man talking in Russian. My mother, a housecoat hastily thrown about her, slowly opens the door and a Russian officer and his orderly walk in; I am peeking through the kitchen door, which has a small window. I don't dare move. The Russian officer explains through his gestures that he and his orderly need a place to sleep overnight, they have been assigned to our flat. My mother, terror in her eyes, points to the only bed we have; she begins to prepare sheets and pillowcases for the officer; the orderly will sleep on a mattress on the dining-room floor. Like a sleepwalker, my mother moves to make room for the two men; her hands are shaking. They watch her. I observe them, they do not look brutal; in fact, they show a certain embarrassment, almost a shyness at having erupted into our life in this way, in the middle of the night.

And then, suddenly, the officer says to my mother in Yiddish: "Ich bin ein Yid! My name is Moishe Abramovitch! Do not be afraid!" My mother, disbelief and wonder on her face, walks to him and shakes his hand. "You are Jewish?!" She is relieved, no longer scared. "My dear, you may come in—the Russian officer is Jewish," she calls to me. And, a smile on her face, she serves him and his orderly tea and biscuits; they can stay, we feel safe, he is our brother, despite his forbidding foreign uniform.

Her stories of a child's terror, courage and liberation are part of my family heritage. From my American father, Jack Yashinsky, I heard stories about life in the submarine corps:

I got into a bit of trouble at submarine school by altering a card that was issued to my group directing us to a mess hall that was a considerable distance from where we took classes. There was a closer mess hall, so practically the whole class changed the card to be able to use the closer one. The training officer got wind of what had happened and announced that he was going to collect the cards in order to inspect them. Everyone got busy changing the location of the mess hall on their card by erasing; I thought that it would be so obvious that the cards had been tampered with that I just turned mine in as it was; I convinced my friend, Frank Yannett, to do the same. Our reward for being honest was thirty days of extra duty polishing floors after training hours. We had to appear before a "Captain's Mast" (a procedure for meting out punishment). The presiding officer—I think he was Admiral Nimitz's son—intimated that the reason for our misbehaviour was fear of being assigned to a sub after our training. I was so offended by his remark that I said he could assign me to a sub that was in dry dock, the USS *Boarfish*, but he just smiled and gave us the extra duty. The USS *Boarfish* was the last sub to be lost during the war.

I was put ashore on muddy Samar [in the Philippines] to wait for assignment to the submarine base up at Subic Bay. It was the rainy season and the whole island was one big mudhole. We were put in tents and told to stake out an army cot to set up housekeeping. All there was were the cots. No blankets, no mosquito netting, not a single dry surface to put anything on. It was miserable. What a place to spend your birthday in, I thought. My eighteenth was coming up and I was feeling down about being away from home in such a godforsaken place. June 14 rolled around and I turned eighteen. I wanted to get a present for my birthday just to cheer myself up. What I needed was a pair of boots. The Navy had only issued me standard black oxfords back in the States, and the mud on Samar was more than ankle-deep. There was an airstrip on the island, not far from my camp. I decided to go to the quartermaster depot there to see if I could talk somebody into giving me a pair of jungle boots. Well, the Airforce QM rating wasn't about to part with any boots for a woebegone sailor—he told me to get lost. But I must have looked really woebegone, because he called me back and asked me why I thought he should give me them. When I told him it was my birthday he laughed, reached under the counter, and tossed me a pair. I tried them on. They fit. And they really cheered me up.

As I was slogging back to the camp, I saw a file of enemy soldiers being led off somewhere. They didn't look very dangerous to me. They were all kind of small and looked as unhappy as I had before the boots.

I spent the following days out at the airstrip watching the B24s and B29s fly in from their bombing raids. A lot of them were shot up, with big holes in the wings and fuselage. A few of them couldn't use their flaps and would go off the end of the strip into the drink. I remember trying to get some of the pilots to take me along on a raid. They wouldn't do it. They thought I was crazy.

I spent a year in Subic Bay, mostly working in the radio shack; in fact, I was on duty the day a message came in announcing that a bomb with the equivalent of twenty tons of TNT had been dropped on Hiroshima; a few days later, another bomb was dropped on Nagasaki and a few days after that the Japanese surrendered. A few months after I had arrived on the sub base, I was resting on my cot in the barracks when I heard the screen door slam and a voice asking if there was a Yashinsky somewhere. The voice belonged to my oldest brother, Ben, who was in the Army medical corps and had been assigned to the Pacific theatre after having spent a couple of years in the Atlantic theatre aboard a troop ship ferrying wounded soldiers back to the States. I didn't know he was anywhere near Subic Bay; but he had been assigned to duty in Manila and found out, I don't know how, that I was not far away. I managed to get a short leave of absence and went up to Manila where we spent a few days together. By the war's end, my mother had four sons on active duty in different parts of the world.

My father became ill in 2000. As his illness worsened over the summer, I reread his memoirs, which thankfully he'd written the previous fall. I also reread every letter and postcard he'd ever sent to me (I'm a packrat, and have many dusty boxes of stuff from the past fifty years of my life). I was searching for the loving, wise words my good father was no longer able to say out loud.

I found this postcard, written when I was twelve years old and away at camp:

July 16, 1963

Hi Din,

How's you? We're all fine except for being a little warm; it's 90 today. There is lot being printed in the paper about the danger of watching the eclipse of the sun coming up this Saturday. Apparently one is not to look directly at the eclipse, even with dark glasses. It seems that even if it is not painful to watch the sun directly, a large amount of infra-red rays enter the eye and can cause permanent damage, burning a part of the retina. I imagine that the camp officials have warned all the boys about this, but, in case they haven't, take this as an official warning and DON'T look directly at the sun in eclipse even for a few seconds. I still haven't found a boat, but I've been looking. Take care, have fun, stay well!

Love, Pip

My father knew from eclipses that particular summer. His eldest brother, the one who'd given him such joy at the submarine base, had committed suicide, there was trouble at home, and he was having a hard time coming back to the used car lot after studying French literature in his spare time. It is the eternal fate of parents to try to shield their children's eyes from the burning eclipses they themselves must face and can't avoid seeing.

The night before he died, the old submariner visited my partner, Carol, and his eldest grandson, Nathaniel, in two separate dreams. Carol told me at breakfast that in her dream my father had been standing next to his hospital bed (after being bedbound for two months in the surreal world of the palliative ward). He was dressed in khaki pants, a light jacket and his favourite sailor's cap, brought back from the French islands of St. Pierre and Miquelon many years before. A screen obscured his waist and legs (where he'd had cancer), but he was cheerful and smiling. "See," he told her, with an understated joy, "I'll be fine." Moments later, our son Nathaniel came up from his bedroom saying he'd had a strange dream about his grandpa. He had appeared at his bedroom door dressed as if for a journey, wearing nice pants, a light jacket and a sailor's cap. "I love you," he told him, then vanished. The next afternoon my father took his last voyage. Five days before, he had celebrated his youngest grandson Jacob's ninth birthday, an event he had looked forward to all summer. He was smiling during Jacob's visit, gave him a present, a kiss and some loving words. Moments after we left, he fell into the gentle five-day sleep that took him to the threshold of death, and then beyond.

Now I believe it is the easiest thing in the world to
tell a story—and the hardest to be a fine storyteller.
RUTH SAWYER, The Way of the Storyteller

THERE ARE TWO EXTREMELY IMPORTANT skills storytellers must learn. The first is how to move furniture. The
second is how to carry cups of tea to old women. The furniture part comes because nine times out of ten, you have
to put the storytelling space in order. Change the lighting.
Move a desk. Shlep the chairs into a circle if, like me, you
like curved lines more than straight ones. I'm quite particular about the space when I tell stories. For example, when
I'm telling to children I never let them stay behind a desk
while they listen. I want my stories to go straight to their
bellies, unimpeded by wood, plastic, metal or textbooks.

But far more important is the ability to carry cups of tea
to old women. This is how you get to hear the best stories.
Exchanging a gift for a story is one of the oldest protocols
of oral culture. Following First Nations decorum, people
will present an elder with tobacco as a prelude to asking a

question or receiving a story. Whenever I visited the Yukon, I would often bring a cup of tea to Angela Sidney, a Tagish elder. Then, her old hands warmed by the tea, she would tell me stories about how Crow made the world. With Angela Sidney, it was tea. With Alice Kane, another of my elders, it was cappuccino, although she never let me pay for it (we were both stubborn, but I had the sense to realize when to concede the field gracefully). I would often drive her on her errands around town, listening to her non-stop storytelling commentary about the city, her friends, her memories of being a children's librarian, contemporary politics (she kept several voodoo dolls in her closet for the politicians she most abominated) and everything else within her far-ranging ken. It was a fair exchange: a ride for a lavish outpouring of oral wisdom. My third elder was Joan Bodger, an American who had moved to Toronto from New York in 1970, two years before I moved to Canada from Santa Barbara, California. We met for occasional cups of tea or coffee (we alternated for the bill), but I think the thing that most pleased her was simply having a young person come to learn with open ears and an eager heart.

Now that my three mentors have left our green earth, I realize how lucky I was to know them. Although later in this book I describe my local library as my main source of stories, the art itself I learned by spending unhurried time with my elders. Whatever I know of the integrity of the art and the depth of oral literature I learned from Alice Kane, Joan Bodger and Angela Sidney. Teachers can sometimes work in strange ways. They may never tell you anything directly about your work, or coach you, or give you explicit instruction. They may never offer a criticism or even a suggestion, but you are learning all the time. Almost every-thing I learned from my teachers came to me indirectly: I observed their art, thought hard about their dazzling skills and knowledge, and brought them many cups of tea; in other words, I was a devoted listener to those who knew far more about stories, storytelling and life than I did.

The Saulteaux elder Alexander Wolfe uses a story to explain why he records and tells traditional stories. The tale has been published in *Earth Elder Stories*.

An old grandfather lived in a large camp beside a great river. There was thick bush across the water, and many trees. He used to go down to the riverbank and build something every day, and one day somebody from the camp asked him what he was doing. He replied:

"You see those trees beyond the river? . . . If you look closely you will see at one place the bush is thin and beyond there is a plain. I am putting together a boat with which my children and grandchildren may cross the river. Once across the river they can make their way through the bush to the open plain beyond. I have come a long way in life. Life has been good to me. I need not cross this river; I am content to live here the rest of my life. There are many, though, particularly the young, who need to go on, through and beyond all obstacles. With my knowledge and experience, it is my duty to help them face their uncertain future. One day my tracks will come to an end and I shall go to my father and grandfathers. You will continue on this path on which we all walk."

This is the philosophy of an elder: he builds the boat that will carry his grandchildren into their future. By telling you about my three elders, I hope you will seek out your own. One day the responsibility of building that boat will fall to you.

Angela Sidney, the Tagish elder, was already old when I met her. One of Canada's most revered storytellers and tradition-bearers, she had come to the Toronto Festival of Storytelling with the anthropologist Julie Cruikshank. When they weren't at the Festival, the two of them cruised the local malls so Angela could buy presents for her grandchildren. After these shopping expeditions, she came to her sessions, took her drum painted with her clan insignia—a double-tailed beaver—and sang and told ancient medicine songs and stories. I met her again when I began to visit the Yukon International Storytelling Festival. She was eighty-nine years old the last time I visited her, and I spent many hours by her side ("Don't tell your wife," she said, laughing). If I followed proper listener's decorum—didn't interrupt or ask too many impatient questions—Angela told me stories.

Angela Sidney knew thousands of stories. She had a story about every creek, mountain and settlement in the Yukon. She knew the history of the Native tribes and the European settlers, stories about old-time doctors (shamans), stories about the Yukon gold rush and stories about the extraordinary men and women of her own family. She could trace the lineage of just about everyone who came up to her with the standard greeting: "Hello, Auntie!" and once she'd brought each face into her nearly-blind focus and placed her visitor's name in its proper matrilineal network, she would half-rise from her wheelchair with an exultant "Gee whiz! It's good to see you!"

(She once asked me, trying to figure out my tribal affiliation, if I was Crow or Wolf—the two largest divisions of the Yukon tribes—and I told her Jewish and gave her a Star of David, which she wore with her Beaver Clan regalia.) And she knew countless stories about Crow.

Crow, in Mrs. Sidney's telling, didn't so much make the world as trick it into existence: through a series of Crowish connivances, misdemeanors and scandalous reversals, the scantlings of the world-to-be emerged. "Crow is always stealing things," she would say (my quotes are based partly on memory, and partly on Cruikshanks's superb study *Life Lived Like a Story*). She often used the present tense in telling of his cosmic accomplishments: Crow steals the sun, the light, the moon, the fire, the fish, the rivers—the earth itself, all the necessities of life—from those stingy chiefs who presume to hoard essential resources. "Someone's always too greedy in these stories!" she'd comment, with a chuckle. And whatever Crow steals he releases into common use. "Go to the skies," he says, tossing the sun and moon up into the heavens. "Now no one man owns the light—it will be for everybody." Crow steals the world and gives it away to us, the creatures for whom it is to be a dwelling-place. When he encounters a greedy sea lion lord who's keeping all the land to himself, Crow kidnaps one of his pups and then trades it back for some grains of sand. "You know how sand'll sometimes float on the water?" Mrs. Sidney would ask her listeners at this point in the story, "That's what Crow does—throws it on the water and some of it floats." And as he casts this sand upon the waters he cries out: "Become a world!"

And there we'd be, me on the grass and Angela Sidney in her wheelchair spinning the tale; and as I listened, sometimes I'd notice a real crow settling nearby on the lawn. Which made me wonder, did she and her Tagish and Tlingit ancestors look at that common, raucous, devious scavenger and see the Bringer of Light, Creator of man and woman, the Worldmaker? Does the spirit of the creator really live on in this embodiment? Is that crow-on-the-grass really *Crow*? And more than that: what would it be like to live in a world shoplifted and bodied forth into glorious existence by a cosmic force they named after an unpredictable black bird?

You couldn't take things for granted in such a world. You could certainly never believe there was only one authorized version of anything important. You wouldn't dream of setting forth on a crusade in the name of Crow to slaughter infidels who happened to believe the world came into being some other way, or that Crow wasn't the way, the truth and the life. It makes no sense to hoard the truth or any other essential resource if you believe the world is a continual and unexpected gift from a fabulously generous, if somewhat unpredictable Creator. Crow-logic is far too open—sometimes ruthlessly so—and spontaneous to motivate the annihilation of your neighbours for the sake of a story. In a Trickster-wrought creation, hoarding is absurd.

So Crow steals the world and gives it into our care, and that squawking, persistent thief of a bird is still around as a daily reminder of the Creator's great and paradoxical lesson: the world belongs to us, the world does not belong to us. This is, of course, like the oral tradition itself, which we own most at the very moment of giving it away. By the time an oral story reaches our ears it has passed through many memories, been uttered by many tongues. Stories passed by word of mouth move through the air from teller to teller, always arriving in new places carrying the whispering voices of ancestors: as we held this tale in our remembrance, they murmur, may you shelter it in yours. And so I would lean closer to my Tagish friend and hear the world being created. Crow utters his words of power in myth-time, but I could hear them in 1991, in the almost-ninety-year-old voice of Angela Sidney, great Yukon elder, proud myth-teller, bearer of the double-tailed beaver's medicine and occasional wearer of a Jewish star. It was her voice that, four weeks before her death in 1991, could still cry out in triumph the words that were first spoken at the beginning of creation: "Become a world!"

I met Alice Kane just after she had retired from the children's service of the Toronto Public Library. She was working as the part-time curator of the Marguerite Bagshaw Storytelling and Puppetry Collection, in a little basement office in the Palmerston Library. Alice Kane had the good fortune to work as a children's librarian when the library was a cultural sanctuary we can barely imagine today. The women in her profession—and they were a formidable sisterhood—were no "information resource workers," or whatever term is used these days. They knew every book in their collection, they knew thousands of stories by heart, and they were able to match a book or story to the individual kids who came to the library after school and for Saturday storytimes. The world outside this haven could be pretty rough. The kids came from impoverished backgrounds, mostly with first-generation immigrant parents. From the Depression to the Second World War, their lives were lived on the edge of hunger, violence, political turmoil. Their older brothers were battling fascist mobs in

Christie Pits park (a little-known part of Toronto history) as Alice's listeners sat on the carpet and listened to Russian fairy tales. The library was truly a good place to be as the world beyond spun towards war.

When I met her, I was a twenty-two-year-old mess. I was heartbroken from a failed romance, I was discouraged about the possibility of ever conquering my paralyzing shyness and becoming a storyteller, I missed my California friends and was finding Canada hard to get used to; I was, in short, a most confused and unhappy young man. Alice was a fine listener, completely unsentimental, always encouraging. Her philosophy was based on her wonder tales, where the heroes, however perilous their obstacles, must face life directly and with the highest spirits they could muster. Almost every time I saw her for the rest of our friendship, she greeted me with a hymn: *Dare to be a Daniel, dare to stand alone, dare to have a purpose firm, and dare to make it known!*

I'd sit in the office and pour my heart out as Alice, her red hair just going to white, listened patiently. Sometimes she wore a magic necklace (at least it seemed so to me). It was the polished, amber-coloured cross-section of a peach pit, which she wore on a simple chain. It looked like a Celtic design, something she might have brought over from her native Ireland—intricately interwoven and very mysterious. My topsy-turvy life shone back at me from the necklace, and I felt that in the world of the woman who wore such a design there would be room for all stories, all destinies, however crazy and desperate they seemed to the ones who inhabited them.

It took a while before I actually heard her tell stories; when I did, I was hooked. I spent the next twenty-five years following Alice Kane, listening to her stories, talking about the art of storytelling, gossiping and sharing countless cups of cappuccino at our favourite Toronto café. We travelled together to England, to the National Storytelling Festival in Jonesborough, Tennessee, and to the international storytelling festival in Whitehorse, Yukon Territory. One of the great encounters of contemporary storytelling was when Alice Kane met Angela Sidney. They immediately recognized each other as spiritual sisters.

We worked together on a ten-year collaboration with the Irish harper Eithne Heffernan exploring Irish myths and wonder tales. Alice was a Northern Irish Presbyterian, Eithne a Catholic from the Republic of Ireland, and we often laughed that it took an American Jew to bring them together.

Every time I heard her tell stories, I wondered how she was able, with the simplest of elements, to create such vivid verbal tapestries in my mind. A good part of her power came from her voice. It still carried the cadence of her Belfast upbringing, and was perfectly suited to the long wonder tales she loved to tell. When I read Jean Mansour's description of the voice of his mother, a traditional singer from the mountains of Morocco, it reminded me of Alice Kane's voice. It had a quality that conveyed the sense of a world glimpsed beyond the horizon of everyday life, a world so fine and full it was impossible—almost—to put into words. "I am not able," writes Mansour of the singing of his mother, Fadhma, the bearer of Kabyle tradition, "to describe to you the moving quality of her voice, her power of incantation. She wasn't even conscious of it herself, and these songs weren't works of art for her, but spiritual instruments she used, just as the weaver uses the wool, the miller the wheat . . . She had a clear voice, almost without timbre, never the least attempt to go beyond the material. Over the long carrying echoes of her voice floated a nostalgia infinitely far off, the feeling of an unattainable yet close-by presence, the presence of that inner land whose beauty is sensed only when one knows one has lost it."

A few years ago, after a series of small strokes, Alice finally retired. She gradually faded into the fragility of extreme old age. In her final years I visited her whenever I could in her nursing home. She sat silent and immobile, her head drooping that once was held so proudly erect. I would read poetry aloud, priming her with old, familiar words: "The time has come, the Walrus said, to talk of many things . . ." and from the ruins of her once-grand story mind a frail voice would sometimes whisper, "of shoes, and ships, and sealing wax, and cabbages and kings." Then we'd chime in together on: "and why the sea is boiling hot, and whether pigs have wings." She once knew thousands of poems by heart, and hundreds of stories, many of them long wonder tales. Alice Kane grew up in Belfast, immersed in oral rhymes, songs, prayers, her father's rather salty sea shanties, Presbyterian hymns, the words of Kipling and the King James Bible. Even in the misty land of her senility, she still spoke the old rhymes with a certain incantatory power. She was frail and fading, but the great House of Story where she once abided had yet a foundation.

One of her favourite stories was "The Wondersmith and His Son," an Irish myth she adapted from Ella Young's telling. When the Wondersmith—known in Gaelic as the Gubbaun Saor—is dying, his son and daughter come to him:

So they went into the house and the Wondersmith, the Gubbaun Saor, sat in his chair dressed as if to receive kings. And the son said to him, "My father, have you a word for us?" "I had the Master Word," he told him, "but I have forgotten it. I have lost it, it is gone." And the son beat his breast and he said, "He will die, he will die, and he will not leave his wisdom to us." And he sat like that, he sat like that, not speaking and barely moving for a whole moon. And the son kept saying, "The time is so short, the time is so short."

When Alice Kane sat in her wheelchair as silent as the Wondersmith, I'd hold her thin, cool hand and ponder: what is the Master Word of a great storyteller? What is the Master Word that can communicate a legacy of stories, a technique for telling them, and the joy of language spoken so unforgettably? But of course with storytelling there is no "master word," only the story, connecting first to one person, then to another and another, in a fragile thread or chain of narrative always at risk of breaking, always in need of the storyteller's powers of remembrance.

Joan Bodger, my third mentor, had a sign on her apartment door: Knock Resolutely! Woe betide you if you knocked with anything less than conviction and courage. I met her at the very beginning of my storytelling career. She was telling stories once a month at a soul food restaurant in Toronto called the Underground Railroad, and when I saw how she held the adult audience I realized it might be possible to take storytelling beyond the realm of children.

She herself knocked with great resolution on every door she faced, and she credited her perseverance and risk-taking to the wealth of stories she heard as a child. Born in Oakland, California, on August 31, 1923, Joan was the daughter of admirals on both sides of her family. Her father was in the American Coast Guard, and her grandfather had sailed under the British flag. She was raised to love the sea. She was also raised by a storytelling mother who filled her childhood with an inexhaustible stream of poems, family lore, folk tales and the classics of English children's literature. In her memoir *The Crack in the Teacup: The Life of an Old Woman Steeped in Stories,* Joan Bodger describes how this story-rich upbringing set her on a path of intellectual adventure: "How did I become a storyteller? We ate and drank stories for dinner. They were our mass, our communion." She shared this passion for literature in *How the Heather Looks: A Joyous Journey to the British Sources of Children's Books* and was very pleased when a retired children's librarian told her it was the book most stolen by retiring children's librarians.

Joan Bodger was a scholar of myth. Her quest for goddess mythology took her to Petra, Jordan, to study the ancient Nabataeans and their goddess Atargatis, and to all the Arthurian sites in Britain, where she told stories of Sir Gawain, Arthur, and the Winter Hag at the very places where the myths began. She liked to see things for herself, to go to the source, to decode secrets. In the Second World War she worked in the code room at the Pentagon. Throughout her work she was fascinated with stories like "Rumpelstiltskin" and "Tom Tit Tot," where the hero or heroine breaks a spell by guessing the secret name of a powerful spirit. She found many echoes in contemporary society, where many of the powers that influence our lives are impenetrable, mysterious or secret: IMF, CIA, al-Qaeda. Just before she died, she was researching the Luddite movement in early-eighteenth-century England. These early revolutionaries had understood the hidden truth behind the machinery: that increasing standardization of labour would inevitably bring with it the destruction of community life. In Joan's view they were the first to resist what we now call the "global economy," and she wanted to tell their story so today's young protestors would know they had active and honourable ancestors.

Joan Bodger was, for me, a real-life version of the Wife of Bath from Chaucer's *Canterbury Tales*. Like her, Joan was independent, high-spirited, generously proportioned, gap-toothed, outspoken and extraordinarily attractive. "The Wife of Bath's Tale," about the knight who must save his life by finding the secret of what it is that all women want, was one of Joan's favourite stories. In Chaucer, the knight discovers that all women desire "sovereynetee." As Joan told the tale, the magic, spell-breaking answer is "to be what you would be, when you choose to be that." She carried this philosophy into every aspect of her personal and professional life, including her response to the cancer she developed in her late seventies.

When she was diagnosed with cancer in 2000, she began making plans to return to the Pacific coast. She chose Tofino, B.C. as her final abode, and was ever on the lookout for whales in Clayoquot Sound, which she could see from the window of Tofino General Hospital. The citizens of her new community welcomed her, appreciated her and were with her through her dying. For a myth-teller like Bodger, whales meant a great deal. She used to savour her father's favourite tall tale, from Benjamin Franklin: "There is no more noble or magnificent sight," Franklin told his credulous French friends, "than that of the Atlantic whales, as they leap up Niagara Falls on the way to their spawning grounds."

Joan Bodger spent her last few days covered by a button blanket embroidered with a killer whale, a gift from a new circle of native friends in Tofino.

On my last visit to Joan, I spent a few days sharing tea and stories in the palliative care unit in the Tofino hospital. I was staying on Vargas Island, a few kilometres across the Sound. One day I walked the trail that cuts across the island to Ahous Bay on the Pacific side. It is a rough trail that barely stays above the rainforest muck on either side. Two-thirds of the way along, I came to an official-looking yellow sign: TRAIL CLOSED—BRIDGES REMOVED. It was a real Joan Bodger moment. I thought of her courage, her willingness to improvise, her open-hearted ability to knock resolutely. Then I climbed past the barricade and, after another kilometre of hiking, pushed through thick green bushes and stood on a vast crescent of beach. Before me stretched Joan's beloved western ocean. It was the essence of her hard-earned wisdom that, even if the trail is closed and the bridges removed, your own passage can become a new bridge for those who follow.

Angela Sidney, Alice Kane and Joan Bodger were my elders. I hope that as you set out on your storytelling journey, you find your own teachers and elders. Bring them tea, carry them cappuccinos; most important, share the gift of your time and listening. Your gifts will come back to you tenfold in their wisdom and blessing.

⟨ SPEAKING STORY ⟩

It is a remarkable story that I have to relate.
GIOVANNI BOCCACCIO, *The Decameron*

PEOPLE ARE DRAWN TO STORYTELLING for many reasons today, and use the art in a wide range of settings. Teachers are finding new ways to make storytelling part of the classroom, public speakers adapt stories for more effective presentations, doctors and therapists use storytelling as part of their healing practice, and activists find that stories give them a new vocabulary for working towards social justice. There are also those who want, as I did, to make storytelling their livelihood. At a less formal level, there is a growing interest in storytelling as an art that flourishes in everyday life—in conversation, family lore and the oral history of local communities.

Alice Kane used to tell a story about a mother mouse who took her children with her when she went for food. She warned them to be very quiet and very careful. A fierce cat was roaming the neighbourhood, and the young mice had to follow their mother without making a peep.

They found a piece of cheese in the alleyway and were just about to pick it up when suddenly the cat sprang in front of them. The cat looked at the mother mouse's children and licked its lips. Just before it pounced, the mother mouse drew herself up to her full height (which wasn't much) and barked: BOW WOW! GRRRR! WOOF! The cat ran away, terrified. They took the cheese home and as they ate, the mother mouse said, "My children, you have learned an important lesson today. You must always know how to speak a second language."

Whatever your mother tongue, every human being speaks Story as a second language. Through the stories they carry and retell, families and communities gain the expressive capacity to speak about the things that matter most to them. Storytellers are the custodians of this language made of stories. They have the dual responsibility of sustaining and enriching the community's body of narratives, and of reminding their fellow citizens that it is to their benefit to speak Story as fluently as possible.

We learn to communicate through metaphor and image at a very young age. We learn by hearing and exchanging rhymes, songs, poems, riddles, nonsense verse, family stories, fairy tales and jokes. In this common language made of stories, we can speak about our unique experiences and feelings, however extreme or surprising they may be. In a living oral tradition, stories are the moral and imaginative frame of life itself. When the anthropologist Julie Cruikshank asked Yukon Indian women to tell their life histories, she found they invariably wanted to begin with myth and legend. "From the beginning," she writes, "several of the eldest women responded to my questions about secular events by telling traditional stories . . . Each explained that these narratives were important to record as part of her life story." Their lives, in other words, were inseparably interwoven with the myths they had inherited and kept alive.

A sense of this profound connection comes through in a comment Angela Sidney made to Cruikshank after a long recording session: "Well . . . I've tried to live my life right, just like a story." Myths helped Sidney understand, express and renew her own life and the life of her people. The stories we keep in our heads and hearts are, as Mats Rehnman and Jenny Hostetter write in *The Voice of the Story,* the "maps that allow us to understand the stream of events that make up our lives." It seems to me that this is true whether the stories you live by are ancient and traditional or spontaneously created and kept alive within families and personal memory. These maps in the form of remembered stories serve to guide us on "the paths between the worlds," in the poet Robert Bringhurst's telling phrase about Alice Kane's stories: "The paths, for instance, between the world of the village and the world of the forest; between childhood and marriage, community and solitude, and the paths between the worlds of life and death, and the worlds of waking and dreaming."

At a very practical level, an immersion in the language of stories is also an education for the tongue. We learn to use words with a heightened sense of their power and music. The words of stories have an energy and beauty that aren't required of them in normal talk. Ted Potochniak, a Toronto storyteller and gifted elementary school teacher, told his grade-four students countless folk tales. One day the worst bully in the school came to Potochniak in tears: he had chosen the wrong person to pick on. His "victim," inspired by a story, had turned on him and said, "Get thee hence, thou wicked wretch!" As Ted pointed out, if she'd retaliated with the conventional schoolyard curse—"Eff off!"—he would have known how to respond, and pounded her; but her ancient and powerful vocabulary completely undid him.

When I teach storytelling workshops, we begin by exploring the students' oral heritage. Who were the chief storytellers within your own families? Through stories, did you get to know a particular place very well, although you never saw it yourself? How did your parents meet? Responding to such questions, you realize that you come with a storytelling lineage. I also like to ask for the proverbs and sayings they grew up with. These comprise the miniatures of oral literature, and are part of our earliest education in using imaginative language. Every family has its own unique sayings and expressions.

In my own family, for example, we like to say "Get out of the car!" if anything unusual happens. As with all family sayings, there's a specific context for this one. When I was growing up in Detroit, my father sold used cars for a living. He also took night courses for many years at Wayne State University, and ended his working life as a professor of French language and literature in Toronto. However, back in his car-lot days, he had a man working for him named Jerry Morgan. Jerry was always getting pulled over by the police (or, as we say in Detroit, the *po*-lice). He was African-American, and in the 1950s that was enough of a reason to get pulled over (and still is, in too many parts of North America). When they stopped his car they'd shout, *"Get out of the car!"* and they wouldn't bother saying, "please" or "sir." Jerry subverted their bullying ways by making this his life-motto. When things went well he'd say it jubilantly. When there was trouble, it became a dirge. Then it passed into our family lore, and you will, as I say, hear it around the house whenever something note-worthy occurs.

A few other favourite examples, gathered catch-as-catch-can over the years:

Much wants more but often meets with less. From a teacher who grew up in a family of six.

Un peu de rien tout nu. (A little bit of naked nothing.) The reply of a French teacher's mother when she was asked what was for supper.

What's for you won't go by you. Friend's family proverb.

You're bored? You should pee in your shoe and watch it go through. From a teacher whose parents didn't think children should ever complain about being bored.

Slowly, slowly the egg grows legs and learns to walk. Chinese friend's family saying.

Nursery rhymes are another essential element in learning to speak Story. Nursery rhymes come with their own sub-lime music and mystery. Even when they veer towards the nonsensical, they are memorable simply because they sing on our tongues. They also evoke countless hidden and untold stories. I recently asked a group at Queen's University to respond to this traditional English rhyme:

How many miles to Babylon?
Three score miles and ten.
Can I get there by candlelight?
Yes, and back again.
If your feet be nimble and light
You can get there by candlelight.

They all caught its evocative mood of night-time or dream journeys, but it was a seventy-year-old woman in the group who said, after a thoughtful silence, "That is the number of years of a person's life." She went on to say that what she'd learned in her own three-score-and-ten-year journey by candlelight was the necessity of keeping your feet "nimble and light," that is, to be spontaneous and creative as you face whatever tragedies life throws your way. She'd caught the echo of one of the untold stories of this unforgettable rhyme.

My own early experience of stories making a frame for everyday life came through hearing and reading tales of Hodja Nasrudin. Hodja Nasrudin rode into my life on my seventh birthday, via a book sent by our Turkish relatives. He was a short, round old man whose white beard should have made him look dignified but didn't quite. He lived in the village of Ak Shahir and liked to ride through its streets on his exceedingly recalcitrant donkey, bestowing opinions, judgments and words of wisdom on his fellow citizens.

Once, for example, the villagers came to him and said, "Nasrudin, you are a 'hodja,' a learned teacher; tell us the answer to this deep philosophical question: if your house was on fire, God forbid, and you could only take one thing out, what would you take?" "I'd take out the fire," said

Hodja. Another time they came upon him contemplating the new moon, and asked, "Hodja, what happens to the old full moon?" "They cut it up," he answered, "and crumble it to make stars."

Once he took his cat to the river, and began washing it in the water. The appalled villagers said, "Hodja, what do you think you're doing? You're going to kill your poor cat by washing it that way!"

"I know how to wash cats," he said, "trust me."

But sure enough, when they came back later, the cat was dead. "We told you you'd kill your cat!" they cried.

Hodja Nasrudin was crying. "I know, I know," he said, "I killed my own cat . . . But it wasn't when I washed it; it was afterwards, when I tried to wring it out!"

Even as a kid I noticed that, although Hodja usually had the last word, it was rarely the final say. His answers and responses tended to raise questions rather than settle them. I mostly didn't get the punch-lines, but I did think Hodja was the silliest grown-up I'd ever come across. Even better, the stories have stayed in my head ever since. Long after he became my companion, I discovered that Hodja Nasrudin is one of the most famous Wise Fools of all oral literature. Stories about his lovable, exasperating, sublimely goofy exploits cross many borders. In the Middle East, tales of the Hodja are recounted by Muslims, Jews, Christians and Sufis. The thousands of stories told about Hodja (who is known by different names in different countries) make up a lexicon of wit and spiritual teaching.

Nasrudin is alive and well in modern times. My friend Mathilde Stephanian came up to me the other day with a recent Hodja story. It seems that a rich man was dying, and he wanted to take his wealth with him into the grave. He entrusted it to the lawyer, the sheik and his good friend Hodja Nasrudin. After he died, the three trustees met at the graveside. The lawyer said, "They say you can't take it with you. What does he need the money for where he's gone? I'm going to keep my share." The sheik agreed. Hodja was shocked by this, and said, "You are betraying your promise to our late friend! I, on the other hand, intend to fulfill my obligation." He took out a cheque-book, wrote a cheque and threw it into the grave.

The last time I was in Israel, pre-Intifada and treaty with Egypt, an Israeli Jew told me a Hodja story. There was a man who owned some land, and he had to go away for a while. He left it in the care of another man. This man took good care of the land. He weeded and watered it, labouring hard to make the land green and prosperous. When the owner returned he said, "You've done your work, and now the land will be mine again."

"No," said the other. "The land belongs to me now. I have made it thrive. The land is mine." They began to fight—"The land belongs to me!" "No, it is mine!"—and finally came to Hodja to solve the dispute. He lay down and put his ear in the dirt.

"What are you doing, Nasrudin?"

"I'm listening to the land," he said.

"What does the land say?" they asked scornfully.

Hodja looked up and said, "The land says that both of you belong to the land."

People have been telling these stories for centuries as an antidote to bullies, dogmas, authorities, pretension, social class. When the theocracy was being established in Iran, apparently the Ayatollah strongly disapproved of his people's love for the irrepressible Hodja. An Iranian friend of mine told me that Hodja Nasrudin was drafted into the Revolutionary Army and put on guard duty to enforce the curfew. He and a fellow-sentry saw a man running like mad through the streets of Tehran five minutes before curfew. Hodja raised his rifle and shot the poor man dead. "Are you crazy?" shouted the other guard. "He still had five minutes before curfew!" "Yes," said Hodja, "but I know where he lives. He never would have made it in time."

Hodja is still with us. I picture him astride his irreverent and unbiddable ass, turban tilting and slipping as he and his mount amble along beside the Information Superhighway. It is said that you should always tell seven Nasrudin stories at a time, so here's one more (mind you, who's counting? Hodja certainly wouldn't). Hodja rode by a computer store and asked, "What are you selling?" The salesman proudly said, "Virtual reality!" Hodja Nasrudin, who is, after all, an old man and rather hard of hearing, called back as he passed, "I'm glad to hear it! We need as much virtuous reality as we can get!"

In a living oral tradition, there are stories available in the collective memory of the community that can illuminate virtually every situation and dilemma that arise. An oral tradition is an entire body of narratives, connected one to another through shared characters, settings, cultural values.

While doing research for her film about the Grimm stories, *The Duration of Life and Other Tales from the Grimms,* the Canadian filmmaker Amy Bodman became fascinated by the inter-connective quality of stories within a tradition:

[A]lthough they are so distinct and varied, when read together they start to seem oddly connected: a character named Hans, for instance, figures in many of the stories (in one, even as a hedgehog)—but after a while, rather than being about a different character with the one name, each story begins to look as if it is about the same character, but in different forms and situations. . . . Eventually, it becomes clear that the stories aren't so much about specific events or topics as they are about the characters in them—and perhaps about those characters in us.

When you immerse yourself in the Grimms' great collection, the stories' patterns and characters start to rhyme, as it were, with the hard-to-perceive forces that shape our lives. Hans My Hedgehog connects to Hans in Luck, which connects to Clever Hans, which connects to the hedgehog-ish, lucky and clever me. Taken all together, the stories become part of a rich and complex language, a verbal tapestry in which human life in all of its complexity can be illuminated. Bodman describes this cross-pollination of life and story as analogous to the familiar experience of hearing a timely tune on the radio:

A story is best remembered when the listener feels it is his or her own story that is being told. A song on the radio heard for the first time may move one simply because it seems to have something to do with one's own life, though what that is may be almost impossible to articulate.

If the radio tunes make the background music of our dramatic lives, the stories we retell are a background narrative.

When real life and Story touch, it is as perfectly timely and moving as when we hear "our" song on the radio.

There are some experiences in life where stories provide the only language powerful enough to touch the unbearable intensity of the moment. In *The Crack in the Teacup,* Joan Bodger remembers the trauma of her daughter Lucy's illness. They had shared countless fairy tales together, and the Narnia books. They were still able to speak Story when other, lesser words failed them:

> Next day, when I visited, Lucy's head was swathed in bandages. She was drinking through a glass straw, bent at an angle. "Just like the Romans," she said, "Lying down and drinking at the same time." She cracked a crooked smile. She was being funny. Then, matter-of-factly, *"Did I almost die?"*
>
> Awful temptation: "Who gave you that idea?" or, "Don't worry. You're going to be all right." Instead: *"Yes. You almost died."* Lucy sighed, satisfied. Perception confirmed! "It was like in 'Childe Rowland,'" she told me. *In the Dark Tower. The big ruby turning and turning in the warm air* . . . I had filled her mind and Ian's with stories for a rainy day. That-which-could-not-be-talked-about came tumbling out in nuggets of imagery—fairy gold! Coin of the realm, it was the only way to make exchange, to communicate the enormity of what was happening to us.

Later, tragically, the cancer returned. A day or two before her death, Lucy told her mother: "I feel as though I'm going on a trip to Narnia . . . I just wish they'd hurry up so I can get on with it and go on the trip. And if I go to Narnia

I'll send you a postcard, 'Having a wonderful time.'" *The Chronicles of Narnia* didn't, as nothing could, mitigate the family's grief, but they did give mother and daughter a language of Story through which to talk about it.

As you develop your storytelling repertoire, it's important to realize that you are building on a foundation that you started creating in childhood. Each story you learn will add a new quality, depth and fluency to a second language you began to master when you first played peek-a-boo.

It's amazing what you see when you're out without
your gun.

Canadian proverb

A STORYTELLER IS ALWAYS collecting ideas, words,
phrases, stories. Only some of them are destined for your
repertoire. The rest are equally valuable, although you
may never tell them in public. These are the stories that
inform your moral philosophy, tune your tongue and ear,
and help stretch your imagination. You find them in
family experiences, in your neighbourhood, in the newspaper. Storytellers dowse narrative material from a wide
range of wellsprings. The story collecting described in
this chapter is more serendipitous than systematic. It is
a matter of walking through life with open ears and a
story-seeking soul.

One of the first things that will catch your attention as
a hunter and gatherer of oral literature is the sheer originality of spoken language in everyday life. Everywhere I
go I hear delicious turns of phrase, hilarious slips of the

tongue, wonderfully imaginative words of mouth. Since I'm a packrat, I always write down what I hear and add it to my ever-growing book of quotes. Just the other day, sitting in my favourite café, I overheard a young woman say this enigmatic phrase to her friend: "'Cause the reason was, my mom had another lover." It was so irresistibly intriguing that it went directly into my quotebook. I imagine countless untold stories held in that one line. I only record phrases and saying that have a certain music running through the words. Here are three recent examples from my own family:

"They taste like shoes and smell like socks." Jacob describing my attempt at mushroom-flavoured risotto.

"You did what? To who? For how many Oreo cookies?" Nathaniel, age 14, to a friend on the phone.

"It's all in the pencil!" Jacob, age 10, writing a story at a Toronto café.

I collect these phrases with all the joy of a gem collector finding a new ruby or emerald. They demonstrate how much spontaneity and creativity can be found in the flow of daily conversation. They also distill entire stories—or possible stories—into miniature form. "Your mother's got *another* lover?" I wanted to ask the woman at Dooney's Café. "Isn't one enough?" But, being discreet, I kept my mouth shut and my ears open.

Sometimes these phrases do wind up in a story. I was once at a youth hostel in London, England. A group of men were playing Arabic music in the common room, and noticed me listening. One of them asked me, "You are an Arab?" "Not exactly," I explained. "I was born in Detroit, I live in Toronto, my mother's Romanian, my grandparents are Polish, Russian, Romanian, and Turkish, and I'm a Jew." He said he was from Algeria, and we started talking, as travellers do. The evening went by quickly. Before going to sleep, I said to him, "See you in the morning." He answered with the traditional Muslim response: "*Inshallah*—Allah willing!" I smiled and said, "Is it necessary to say 'God willing' even for one night?' He gripped my arm and said, with real intensity, "A man does not know the hour of his own death." I never forgot his proverb, and it became part of the Storyteller's final speech to the King in my tale "The Storyteller At Fault" (see the Stories section of this book, page 251).

In this realm of oral poetry, every schoolyard in the world becomes a mini-festival of rhymes, poems and songs at recess time. Iona and Peter Opie begin their famous book *The Lore and Language of Schoolchildren* by stating, "The scraps of lore which children learn from each other are at once more real, more immediately serviceable, and more vastly entertaining to them than anything which they learn from grown-ups." Storytellers would do well to listen in on this daily and exuberant linguistic celebration. For one thing, these rhymes help tune your tongue and can add new music to your telling. For another, they connect you directly to one of the few sources of living oral tradition in our society. Lastly, they are windows back to your own childhood.

The children in my neighbourhood grew up chanting this inspired bit of nonsense:

Ladies and jellybeans
hoboes and tramps
cross-eyed mosquitoes
and bow-legged ants
I come before you
to stand behind you
to speak of something
I know nothing about!

The mock introduction was often followed by a speech:

One fine day in the middle of the night
Two dead boys got up to fight
Back to back they faced each other
Pulled their guns and shot each other
A deaf policeman heard the noise
And came and shot those two dead boys,
If you don't believe my story's true
Ask the blind man, he saw it, too.

We counted out with:

Engine, engine number nine
Goin' down the Chicago line
If the train should jump the track
Do you want your money back
Yes, no, maybe, y-e-s spells yes!

For a sense of how these rhymes and sayings can enrich a child's life and provide a background for anyone who loves literature, read Alice Kane's *Songs and Sayings of an Ulster Childhood,* edited by Canadian folklorist Edith Fowke. It is Kane's memoir of growing up in Belfast, her childhood framed by an extraordinary wealth of oral poetry, proverbs and music. Alice Kane writes, "It's impossible to describe the riches poured on the children of my day. Every grown-up in the family contributed riddle or joke or book or story to inform or amuse or correct." Describing her own belief that life must be faced courageously and with a high heart, she would often quote her favourite childhood saying: It is a poor heart that never rejoices.

I was walking along St. Clair Avenue once, with two five-year-old boys and a seven-year old girl trailing behind. They were chanting an innocent-sounding verse and laughing hysterically. I turned to see what all the commotion was about. The rhyme said: Milk milk lemonade / Push the button, chocolate cake. As they sang, they touched their chests, then where they pee, and finally the place out back where, as we say around here, "the sun don't shine." As children master their inheritance of oral lore, they quickly learn that one of its uses is to mock and experiment with the mysterious rules and taboos of the adult world. At the age of six, my youngest son came home from school delighted with a new poem:

> In the land of Oz,
> where the ladies wear no bras,
> the men don't care,
> they're not wearing underwear,
> there's a hole in the wall,
> where the children see it all.

This same child, at three, discovered riddles. He didn't know how they worked yet, but he revelled in the fact that he could stump a roomful of adults with a peculiar-sounding question. He made this one up, and it worked every time: *What's brown and red and pink and blue and black and white and red and yellow?* What? we asked with futile hope. *A donkey,* he chortled gleefully.

I love riddles, myself, and often use them to start story-telling sessions. Riddles are wonderful collector's tools. If you pose a riddle to a group, especially of children, chances are you'll hear a few back. Here's one of my favourites, collected from a Jamaican boy in a suburban school:

> The schoolhouse is green,
> the hallway is white,
> the classroom is red,
> the students are black, brown, and white.

The riddle is particularly timely in a multicultural society. The answer is: *A watermelon.*

As storytellers, the value of revisiting these rhymes and riddles is first of all the sheer pleasure of hearing such glorious oral poetry bubbling up in playgrounds, kitchens and backyards. We also learn that language is by its very nature a musical experience. The meaning of words cannot be separated from the tune that carries them from tongue to ear. Storytelling is an oral medium. Your voice and the language of your story must engage and hold the ear of your listener as fully as a sonata, a jazz riff, a gospel song or a piece of hiphop. If all the language in your story sounded the same, how would the listener's ear distinguish the prelude from the climax, or the moment of greatest suspense from the casual throw-away line?

Storytellers often read their daily newspapers with a pair of scissors close by. I'm always on the lookout for old tall tales, ghost stories and yarns that resurface as modern news reports. I have a whole folderful of such clippings. I collect them because they represent traces of living oral tradition in our everyday lives. Here are three from the files, collected most unsystematically over the years.

Nova Scotia Woman Finds Froggie Surprise in her Frozen Peas (Sherbrooke, Nova Scotia—Canadian Press): Jackie Silver isn't making her children eat their greens any more. Not after finding a dead frog mixed in with a bag of frozen McCain's peas a short time ago. "I went to stir them when they were halfway through cooking and I saw this thing," Silver said. "Most of the kids started crying. Most of them will only eat peas so I don't know what I'm going to do now." Silver hasn't had much of an appetite since finding the little fellow, she said. "The sad thing is it's missing its legs, so I don't know if it's in the peas somewhere or if it's already been consumed. . . . I didn't want to know for sure." A spokesperson for frozen food giant McCain's said the company was investigating.

Kitty Mauls Senior (Trois-Rivières-Ouest, Quebec—Canadian Press): Four carloads of police, two ambulances and an animal control officer were needed to control a cat that mauled an elderly man. The commotion in the apartment was so great that police responded in force believing they were dealing with a domestic dispute. They found Gerard Daigle and Francine Gagnon, both in their eighties, cornered in their bathroom by Touti, a caramel-coloured feline. The cat was spooked by water when

Daigle turned on the shower to bathe his parrot, the animal control officer said yesterday. Guy Theriault, who finally captured the cat, said it was scared and reacted with force. "It was scared of the water," he said, "It felt threatened." Daigle was jumped by Touti on Tuesday just after he had given his parrot a shower. Hearing her husband's cries, Gagnon beat the cat off him with a broom as it clawed him in several places, inflicting deep scratches. The couple barricaded the bathroom door with a broom and cowered there. The cat, which weighed about four kilos, was put down and an autopsy was ordered.

Girl Turns Orange from Drink (from *The Globe and Mail*): A 5-year-old girl in north Wales has turned orange after over-imbibing Sunny Delight, a popular fruit drink that contains significant levels of beta carotene. The child's face and hands turned orange after she consumed three litres of the drink per day.

I read all of these in my morning newspaper. Each story has something memorably absurd in it. The fact that a family whose children eat only peas has the misfortune to find a frog in their pea package, or that the poor senior citizen was "jumped by Touti on Tuesday"—you have to laugh. On the other hand, if I ever read these clippings aloud to groups of adults, someone invariably has known somebody whose kid also turned orange (or green, or purple) from drinking too much pop, or who found a mouse/frog/rat or other inappropriate visitor in their fast food. Often cautionary in nature (don't drink too much Sunny Delight, don't eat too much fast food, and mind the cat when you're cleaning your parrot), these stories, true or not, are part of the oral literature of everyday life. They are, in their wonderfully weird way, a tribute to the irrepressible strength of the spoken word. Scholars like Jan Brundvand, author of *The Vanishing Hitch-hiker,* and Gail de Vos in her collection *Tales, Rumors, and Gossip: Exploring Contemporary Folk Literature in Grades 7–12,* have shown that virtually all of our modern urban legends have an ancient lineage. There were undoubtedly rumours circulating around Rome about a rat found in an amphora of wine, and scholars have shown that the Roman soldiers around their campfires were already telling versions of the Ghostly Hitchhiker. It reminds me of the old proverb about the bad penny always showing up. So it is with the oral tradition, even here, even now.

In 1995 I attended the war crimes trial of Imre Finta. Courtrooms are fascinating places from a storyteller's perspective. A person stands up in court and has the chance to tell his/her version of the truth. A prisoner can give her word and be granted "parole," from the French for "spoken word." Finta was the first person to be tried under Canada's war crimes legislation. He was accused of being in charge of the gendarmerie in his small Hungarian town. On his watch, close to nine thousand of his fellow citizens—Jews and inmates from the local asylum—were corralled by his officers in a brickyard conveniently located by the train tracks. These "undesirables" were loaded under his supervision onto trains bound for Poland and Germany. Very few of them ever came back.

He was eventually acquitted, though, as far as I could tell, the jury didn't seem to doubt that he was indeed the man who did the appalling deeds. But it is far easier to convict a mugger than someone like Finta, who was, after all, the most minor cog in the machinery of the Third Reich. Apparently he carried out his duties with no special anti-Semitic enthusiasm or Nazi fervour. He wasn't even a member of the party; just a small-town policeman who followed his conscience. Unfortunately, his conscience said *Obey*. The consequence of this kind of obedience was, as we know now, the destruction of several thousand lives from his town, and several million more across Europe.

I went to the trial because I wanted to hear the stories people told. At times, it seemed that memory itself was the real defendant, not the feeble, harmless-looking ex-captain. Each witness took the stand, testifying in Hungarian-accented English or through a translator about things they'd seen or experienced almost fifty years before, mostly in a state of paralyzing terror. The bridge of remembrance seemed rickety indeed as the defense lawyer questioned every detail: "Eight bodies in front of the police station? But in your first deposition you mentioned only six. I submit that you are not able to accurately recollect the events of that particular day." Even so, piece by tortured piece, the story slowly emerged. The brickyard was a hellish place, filled with women and children and mental patients. Their men had already been taken away. They had little food, no shelter, they'd lost their homes; most of them would end up in the death camps that lay at the end of the track.

Curiously, there was one detail that appeared in almost every testimony. The captain, rather vain as he lorded it over his brickyard empire, liked to wear beautifully polished black riding boots. He'd stand on a platform in the middle of his heartbroken charges, and even decades later they all remembered him by those impossibly brilliant boots. The black boots shone so that you could almost see your reflection in them. The witnesses were as old as their former nemesis. They told their stories patiently at the trial, knowing, I suppose, that soon enough they'd be gone and the story would be the only thing left. And perhaps that was the real value of the trial—not to convict or acquit, but to bear witness: remember and retell.

The stories of people's life-experiences make a rich and inexhaustible source of inspiration for storytellers as I find each time I do another Telling Bee. Life itself is, of course, one big Telling Bee. Extraordinary stories are exchanged constantly—at work, around the kitchen table, on long car-rides. Storytellers keep an ear cocked for these sagas and legends of human life, including their own; they are often able to make them memorable in conversation. The Israeli storyteller Shlomo Abbas once told me the mark of a great storyteller was that he or she could keep him entertained not only from the stage, but also during the cab-ride on the way to the concert hall. "Experience which is passed on from mouth to mouth is the source from which all storytellers have drawn," wrote Walter Benjamin in his superb essay "The Storyteller." Of all the arts, storytelling is perhaps the one that draws most deeply from this pool of shared human experience.

If your hunting and gathering takes you near the story traditions of aboriginal peoples, it's wise to remember that oral culture has its own decorum and unwritten principles. Although many Native stories have been published in books, both by Native writers and by non-Native anthropologists, ethnographers and writers, there is still a strong feeling, at least in Canada, that these stories should be approached with great respect by people from outside the tradition. It's not enough to simply learn a First Nations story from a book. Go spend time with the elders. Sit and listen. Pay attention to their stories, even if you don't always follow the narrative thread. Elders have a way of leading you not to where you think you should get to but to where they think you need to go. Above all, don't interrupt!

On visits to the Yukon, I'd sometimes hear Angela Sidney tell old-time stories from her Tagish and Tlingit traditions. If I, running on big-city time, jumped in with a question, she'd shush me and retell the parts she was afraid I might have missed in my impatience. When I was editing *Next Teller: A Book of Canadian Storytelling,* the Anishnabe storyteller Gilbert Oskaboose allowed me to include some of his stories about Nanabush. In doing so he warned me eloquently and in no uncertain terms not to change the stories in any way: "These are ancient and sacred tales of the northern Ojibway and I hold them in trust—temporarily." As they were passed on to him, so must they be kept intact for the next reader or listener.

If you do learn about Native oral traditions only from books, you should know that in Canada and around the world there has been a recent flourishing of creativity by aboriginal authors, editors, historians and filmmakers. Tellers from many different First Nations have found a way to bring their living oral traditions into literary form. Alexander Wolfe, in the preface to his extraordinary book *Earth Elder Stories,* explains the difficult path that led to his decision to write in English, not Saulteaux, the oral stories of his people:

To be responsible for retelling the stories of the grandfathers today, the Anishnaybay must renew their commitment to the oral tradition. At the same time, we must turn to a written tradition and use it to support, not destroy, our oral tradition. The structure of our society in the days when the grandfathers were still with us was very different from what we have today. Information and instruction were transmitted to us orally, in story form, by our old people. Listening and absorbing what was told required great lengths of time. The use of the mind and memory were important; this is why the stories were told over and over again. The environment of that time held nothing to distract the listener and the storyteller. Today many things distract the listener and disrupt the storytelling. Radio, television, video, and printed material take precedence in the everyday lives of many children, and even the adults, in our present society. We are ceasing to be storytellers and listeners, and in so doing we are losing that great virtue called patience, so strongly emphasized by the grandfathers. If we are to preserve the stories that contain our history we must restore the art, practice, and principles of oral storytelling. We must also commit our oral history to written form. That written form, however, must still comply with the wishes and aspirations of the grandfathers, now long gone from our numbers.

After long consideration, Wolfe created a written record that he felt honoured his tradition: "The prime responsibility of the storyteller or oral historian, therefore, is to ensure that the stories are preserved intact and unaltered. To take out or add content to these stories destroys the truth found therein." However much non-native storytellers love these splendid creation myths, histories and teaching stories, they must not assume that their affinity guarantees the right to retell them. And if you do work with traditional Native narratives, whether you meet them orally or in print, remember Alexander Wolfe's warning and take the care necessary to preserve and respect them.

One of the deepest impulses of a story collector is to keep stories alive that might otherwise disappear unheard. Yaffa Eliach, in her collection *Hasidic Tales of the Holocaust*, described both survivors' desire to tell their stories and her own impulse to record them as a powerful imperative. "Many a time, on a New York subway or on an international flight, strangers have walked over to say how grateful they are for the opportunity to tell their children, and posterity, of their suffering during the war. Some speak in torrents, others in a few restrained sentences." As a collector and editor of these stories, Eliach "constantly sensed that the tale entrusted to me was a living witness, a quivering soul. The painful spoken words were a memorial to a family, to a mother, father, brothers, sisters, the only testimony to their ever having existed on this blood-soaked earth. Now the responsibility rested with me, to pass on the legacy of their lives and deaths. If the tale fails, the only imprint of their existence will be a patch of blackened sky and a handful of scattered ashes." This instinct to give voice to what must never be forgotten lends extra purpose to every storyteller who ventures forth to hunt and gather the world's stories.

There's an old Jewish joke about a rabbi who was renowned for his storytelling ability. He always seemed to have the right story for any moment that arose in life. His student, marvelling at the rabbi's great skill, once asked him the secret. How did he know what story to tell, and when, and to whom? The rabbi, not surprisingly, answered: That reminds me of a story!

There was once a young man who went off to become a great sharpshooter. He studied for years, mastering every skill of marksmanship. Finally, after graduating at the top of his class, he wanted to ride home and show his parents and friends his fantastic ability. As he was riding along, he passed through a little village. On the side of the road was a broken-down barn. On the side of the barn somebody had painted one hundred targets. And, to the young man's amazement, in the middle of each target someone had shot a perfect bull's-eye. He couldn't believe his eyes. Reining in his horse, he stared and stared at this incredible sight. Then he looked around the poor village. He called out, "Who has done this great feat? Where is the world's greatest sharpshooter?" A little girl walked across the road. "I did it," she said, scuffling her shoes in the sand. "You?" he said. "I can't believe it. I've studied for years, I've learned every skill of sharpshooting; but even I could never do such a thing. What's your secret, little girl?" "Let me explain," she said. "You see, I don't draw the target first. First I shoot, then I draw the target."

Where the joke ends, the commentary begins. In the American storyteller Penninah Schram's telling, it is the Dubner Maggid (a famous travelling rabbi and teacher in the eighteenth century) who tells the parable. He explains, "I don't always know the right story for the subject being discussed. What I do is read many stories, and listen to many stories, and remember all of these stories. Then when I find a story I want to tell, I introduce the subject that leads me into telling that perfect story."

The message might equally be that when you go through life with a headful of good stories, it's never hard to find a moment that seems to call for that story, whether you plan it or not. The stories are there, waiting to be heard and overheard. Our mission as storytellers is to gather them, story by story, until one day you find you have, indeed, a story to tell for every occasion.

⋞ THUNDER OVER THE LIBRARY ⋟

A story is a letter that comes to us from yesterday.
Each man who tells it adds his word to the message
and sends it on to tomorrow.

G. AND H. PAPASHVILY, Yes and No Stories

FOR MOST CONTEMPORARY STORYTELLERS the local library is our elder. Much of my repertoire has been harvested and adapted from written sources. As the storytelling renaissance grows, there are more and more stories to be gathered from other tellers' books—always with their permission, of course. But there are also more and more live sources, traditional tellers active in many parts of the world, and they usually welcome new listeners and even apprentices. A story that comes to you that way, directly via the oral tradition, will often set deep roots in your life and repertoire.

I remember hearing the great Anishnabe storyteller and historian Basil Johnston telling a story nearly thirty years ago. Somehow, even though I don't have a particularly good memory, his words went straight in, and I've been able to remember the story verbatim ever since. Mind you, even when you remember a story perfectly, it's no guarantee you'll be able to tell it. Augusta Baker, one of the finest tellers of the twentieth century, came to a library where I was teaching a class. She told "The Woodcutter of Gura," an Ethiopian story by Harold Courlander in his book *The Fire on the Mountain*. She reduced—or elevated—us to helpless laughter with her deadpan rendition of the story. I swore to myself I'd learn it, and I've tried and tried—but it just won't come to my tongue. Yet I've got her telling deeply and unforgettably inscribed in my soul.

Besides these rare experiences of direct oral transmission, most of us contemporary tellers find our stories in books. In an oral culture you have the chance to hear many tellers tell stories on many occasions, but in the library it's different: you must develop your own strategies for finding, sifting, evaluating and choosing stories. I've included a brief compendium of my own eclectic sources (including full information on all the books mentioned and quoted) at the back of this book, but any comprehensive 398.2—folk and fairy tales—section will offer a treasure house of traditional oral literature.

The most important thing to remember as you search through old and new books is that there are no official editions of traditional stories; only versions upon versions, a multiplicity of tellings and translations and adaptations. From this wide-open field you may select the ones that best suit your own telling style and philosophy. I'd like to suggest a certain approach that, while it isn't particularly methodical or scholarly, does give an inner sense of a story's quality. This approach is based on paying attention to pattern. The question to ask is this: Does the author present his/her story with the pattern intact, or are you getting a diminished, less-realized telling? To make this question useful, you need to know several versions of the story you're thinking of learning. While this doesn't necessarily mean becoming a folklorist or scholar, it does mean spending unhurried time in the stacks, following the trail of the story wherever it leads.

As you skim, browse and make your way around 398.2, you will notice that the boundaries of the books you find there are amazingly porous. The same story pattern shows up in a collection from China and in an Irish variant, translated from Ashanti and in a Yiddish accent, told by Scheherazade and by an Ojibway elder. Hodja Nasrudin from Turkey reappears as Juha in Morocco, one of the fools of Chelm in Poland, and, with more wisdom than foolishness, as King Akbar's counsellor Birbal in India. The story is never exactly the same, of course—the words change, the names of the characters vary, the events take on local colouring—but enough of the pattern remains intact for you to recognize the story across the range of its various expressions. It is like a slipknot on a much-spliced rope: hemp or nylon, the knot keeps its own integrity. Not only that, but within a specific national tradition the same story title can bespeak a surprisingly diverse set of tellings ("Cinderella" by Perrault, for example, differs mightily from the earthy French peasant version). And even within the work of a single author—Wilhelm Grimm is the most famous example—a story can be rewritten through succeeding editions (see *One Fairy Story Too Many* by John Ellis for a critical perspective on the Grimms' propensity for rewrites). The patterns of traditional stories seem designed to outlast any particular interpretation of them.

They act as narrative force-fields, generating and defining a number of possible tellings.

A. B. Lord, in his classic study of the bardic tradition *The Singer of Tales*, refers to the "multiformity" of oral literature. He and Milman Parry travelled through the highlands of Yugoslavia exploring a still-living world of epic storytelling. They observed that in an oral milieu there was no fixed and standard text of a given tale, no "authorized edition." There is a living and interconnected web of all the stories a teller has heard, heard of, and performed. The essential pattern of an oral tale lives not as a static entity but, in Lord's telling phrase, through the "constant re-creation of it." A traditional storyteller learns, perforce, to cultivate a tenacious regard for these patterns, which underlie and unify his/her tradition. David Bynum, in his book *The Daemon in the Wood* writes, in the same vein as Lord: "The text of oral narrative is the whole tradition, not the single tale." Only by hearing the same story told in several ways by several tellers do you come to understand its deepest patterns.

Lord describes the working conditions of his Yugoslavian bards, and one can sense the power of their commitment to pattern as the basis of their art. They typically performed in roadside cafés: "The farmers of the nearby villages drop in . . . They come and go. The townspeople join them. There are shopkeepers and caravan drivers who have come in with merchandise . . . They are a critical audience." Critical, gossipy and restless—with an audience like that it's no wonder each telling was different. These epic singers had to be masters of improvisation, able to reweave strands of narrative, to stretch or condense, to bring on the battle scene when the inebriated shepherd started calling for a round of double rakis—and all without missing a beat on the gusle. Half the time they didn't even get to finish; as Lord drily notes, the reason why "different singings of the same song by the same man vary most in their endings is that the end of a song is sung less often by the singer."

Yet despite (or more likely because of) this lively and sophisticated multiformity, the Yugoslav bard would always claim to be faithful to his source, namely, to the traditional form of his tale. As Lord says, "His idea of stability, to which he is deeply devoted, does not include the wording, which to him has never been fixed, nor the unessential parts of the story. He builds his performance . . . on the stable skeleton of narrative." The traditional narrator holds firm to the belief that the story must be passed on undiminished. This commitment to the idea of the story's integrity is affirmed by the contemporary Scottish storyteller Duncan Williamson: "You may think it strange that I don't make up any stories. I couldn't, suppose you paid me for it. I can make up a song of the present day but it's just not within me to make up a story. I wouldn't believe it!" Williamson's book is titled *The Broonie, Silkies, and Fairies.* "For this ye knowen al so wel as I," writes Chaucer for his still-oral audience, before recounting the tales of the Canterbury pilgrims:

> Whoso shal telle a tale after a man
> He moot reherce [as near] as ny as evere he kan
> Everich a word, if it be in his charge,
> Al speke he never so rudeliche [rudely] and large
> Or ellis he moot telle his tale untrewe,
> Or feyne [feign, pretend] thing, or fynde wordes newe.

That is, the storyteller must retell every word as closely as he can, or else he's just fabricating the whole thing. And Lord again: "If the singer [or storyteller] changes what he has heard in its essence, he falsifies truth."

Devotion, belief, truth, falsehood—it's clear that more is at stake than mere telling styles. Let me take these ideas from the world of the bards back to 398.2, my world of books. As I search for a story to make my own, I read a host of translations, adaptations, transcriptions; and I'm faced with the problem of choosing (or sometimes reworking) one version above the rest. How can one decide which author or editor does the best justice to a story's stable skeleton of narrative when you meet its multiforms in print?

Take "Ali Baba and the Forty Thieves." You can find many versions of this story in the library. I'll use two of them as my examples; both are by contemporary writers who have adapted their stories from previously published English translations.

The authors, Laurence Housman and Geraldine McCaughrean, agree on the main sequence of events, but they differ on what happened in Ali Baba's courtyard on a certain dark and dangerous Arabian night. Here is the background: A travelling oil merchant has begged Ali Baba to put him up for the night. He is none other than the notorious chief of the robbers, come with his men to wreak a bloody vengeance on the man who discovered their secret treasure cave. After the false villain goes to bed, Ali Baba's servant girl Marjanah goes out to borrow a measure of oil from one of the jars. She discovers that they contain not oil but thirty-seven robbers (there used to be forty, but two have already been executed by their colleagues, and the chief is asleep in the house). Finding one jar with real oil and knowing any alarm would be futile, the resourceful Marjanah fills a cauldron with oil from the genuine jar and boils it in the kitchen. She returns to the courtyard and, in Housman's spare telling, pours into each jar "a sufficient quantity of the boiling oil to scald its occupant to death."

This is the customary way of recounting the scene, dating back to the story's appearance in Antoine Galland's French collection of 1704. Marjanah's actions are extreme, cruel, efficient—but one must not forget that these men were no cupcakes. They were crouching in the empty jars with drawn daggers, awaiting their chief's signal to commence their bloody attack.

In her version of the story, McCaughrean tells the scene differently. On finding the hidden robbers (here numbering thirty-nine, the two executions having been deleted), Marjanah "fetched a large cream cheese from the kitchen and stopped up the breathing holes in all the thirty-nine jars which spoke."

It is a small detail in a long and complex story, this substitution of cream cheese for boiling oil as Marjanah's instrument of retribution. McCaughrean doesn't explain why she makes the change. One can only wonder if a squeamish editor suggested that today's readers would find the traditional method of robber elimination too violent, and that death-by-dairy-product is somehow more humane and palatable.

Even though it seems like a small change, it affects the deepest patterns of the story. Marjanah becomes for that moment not a strong, courageous, smart heroine, but a character in a cartoon. The scene becomes self-consciously ludicrous. Oil might have done the trick, but you will never get me to believe that a big, mean robber would simply wilt into oblivion under a suffocating mass of cheese. Unless, that is, the author wants me to think the whole thing's just a joke. But I don't want to laugh at Marjanah, I'm drawn to her adventurous charm. I like her fierce and implacable. She reminds me of other characters in Story— Odysseus, Anansi, Brer Rabbit, Coyote, the English Molly Whuppie, even Hodja Nasrudin. She is cut from the same cloth. Like all tricksters in oral literature, Marjanah prefers to turn evil against itself, using her enemy's strength to destroy him. Earlier in the tale, on finding a strange mark on her door, she marks all the doors on the street in the same way, thus turning the thieves' sign into her own best camouflage. Here in the courtyard it makes perfect trickster sense to kill the robbers with the very oil they have displaced.

By giving Marjanah a silly, implausible deed to perform, this teller makes her less heroic, less consistent within her own story, and therefore less connected to her trickster colleagues throughout oral tradition. Even such a small detail as how to get rid of a gang of robbers turns out to be part of the story's "stable skeleton of narrative." I do not choose to tell this version.

Another collector, Ethel Phelps, wrote in the introduction to her book of stories, *The Maid of the North*: "In giving the older tales of our heritage a fresh retelling for this generation of readers, I have exercised the traditional storyteller's privilege. I have shaped each tale, sometimes adding or omitting details, to reflect my sense of what makes it a satisfying tale." A small alarm bell went off when I read this: it sounds like a "privilege" or prerogative no traditional teller would ever claim, let alone publicize. They would make the quite different assertion that they are faithfully passing along the story exactly as it had been given to them. Phelps describes her version of the Russian wonder tale "Maria Morevna" as being "compressed to make a smoother flow of narrative." It is worth comparing Phelps's telling to the older version collected by the great Russian folklorist Afanas'ev, which I read in a translation by Norbert Guterman.

In Afanas'ev, the story begins with the dying wishes of an old Tsar and Tsarevna. They summon their four children—the princesses Olga, Anna, and Maria, and Prince Ivan—and they ask Ivan to be sure his sisters find good husbands. When the parents die, this rather patriarchal premise is immediately put to the test: three supernatural suitors come courting—Falcon, Eagle and Raven. They ask Ivan to give his sisters as brides. Ivan refuses to exercise the authority his parents seemed to confer on him, and which the bird-knights expect him to possess. He avers that he cannot choose on behalf of his sisters. The three sisters choose on their own to depart with their respective bridegrooms, and Prince Ivan is left alone.

Later, Ivan sets off to visit his sisters, and comes to the battle camp of the warrior queen Maria Morevna. Maria Morevna has just slain an entire army of male soldiers. When Prince Ivan shows up in front of her tent she greets him with a curious challenge: "Hail, prince. Whither is God taking you? And is it of your own will or by compulsion?" To which the young seeker responds, "Brave knights do not travel by compulsion"—which is surely the proper heroic answer to give a beautiful warrior queen, even though our young hero is about to spend the rest of the story discovering that brave men and women travel both by compulsion *and* according to their freely chosen destinies. Maria Morevna replies in her matter-of-fact style, "Well, if you are not in a hurry, rest in my tents," and so makes her own free choice of Ivan as her lover.

Before the Afanas'ev version allows Ivan to reach intimacy, he has been made to pass a sequence of tests. He is shown refusing to exercise power over women, although it is expected of him, and the consequence of his refusal is to find himself sisterless and alone. He is shown in the roles of a son, a brother, a man who doesn't force his will on women, a man connected through his sisters to supernatural beings, and a seeker on his own behalf. All of this qualifies him for his encounter with his mate-to-be.

In the Phelps version this complex prologue is missing. As she tells it the story begins with Maria Morevna's succession to her father's throne:

> She had inherited her kingdom from her father, and her father, very wisely, had trained her not only to govern well, but also to defend the kingdom against enemy armies. Many princes sought to marry her, thinking to gain control of the country. Maria Morevna refused them all. One day the young Prince Alexey rode in from the south and said he wished to serve in the army of Maria Morevna. The long and the short of it was—they fell in love, and the marriage took place three months later at the palace . . .

I notice small changes first. Maria Morevna is portrayed here not as a full-blown warrior queen but as the product of her father's training. Phelps doesn't let her choose the boy ("they" fall in love), nor does she let them hop into her tent *tout de suite;* she interpolates a more decorous period of three months.

The big change here is that she truncates the prince's rite of passage. In Phelps, Prince Alexey simply rides in "from the south." He has no history. He does not earn the right to his intimacy with so formidable a heroine as Maria Morevna. Because the prince has made fewer and less significant choices, Maria Morevna's choice of him as her husband seems also diminished and trivial.

Later in both tellings of the story, the prince is put to the ultimate test. In Phelps and Afanas'ev, Maria Morevna is abducted by her erstwhile prisoner, Koschey the Deathless Wizard (who was liberated from her dungeon by none other than her own unsuspecting, kindhearted husband, Ivan/Alexey). The prince rides forth to find her again, but Koschey proves to be a most dangerous foe. In the Afanas'ev version, he kills Prince Ivan on his third attempt to win back Maria Morevna: "Koschey galloped off, overtook Prince Ivan, cut him into tiny pieces, and put the pieces in a tarred barrel, reinforced it with iron hoops, threw it into the blue sea, and carried Maria Morevna off to his house." Having read my way through 398.2, I'm not worried about the difficult straits the pieces of our hero find themselves in. Death is only a temporary obstacle in a wonder tale, and Ivan is, after all, connected to those powerful brothers-in-law. Earlier in the story Ivan had found his sisters again, and left with them silver tokens to remember him by. At the moment of his death these tokens turn black. Falcon, Raven and Eagle fly forth to rescue and restore the young hero, literally re-membering him with their magic powers, and so making possible his continued search for Maria Morevna.

In Phelps, because her prince has no history before marrying Maria Morevna, he has neither sisters nor supernatural helpers to come to him in his moment of need. Three unusual, pattern-breaking things happen in her telling of this scene. The first is that Prince Alexey does not die. He begs for his life and is spared: "As the wizard swung his sword high, Alexey cried out, 'When I gave you the third jar of water you promised me my life!' The sword stopped in midair. 'Very well,' snarled the wizard. 'I will not kill you.' And he gave orders for Alexey to be put into a large cask . . ." I find these are strange things for a hero and an evil wizard to do. Fairy-tale heroes and heroines don't often beg for their lives. In fact, in the whole Folk and Fairy Tales section of the library, this is the only case I've ever come across. It is simply not done. Oral tradition likes its heroes courageous, uncalculating, spontaneously generous and, most of all, ready to die for their deeply held beliefs. Prince Alexey, by putting a value on his own life, by showing himself unwilling to die for his love, by having second thoughts about the whole affair, is just plain craven by the standards of traditional wonder tales. Phelps has broken the pattern that connects her prince to the other passionate and noble seekers, warriors and lovers of oral literature. As for Koschey, there, too, the pattern falters. No evil ogre, wizard or bad guy in 398.2 has ever spared his enemy's life, no matter how hard they begged.

The prince still winds up inside the cask, however, and this leaves Phelps with the problem of narrating him out of it. This is the third and strangest moment of all. Her Prince Alexey has no organic and familial link with the world of magic. Who will extricate him from the barrel?

As she tells it, "Now, it happened the next day that a hawk, an eagle, and a crow, seeing the cask floating in the sea, became curious and pulled it to shore." In 398.2, magic never "happens" to happen. Magical beings, or even a trio of birds, do not simply float across the scenery looking for heroes to rescue. Though these are called wonder tales, the "wonder" appears sparingly and always with strong reason. If beings with supernatural power do appear, however suddenly and unexpectedly (a magical wolf, a horse of power), they stick around long enough to turn into real characters, not simply to serve as creaky deus ex machina. Magic is more than a device to advance the plot, or peel open a barrel.

In making what she claims is a "smoother flow of narrative," this writer has muffled the story's voice and reduced its range of expression. Her prince is less heroic, her heroine less compelling for choosing such an inconsequential, unmagical man. As for Falcon, Eagle and Raven, they are cut off from their magical roots, deprived of their mysterious and magnificent power.

And who are these strange creatures, these bird-men who flash down in a thunderburst to court Prince Ivan's sisters? They initiate the hero's journey towards desire and intimacy; they console and succour him along the way; and they restore him when the enemy of love has shattered and destroyed him. Who are they?

I was telling the story of "Maria Morevna"—the Afanas'ev version—to Ron Evans (my Metis storm-fool friend) one night. He grew up in the Chippewa–Cree tradition of northern Saskatchewan, and he smiled as he listened to the story. Afterwards he said, "We tell stories about them, too. We call them the Thunder Beings, and they're always trying to find earthly men and women to marry. They are very powerful spirits."

How did Cree Thunder Beings find their way to the sky above Prince Ivan's Russian palace? Does the same sky of wonder and possibility vault over all heroic destinies? Does the search for intimacy always commence with a thunderous, roof-cracking intervention, connecting us to the mysterious forces that smash and remake the everyday world? There is no answer to these questions, at least none as entertaining as the questions themselves. What I gather from this play of stories is that, unless the pattern is given in all its details, unless the teller passes along as much as he or she has been given, the story cannot evoke its fullest range of response.

The next time you visit the library looking for stories to learn by heart, keep an ear out for thunder. That rumbling sound above your head may be the Thunderbird reminding you that when you put a traditional story together, you should put all the bones in the right places.

A story is not good unless you add something to it.
Tuscan proverb

STORYTELLING IS A CREATIVE ART. Working with old patterns, storytellers are free to use new yarns, so long as we don't damage or diminish the tale in the reworking. Many traditional storytellers I've known might well disagree. They would say that originality is vastly overrated, their artistic practice and purpose being to serve and preserve a narrative inheritance. But for storytellers who are part of the contemporary renaissance, invention and experimentation are essential ways to rediscover the art. And even among traditional storytellers, despite their claims of fidelity, they never treat their stories as museum pieces to be kept safe and carefully handled. Traditional storytellers often have a great ability to respond to the moment, to include the audience, to make up new details as the story requires; that is, to play with the material.

Robert Munsch, a Canadian children's writer, gives a good example (I included it in my book *Tales for an*

Unknown City) of how a new audience made him find something new in his own story. He was travelling in the far north and he tried telling his story "The Mud Puddle" to an audience of Inuit children. The story, which has become practically a folk tale among North American children, is about a girl who is repeatedly assailed by a mud puddle in her backyard, despite the best efforts of her mother to keep her clean and out of trouble. The story, he claims, had never failed to grab any audience of kids. Up north, nobody laughed. "It was a dud," he reports. At the end of the story, he realized what was going on: "When I was done a kid put up his hand and asked, 'What's a mud puddle?'" The ground in Inuktitut had never been warm enough to turn into mud. The kids had never seen it, and had no idea why mud puddles could behave so capriciously and unsanitarily. Munsch turned the mud puddle into a snowdrift and the Inuit kids now found it hilarious.

Sometimes the originality lies in recognizing a new use or context for a traditional story. Angela Sidney's son left the Yukon to join the Canadian army and fight in the Second World War. He was gone for five years. When the war ended he sent a telegram from Europe to the Yukon. As Julie Cruikshank writes in *Life Lived Like a Story*, "She began planning his homecoming at once, estimating the number of days it would take for him to travel across the Atlantic by boat, across Canada by train, up the west coast of the country by boat, and inland to the Yukon on the narrow-gauge White Pass and Yukon Railway. She arranged a party to welcome him and as a special gift she gave him the song of Kaax'achgook . . ." The song comes from a Tlingit story given to Angela Sidney's clan by another Crow clan. It is the story of a man who is lost at sea. He is able to return from the island on which he is shipwrecked by calculating the position of the sun at the summer's solstice. In Angela Sidney's words:

> That man, Kaax'achgook, he always goes to northwind side every day.
> He goes out on the point—never tells anyone.
> He marks when the sun comes out in the morning.
> Marks it with a stick.
> In the evening, he goes out again.
> Marks a stick where the sun goes down.
> He never tells anyone why he does this.
> He just does it all the time.
> Finally, that stick is in the same place for two days.
> He knows this marks the return of spring.
> Then the sun starts to come back in June, the longest day.

Using the sun as his navigational aid, he is able to paddle home with his eight nephews. He had been gone for a year, and long since given up for dead. As he nears his home shore he begins to sing three songs:

> *I gave up my life out on the deep for the shark.*
> *The sun came up and saved people.*
> *I gave up hope and then I dreamed I was home.*

The story and the three songs were the present the joyful mother gave her soldier son at the potlatch where she welcomed him home. The story and the song of Kaax'achgook brought the young man's own perilous journey full circle—life and story completing each other in her extraordinary gift. Odysseus-like, the young soldier hears his life framed by a myth.

Ruth Sawyer said storytellers should make "a determined effort to write at least one original story every year, using some folk-source." I'd like to describe the process of rewondering traditional tales, using my own stories and Kay Stone's "The Curious Girl" as examples.

For many years, I happily told the "The Devil with the Three Golden Hairs," from the brothers Grimm. It features an absurdly greedy king who, when he hears a prophecy that his daughter will marry a poor child born with a lucky caul, sets out to destroy the young man. It occurred to me, after many hundreds of tellings, that I knew this king very well. Just as the king's mad and unrelenting greed for control cannot let his daughter find her own future, so I live in a world where individual creativity is squelched, where an insidious force insists on making everything the same, on standardizing hamburgers and funeral homes, on microsoftening our very capacity to share data. This new take on the story launched a retelling set in modern times ("Mr. Globus and Laughing Boy" is included on page 230). The king transformed into Mr. Globus, the CEO of a multi-trans-international corporation that makes, not only handheld remote-control electronic channel changers, but also the televisions that have the channels you can try to change. Same greed, different villain.

I was telling "The White Snake," also from Grimm, when a group of listeners opened a new window into the story. It is a story featuring a young man who learns the language of the animals. He steals this knowledge by tasting of the King's secret and forbidden dish: a white snake. On the journey he undertakes after leaving the King's service, he meets fish, ants and ravens, all of whom he helps after understanding their language. He is riding a horse that, in the Grimms' version, is the only animal in the story that doesn't speak. When the baby ravens ask for meat, this is what happens: "So the good young fellow alighted and killed his horse with his sword, and gave it to them for food."

I always found this scene hard to tell, not because it was violent but because it broke a thread of suspense in the story. It never made sense to me that a man who could speak the languages of all the animals had no connection to his own horse. Because in the traditional version there is no intimate relationship to the horse, his sacrifice of it seems superficial. As I was strolling up and down the hills of Cape Clear, Ireland, with a group of storytellers, I asked them what they thought about the story. They found this scene as jarring as I did. It was as if the story turned its back on its own magic. I admitted that I had always been bothered by the relationship, or lack of it.

The story began to evolve in a new direction. In the version I've included in the Story section of this book, "Strange Voices," (p. 201) when the young man goes to choose his horse, it is the horse that claims him. When the time comes to make the sacrifice for the baby ravens, it is the horse that offers itself. The man resists, but the horse's wisdom prevails. Upon her death, his sacrifice is losing his magical power to understand the language of the animals. Later, he receives a reward for his acquiescence to the greater wisdom

Kay Stone, in her book *Burning Brightly: New Light on Old Tales Told Today,* studies a number of storytellers who work with traditional material in inventive ways.

Drawing on her own experience as a teller, she reports on how she recast the Grimms' story "Mistress Trudy" into a story she calls "The Curious Girl." "Mistress Trudy" ends when the disobedient heroine winds up turned into a log and tossed on the fire after she has beheld the "witch in her true form." The burning girl makes "a bright light." Stone's first encounter with the Grimms' version was upsetting:

> When I first met Mistress Trudy in my own copy of the complete Grimm tales she did not offer pleasant company. I was enraged. So much so that I threw my book across the room—something I have not done since I was a child. It split neatly in half. The story inflamed me. I was too sympathetic with that overly curious and disobedient girl who set out so boldly on her path into the woods, and who was eventually overwhelmed and destroyed by the witch she sought out. It was an ugly story . . .

After this unpromising beginning, the story somehow set deep roots in Stone's imagination. Over a period of many years, she kept revisiting its themes, images and characters.

> What continued to push the story into new growth was my own stubborn curiosity. I wanted to know what happened to the girl after she was thrown into the fire. How did she survive, and why? I knew there was something about to happen next but I did not know what it would be. Every time I told "The Curious Girl" I trusted that I would discover at least one thing that I had not noticed before, and each discovery gave its energy to the next

telling. In this way the story grew on its own and it became easier and easier to tell as I became more willing to enter Mistress Trudy's door.

Stone developed a new story from the bones of the traditional version. As she tells it, the Curious Girl is transformed into a bird by the witch's fire, and is promised a restoration to human form when she brings back a story the witch has never heard before. She travels the world, gathering stories from all creation. Even so, when she returns to tell them, Mistress Trudy says, "Excellent, excellent! But I heard every one of those stories before you were even born. I hope you have another." The bird/girl isn't sure what to do. She has, like Odysseus in Phaiakia, truly landed on the shore of her own destiny. "She opened her mouth to say 'No!' But a story began to come out on its own. It sounded familiar: 'Once there was a girl who was curious, and stubborn, and always disobedient to her parents . . .' Indeed that was the story that had never been heard, and as far as I know, it is still the story with no end."

Sometimes I tell stories in the "first person fabulous." This is a narrative voice that lets "me" wander through fantastic realms, encounter mythic beings, and slip through the frontier between real life and magic. In other words, it lets me tell lies. Alice Kane used to recite this poem by Ida Zeitlin by way of reminding her listeners that story-wisdom comes via unpredictable routes:

> The Dreamer awakes,
> The shadow goes by,
> The cock never crew,

The tale is a lie;
But ponder it well,
Fair maiden, good youth,
The tale is a lie,
But the teaching is truth.

Story lies are, of course, different than pernicious everyday lies. Call them "fiction" and they become art; call them narrative inventions, and they sound noble, even wise. The first person fabulous is the voice of tall-tale tellers, but also of philosophers and purveyors of parable. It works as a passport for travelling quickly between everyday life and the dimension of legend, letting the storyteller use the energy and intimacy of a real-sounding account to create an utterly fictional world. I like it because, although I'm reluctant to use my personal life as material for stage performances, when I tell stories in the first person fabulous, I can have my privacy and perform it too.

In "The Devil's Noodles" (p. 209), I use the first person fabulous voice to set the scene in Toronto's Little Italy, my old neighbourhood. The story-pattern comes from a traditional tale often titled "The Blacksmith and the Devil." I used to tell Richard Chase's wonderful version "Wicked John and the Devil" from *Grandfather Tales,* his classic collection of Appalachian oral tradition. My friend Renato, who ran a café around the corner from my house, always struck me as larger than life. He was generous, funny, brusque, irreverent. He never paid his taxes and he sold wine illegally to customers he knew well. And he was the most tender and kindhearted man in the whole *quartier.* I didn't set out to modernize Wicked John, but meeting Renato let me imagine how the story could evolve.

Another example of my use of the first person fabulous comes in "The Devil in Don Mills" (p. 220). The inspiration for this contemporary Faust tale came from two sources. One is a novel by the Russian writer Mikhail Bulgakov titled *The Master and Margarita,* in which the devil is a paradoxical power: he reveals truth by fabricating deceptions. The other source is a poem by Charles Baudelaire that depicts a Parisian roué meeting Satan in a café. The promise of modern technology—for example, to give us speed and ease in finding data—has proven to be a deal with the devil; as our data-hoards grow, our story-memories weaken. Instead of Stalinist Moscow or 1890s Paris, my natural setting for a Faustian encounter turned out to be a suburban shopping mall, full of standardized doughnut shops, hamburger joints, clothing stores and computer outlets. But the story-pattern hasn't changed, and neither the moral dilemma it poses; only the scenery and the characters look a little different.

It is no accident that the first person voice has become part of contemporary literature, both written and oral (and televised, if you watch Oprah). Walter Benjamin, in his essay "The Storyteller," written after the First World War, observed that soldiers back from the battlefield were shockingly silent, unable to find words to describe the horror and absurdity of the mechanized slaughter they had witnessed. They were "not richer, but poorer in communicable experience." The war's insane violence undermined the very value of experience itself—moral, emotional, physical, communal. Benjamin believed this loss, this growing silence, threatened the very possibility of storytelling as a human activity because "experience which is passed on from mouth to mouth is the source from which all storytellers have drawn," and he went on to say, "It is as if something that seemed inalienable to us, the securest among our possessions, were taken from us: the ability to exchange experiences."

Benjamin wrote his elegy in 1936, three years before the world entered a period of unimaginable atrocities, and four years before he himself, pursued by Nazis, entered the silence of suicide. He chose to give up his own ability to exchange experiences, and so entered the very history he had so eloquently chronicled: the twentieth century silencing of the storyteller's voice.

In the storytelling renaissance, the first person, the witness, the real-life hero telling the chronicle of his/her own adventure has an urgent appeal for those hungry for an unmediated contact with life, starved of direct experiences. Storytelling has become one way to reclaim the ground of human experience as a source of understanding and communication. The first person voice, fabulous or real, is a route back to a world where our personal experience is primary. Benjamin would be surprised and probably pleased to know that storytelling has returned after what he thought was its final exile.

There are certain protocols involved in working with traditional stories, particularly if you find them in published sources. When I was working on "The Storyteller At Fault," I wanted to include my adaptation of Harold Courlander's famous story, "The Cow-tail Switch." I wrote to Courlander asking for permission.

The great folklorist and writer felt that my reworking had lost too much of his story and reminded me in no uncertain terms that it is essential to respect the traditional pattern that once anchored the oral multiforms of traditional tales. In the end my story evolved in a completely different direction.

This kind of experimentation, whether it meets with success or failure, is part of the contemporary storytelling renaissance. It springs from the borderland between literate culture and the emerging arts of orality (storytelling, spoken word, rap). For as long as humankind has been literate, there have always been raids back and forth across this frontier. Authored stories and poems often turn into folklore, and oral sources inspire written versions. Most Canadian schoolyards resound with children chanting "Alligator pie, alligator pie, if I don't get some I think I'm going to die . . ." They may or may not know that the Canadian poet Dennis Lee wrote this poem; it has already become part of their oral lore.

The distance between the two worlds of oral and written tales changes from one epoch to another. In the fourteenth century, for example, a rich oral tradition prevailed. The streets of Oxford, London, Florence, Baghdad and Cairo were filled with countless *gestes* of saints, knights, amorous clergy, lusty maidens, ridiculous bureaucrats, craftsmen, kings and peasants. Chaucer, Boccaccio and the editors of the *Thousand and One Nights* must have absorbed these legends, wonder tales, religious fables, tall tales, all the "urban myths" of the day. From this speakable feast, they fashioned some of the worlds greatest narrative literature. The historian Barbara Tuchman calls this period a "distant mirror" of our own time. As a storyteller, I look back and see a curiously inverted image. If Chaucer wrought *The Canterbury Tales* in the midst of a living oral tradition, six hundred years later contemporary storytellers are trying to create a new spoken literature drawn largely from the shelves of our local libraries.

What makes this inventiveness possible is the fact that stories have an inner life that allows them to sustain their meaning through myriad expressive forms. Robert Bringhurst, in his introduction to Alice Kane's *Dreamer Awakes,* writes, "[I] am amazed by the way stories and songs, and the words of which they are made, preserve their forms over hundreds of years and thousands of miles, just as animals and plants do over many generations. Stories are not *copied;* they are *reborn,* and each succeeding individual is different, yet the species, for long stretches, is substantively the same." The landscape of "The Devil's Three Golden Hairs" transforms, in my telling, into a world where the poor live so far away that they only get one channel, and the hero gets pulled from Wild River by a lesbian couple; still, if I've done any justice to the story's underlying pattern, it is essentially the same tale the brothers Grimm collected and wrote. Munsch changes his mudpuddle into a snowdrift but the story, that is, the part that makes it worth remembering, is unchanged. Stories are not museum artifacts.

Bringhurst describes this process as an organic one: "Stories find the tellers they need. They nest in us like saw-whet owls and wood ducks nest in trees. . . . [T]hey use us to reproduce themselves." As they are re-created in each generation, the details may change but the story can, with the Muse's and teller's help, continue to speak with undiminished force.

But you know, what amazed me was that the good
hakawatis didn't have flying carpets constantly
whizzing around, or dragons spitting fire, or witches
concocting crazy potions. They kept their listeners
just as spellbound with the simplest things . . .

RAFIK SCHAMI, *Damascus Nights*

THE AUSTRIAN STORYTELLER Karin Tscholl describes
storytelling as the art of "juggling with a knife and a balloon." The balloon part is the gentleness needed to create
a shared reverie with the audience; the knife is the edge of
suspense as the story unfolds, the irresistible energy that
makes you want to hear what happens next. Both forces
must be balanced to make a story memorable from the
first word to the last. So a story must be as light as a
balloon and as sharp as a knife. This is helpful, but
a beginning storyteller may wish for some more specific,
hard-and-fast rules—the Top Ten Tips of Unforgettable
Storytelling. Unfortunately, they don't exist! There is no
one right way to tell stories. I have, however, worked out

some useful principles, which I keep in mind whenever I tell stories. These aren't tips or methods or systematic ways to improve your storytelling technique, but simply four important ideas that have guided me in my own explorations.

Anne Pellowski, in her splendid study of international storytelling, reports a telling by Sabadu, an African story-teller: "To the rabbit, of course, he gave a wee voice, to the Elephant he gave a deep bass, to the Buffalo a hollow moo-ing . . . when he mimicked the dog, one almost expected a little terrier-like dog to trot up to the fire, so perfect was his yaup-yaup." At the other end of the performing spec-trum is someone like Alice Kane, who with her quiet voice and her stillness can hold five hundred people spellbound. I saw her do so in a tent at the big storytelling festival in Jonesborough, Tennessee.

The only style worth pursuing is your own, however long it takes you to discover it. As you search for your own voice and storytelling way, as you experiment, copy, turn back, and sometimes make triumphant and original breakthroughs, it's worth remembering the story about Reb Zusya, one of the great Hasidic teachers. I once heard the late Reuven Gold tell of the time Zusya said to his stu-dents, "When I die, I'm not afraid of the angels asking me if I was as wise and virtuous as Abraham, or Isaac, or King David, or Solomon. I know that I could not be like them. I'm much more afraid that they will ask me if I had been as good as Zusya could have been."

I take from this Reb Zusya story the encouraging notion that if you are patient, and willing to make many mistakes, and willing even more to start over when you've fallen down, one day you'll find that both your stories and the voice in which you utter them are entirely your own. I say that from experience. I think I've probably made every mistake in the book. I've chosen inappropriate stories, interrupted my elders when I shouldn't have, lost the thread of a tale, recited a text from memory when I should have been spinning a tale, even bored an audience or two over the years. The good news is that they were all helpful mistakes.

After that first summer at Bolton Camp as a counsellor, I made the most important phone call of my life. I knew I needed a teacher if I was going to go further with this utterly intimidating art I had chosen to pursue. I went back to Boys' and Girls' House and asked if they knew anybody who told stories. They told me I should call Alice Kane, a recently retired librarian who knew something about the art of storytelling.

I gathered my courage and made the call. I introduced myself, and explained all in a rush who I was and what I wanted, that I had tried storytelling and that it was the hardest thing I'd ever done but I wanted to do it for a living, and did she know anybody who would be willing to teach me? There was a pause at the end of the phone line. Then she said, with a hint of iron challenge in her voice— a voice that still carried the cadence of a northern Irish childhood, "You're not an *actor,* are you?"

Me, an actor? Absolutely not. At twenty-two I hadn't even learned to play myself, let alone any other role. I answered, "No." Then I made bold and asked her, "Why?"

In a soft, clear voice she replied, "Because actors can't tell stories. An actor puts himself between the story and the listener. A storyteller has to let the story through directly."

I've thought about her Zen-like statement ever since. It haunts me, puzzles me, exhilarates me. It reminds me of Homer's invocation at the beginning of the *Odyssey*: "Sing in me, Muse, and through me tell the story . . ." When I hear a great story, I can't tell you afterwards what the storyteller was wearing, or how they used or didn't use their hands, or anything else. All I saw was my own mind-movie as the story was being told.

Alice's own favourite example of this was the time Helen Armstrong, a children's librarian, was telling hero stories to other librarians.

> She was telling us the story of "Olaf the Glorious." And she got up and her friend Dorothy said to her, "Don't button and unbutton your jacket all the time." So she got up and she stood in a little bright patch of sunshine, and she unfastened her jacket all the way down, and then she buttoned it all the way up. And then she unfastened it all the way down again, and she kept on doing this. And she started the story, and you watched her doing her jacket. At some point—I don't know when—she was gone. She was totally gone from that patch of sunlight, and in its place was the Norwegian ship on a blue, blue sea. The sky blue above, and the waves breaking around it. The colours were all blue and white, with a touch of red. It was full of shouts and cries, and suddenly young Olaf with his shield in his hand leapt up and over the edge of the ship and into the water and the waves closed over his head.

The story had come across, vivid and intact, through the teller. And that is the first of my four guiding ideas: *It is more important for the listener to see the story than to see you.*

And how do you do that? In Ms. Armstrong's case, it was probably the intensity of her own vision of the story, the perfectly chosen language and her deep emotional connection with the heroic protagonist. In other words, it was the same mix of skill, inspiration and purpose that makes all great art possible. She herself, many years later and long after she stopped fiddling with her buttons, accounted for her art in two ways. First, she worked with the very best versions and translations of epic that she could find. Secondly, she had a deep affinity for the world of "deliberate valour" that the heroes of epic literature inhabit: "I am a natural hero-worshipper. I cannot help giving my whole-hearted devotion to people like Don Quixote, Hardy's Gabriel, Trollope's Dr. Harding and Harold Godwinson, the Golden Warrior; not to mention a doll called Totty, a spider named Charlotte, and Sam the hobbit; so I suppose it is only natural that I should specially like those most heroic heroes of all, the epic heroes. . . . There is an element in the epic stories that is unique to them and that generates what is almost a compulsion or at the least an obligation to pass them on."

The second insight I have to offer you follows directly from the first: *When a witch screams in a story, the storyteller doesn't have to*. The audience is better able to imagine the witch's scream without the teller acting it out. I've read many how-to books about storytelling. These books like to provide "helpful" coaching tips in the margins of the stories: "Stand up here." "Wave your arms like a bird." "Whisper this part." "Make eye contact." This is dreary and discouraging advice. Eye contact? But Homer himself was blind! If anybody tries to sell you one of these tell-by-the-numbers books, take my advice—save your money. The audience doesn't need to look at you.

The third of the four ideas that have guided me is that *storytelling is a dance between suspense and revelation*. We start learning about suspense when we play peek-a-boo. Babies are pretty sure the big face is only temporarily concealed, but they still thrill with joy when it BOOS back from behind the finger-curtain. This could be the secret of all storytelling: the hidden part is what makes the story. From then on, we're hooked. We have entered the storyteller's shire and there's no turning back. We will spend the rest of our story-listening lives giving soul's welcome to the storyteller's voice, hungry to hear what happens next, and hoping with equal force the secrets will be revealed as slowly and deliciously as possible. The teller's art is to move gracefully between suspense and climax, between clearly spoken words and well-kept silence. When you're learning a story it is always valuable to think about the moment of maximum suspense, the moment Scheherazade would have chosen to stop her telling and save her life for one more Arabian night. You can't build suspense in your telling unless you know when you're *peeking* and when you're *booing*.

I once saw an astonishing wolf drawn by an eight-year-old friend. It galloped across the page, mouth slightly open and eyes full of spirit and ferocity. When I admired her artistry, the girl gazed at her own work for a moment, and then explained, "It took a strong *eraser* to make that." A good storyteller, like this wonderfully intuitive young artist, uses just enough words—not too many, not too few—to sketch a wolf that can run straight into the listener's mind.

My fourth piece of counsel seems almost heretical to say. *Storytelling is the most boring art in the world*. To redeem

myself, I'll immediately claim that it is also—or can be—
the most thrilling. A good story well told is absolutely
enthralling. We are willing to wholeheartedly entrust our
imagination, feeling and intellect to a storyteller who can
hold us as they tell their tale. The Cape Breton storyteller
Joe Neil MacNeil remembers the master storytellers of his
youth: "[T]he tale was so enjoyable and would please you
so well as it progressed that you would find yourself hoping that it would not end for a long time, that there would
be a great amount of working around it so that the storyteller could make it very, very long before he arrived at
the end of the tale." MacNeil, you'll notice, didn't say the
tale *was* long. He says the listener *wanted* it to be long,
because they found it so compelling. To achieve that, you
must remember that human beings do have notoriously
short attention spans. It has never been easy for people to
sit and listen for long periods of time to one person who's
doing all the talking. (Mind you, I've spent many hours
listening to tellers speaking languages I didn't understand, held simply by the music of their voices.)

Traditional cultures around the world have always
known that boredom is an ever-present risk when a teller
opens his/her mouth. That's why the Haitian storyteller
cries *Cric?* and Homer played a lyre, and Africans run
riddle-games with the audience. It is why Scheherazade
stopped her stories at the most suspenseful moment. It is
why Tuscan storytellers always made sure of a warm welcome before starting: "The old storytellers would never
begin on their own initiative. They would not want to err,
as did the blindman of Peretola, 'who needed a coin to
begin, and ten to stop.' Even though everyone knew they
would finally concede, and happily, they still looked for a

lot of coaxing first. It seemed to be part of the performance itself, not just a happy prelude but a way of establishing the proper mood and the right way to frame the scene," writes Alessandro Falassi in *Folklore by the Fireside.* And according to Rafik Schami, in *Damascus Nights,* "A story has to taste every bit as good as the food, otherwise most of my guests would get up, pay for their waterpipe, and leave . . ."

How boring can storytelling get? I was once at a friend's house when somebody came by with a slide projector and some carousels of slides. He had been to Calgary and Banff, Alberta, for the Winter Olympics. He said he had a few slides to show. After about thirty, the children had fallen asleep on the rug. By the time he started on the second carousel, his wife was nodding. As for me, I heard the click of the third carousel starting, but I didn't wake up until the door opened and he said goodbye. He had bored an entire roomful of people into utter oblivion. One of the problems, of course, was that every picture was more or less the same: he was standing on a snowy hill; or his wife was standing on a snowy hill. He could happily have shown his supine audience another three hundred slides. Why? Because *he was in them.* It was his life and personal memories being reflected. We humans have limited patience with the display of somebody else's life on a screen, but we find our own lives infinitely fascinating.

And there are many other ways of boring a listener. Dr. Samuel Johnson and his sublime chronicler James Boswell were once travelling together, and they fell in with a certain man, who tried to relate a story. As Boswell reports, the story didn't exactly keep Johnson on the edge of his carriage seat:

A learned gentleman who in the course of conversation wished to inform us of this simple fact, that the counsel upon the circuit at Shrewsbury were much bitten by fleas, took, I suppose, seven or eight minutes in relating it circumstantially. He in a plenitude of phrase told us that large bales of woollen cloth were lodged in the town-hall;—that by reason of this, fleas nestled there in prodigious numbers; that the lodgings of the counsel were near the town-hall; and that those little animals moved from place to place with wonderful agility. Johnson sat in great impatience till the gentleman had finished his tedious narrative, and then burst out (playfully however), "It is a pity, Sir, that you have not seen a lion; for a flea has taken you such a time, that a lion must have served you a twelvemonth."

One of the stories told in Boccaccio's *Decameron* features a similarly leaden-tongued raconteur:

[O]ne of the knights turned to her, and, perhaps because they were having to travel a long way, on foot, to the place they all desired to reach, he said, "Madonna Oretta, if you like I shall take you riding along a goodly stretch of our journey by telling you one of the finest tales in the world."

"Sir," replied the lady, "I beseech you most earnestly to do so, and I shall look upon it as a great favour."

Whereupon this worthy knight, whose swordplay was doubtless on a par with his storytelling, began to recite his tale, which in itself was indeed excellent. But by constantly repeating the same phrases, and recapitulating sections of the plot, and every so often declaring that he had "made a mess of that bit," and regularly confusing the names of the characters, he ruined it completely. Morever, his mode of delivery was totally out of keeping with the characters and the incidents he was describing, so that it was painful for Madonna Oretta to listen to him. She began to perspire freely, and her heart missed several beats, as though she had fallen ill and was about to give up the ghost. And in the end, when she could endure it no longer, having perceived that the knight had tied himself inextricably in knots, she said to him, in affable tones: "Sir, you have taken me riding on a horse that trots very jerkily. Pray be good enough to set me down."

The Irish storyteller Padraic Colum would have advised unfortunate narrators that they need not describe the entire sea, but rather must give their listeners "the flash of the wave" ("Storytelling New and Old"). My son, Nathaniel, after seeing the movie *Finding Forrester*, commented, "They left too little unknown."

Those are my four counsels. Although they won't save you from your own stumbles and they probably won't speed your own discoveries, they are useful things to remember as you work with stories.

Besides those four overall guiding principles, there are a few practical thoughts I have, especially for the beginning storyteller. Whenever I work with teenage storytellers, I insist they learn their stories by heart. "Word for *word?*" they ask, incredulous that anybody nowadays would demand such a preposterous chore of a teenage brain. Yes, I tell them. A musician doesn't ask if he or she needs to learn *every note* of a Mozart sonata. The right notes give the music its fullest expression. So too with the words of a story. What I know—but don't usually explain to the high school kids, because I'd rather they discovered it for themselves—is that by the time they've told the memorized text a few times, they will have unconsciously started to adapt the story to their own voice. They move from classical to jazz mode, so to speak. And because they worked so hard to get the words right in the beginning, their tenth telling has all the confidence and spontaneity and precision of language that their first telling may lack.

There are, of course, many points of view in the storytelling world. I've heard very fine storytellers argue that it's better to learn stories from their images, and not worry so much about the exact words. Ruth Sawyer is adamant that it is better to learn stories this way, that it frees the teller from sounding like a mere reciter and turns them into more creative artists. But Nancy Woods, a high school teacher I've collaborated with many times, always has her storytelling students memorize their stories, some many pages long. These bright teenagers begin by thinking storytelling will be a breeze, but having to master a text filled with very particular turns of phrase "stops them cold," Nancy says, and makes them realize this is not such an easy art after all, but one that will take all of their resources of attention, memory and imagination. Storytelling is the favourite unit among Wood's tenth-grade students, she reports, because they are invariably pleased with themselves when they discover what they can do.

However the words come to you—learned by heart from a literary source or text, or improvised from a basic plot—the aim must be to make the story sound fresh every time you tell it, as if you were discovering the story's people, dilemmas and landscape for the first time along with your listeners. When I tell the stories at the back of this book, I probably don't stray far from the text as it's printed. But if you heard me tell them, you might well think I'm making them up fresh just for you, and just for the occasion. At least, that's the effect I'm aiming for.

Rehearsing can be a problem for storytellers, especially if, like me, you do your best thinking out loud on long walks. Storytellers should carry a sign that says Rehearsal in Progress. I'll often stroll throught the ravine near our house, mumbling and declaiming a story I'm working on. It's a dangerous habit. If you do it in your car in the middle of rush-hour, other drivers pass you with alarm in their eyes. If you do it on a city street, people think you're a little nutsy-fruitsy (my mother's expression).

I was once trying to prepare "The Princess and the Pea." It was a foggy night and I was walking down Brunswick Avenue, just south of Toronto's most famous beer hall, and I said out loud, with feeling, "But she must be a *real* princess!" A young woman loomed out of the fog at that moment, and looked at me with great alarm. She probably thought I'd just staggered out of the Brunswick House somewhat over-refreshed with ale.

When you are telling a story, don't get distracted. I was once telling a funny story to a grade-five group, and one boy laughed so hard he fell off his chair and let out a loud fart at the same time. It took a while for the group to calm down, and longer for him, but I didn't stop telling the story for more than a moment. Once the flatulent echoes died away and the boy stopped quaking with laughter, calm was restored. Almost all questions the chldren may have for you can wait until the end of the story. Ever since my run-in with Farting Frankie, nearly thirty years ago, nothing except a fire drill can stop me from telling the story right through to the end.

The one imperative of storytelling is that the audience must long to know what happens next. Tell your story as if the garbagemen of Jalandhar were in the audience; I read the tale of these great listeners in a Canadian newspaper, and they've been my heroes ever since. The dateline is New Delhi, 1988:

> The garbagemen of Jalandhar have gone on strike in this city in the Punjab to protest the cancellation of a popular television series. The series is based on the Hindu epic the *Ramayana* and is the most popular show on Indian television. Its seventy-eight week run is scheduled to end this month, but the Jalandhar garbagemen demand an extension to show what happened to Lord Rama's two sons. Municipal officials fear the workers' refusal to collect garbage could spread disease.

My friends in India tell me this report is true; while the show was on, the whole country came to a standstill. What an honour it would be to tell stories for an audience willing to go on strike for the sake of a beloved story. For such noble listeners we must be ready to juggle with the lightest of balloons and the sharpest of knives.

EMERGENCY STORYTELLING

Never say "whoa!" in a mudhole.

Canadian proverb

I WAS TRAVELLING in Devon many years ago when I needed to find the right story for a difficult moment. My friend Ken Sprague took me over the hills to meet his neighbour, a farmer named Edward who'd recently suffered a calamitous loss. His only son had an unsuspected heart condition, and one day when Edward had been urging him to work harder in the fields, the boy had keeled over and died in front of him. When Edward and his wife heard I was a storyteller, they poured the tea, and asked if I could tell them one of my stories. I wondered what story I could possibly tell in this grief-stricken farmhouse. Then this one (which I had heard from the American teller Barbara Freeman, but had never told myself) popped up:

A man was away from home for quite a while. He ran into a neighbour as he walked into town. "How ya' doing?" he asked.

"All right. How 'bout you?"

"Not bad. I've been away a while. Any news?"

"Nah, it's been real quiet around here."

"Are you sure nothing's happened while I've been gone?"

"Well, now that you mention it, your dog died."

"My dog? How did that happen?"

"He got into the barn and ate some burnt horse meat."

"What was burnt horse meat doing in my barn?"

"When your barn burned, all the horses died in the fire."

"You mean to say my barn burned while I was away?"

"Yep. Apparently a spark from the house caught it."

"My house was on fire too?"

"They say it was the candles in the living room burning the curtains."

"But what were candles doing in my living room?"

"They were all around the coffin."

"You mean someone died while I was gone?"

"That would've been your mother-in-law. The shock carried her away."

"What shock was that?"

"Hearin' the news about your wife."

"And what happened to my wife?"

"Oh, I guess she ran away with the gardener."

"My wife ran away, my mother-in-law died, the house burned, the barn burned, the horses died, my dog died—and you said there wasn't any news!"

My listeners laughed when they heard this tale of woe. Did they find in it a reflection of their own tragic history? Did hearing of someone else's troubles make them feel less alone? Did they forget their sorrow for a moment with the story's preposterously backward revelation of the news? Perhaps for all of those reasons, it seemed to be the right story for the occasion.

All storytellers are children of Scheherazade. Like her, we must be ready to tell stories in case of emergency. She was the great storyteller in the *Thousand and One Nights* who risked her life telling stories to her mad husband, King Shahriyar. Every night this deranged monarch sought revenge on all womankind by taking a virgin bride and chopping off her head in the morning. He was afraid they would betray him as his first wife had done. When Scheherazade married him, she used the most famous storytelling ruse in world literature to save her life. Each night Dunyazad, the storyteller's little sister, would kneel by the bedside and ask for "a tale of wonder to make the hours of night pass pleasantly." Scheherazade, with superb courage, as if she had all the time in the world to spin her yarns, answered:

> Come, little sister, come near
> Leave behind all of your fear
> Darkness comes and night is near
> But dawn shall find you sleeping here.

Then she would begin her story. But every night she stopped her stories at the most suspenseful moment, and the king, eager to hear what happened next, spared her life for another day. For a thousand and one nights she spun her marvellous yarns. One or two or even a hundred tales wouldn't suffice. King Shahriyar needed to hear a vast range of stories, reflecting all of the permutations of human desire, dread, hope and dreams. He heard about the high ones and the lowly ones of this earth, each with his or her own destiny. He heard ancient histories and modern spoofs. Most of all, he heard about the immense, pervasive power of magic to utterly transform both kings and peasants, fearful husbands, curious wives and all who walk on the green earth by the light of day. It took the cumulative wisdom of an entire oral tradition for Scheherazade's mad listener to be healed.

On the one-thousand-and-first night, Dunyazad brought in the three children her sister had borne (Scheherazade and the king had clearly found time for other, non-narrative activities during those three years).

"Spare my life for the sake of our children, husband of mine. My stories are ended," said Scheherazade.

"Your tales, O Queen, beloved wife, have healed my madness," he replied. "You have shown me that women are wise and tender, chaste and eloquent. My grief and rage are ended, for I see now that the two things men cannot control are destiny and a woman's soul. May all your ancestors be blessed and may your descendants find favour with Allah; for me, this one-thousand-and-first night is more radiant than the day itself. . . ." (and so on in like manner, for Shahriyar had become a storyteller himself by now).

The story of Scheherazade's heroic storytelling reminds me that every time a tale is told, the souls of both teller and listener may be in the balance. Storytelling is not only an entertaining way to pass the time. It is also an art that can mend broken souls.

In a speech given at York University in Toronto, the great Hungarian poet George Faludy recalled that in

Recsk labour camp in Stalinist Hungary, he and his fellow-prisoners were near death from starvation and disease. Every night the men gathered around Faludy as he told them stories, recited opera libretti, discoursed on Renaissance art, shared all the poetry he knew by heart. The prisoners who scorned these whispered narratives and went off to catch an extra hour of sleep were the ones who died first. Faludy's circle of loyal listeners survived. "I cannot claim," he said, "that this saved us from death, but it did undoubtedly save us from the despair that inevitably resulted in death."

Because storytelling is portable, requires no props, and can be activated immediately, under any circumstances, it is wonderfully adapted to emergency situations. The American storyteller Laura Simms has been very active in helping African children who were kidnapped and forced to become soldiers. One fifteen-year-old boy was brought directly from the battle zone in Sierra Leone to address a conference at the United Nations in New York. Without a visa, he couldn't stay. He was utterly terrified at the prospect of returning to his war-torn land. In the taxi to the airport, Simms asked the boy what she could do for him. "Please tell me a story," he replied. This is the story she told:

> There was once a poor boy who went to a market. He had no money to buy anything. He wanted everything. In the market was a magician performing a magic act. He had a magic finger. Anything he touched turned to gold. The boy watched the magician with amazement. The magician asked, "Would you like some gold?"
> The boy said, "Yes."

The magician turned a mouse to gold. But the boy refused it. He said, "I want more." The magician turned one thing after another to gold. Each thing larger than the last. The boy continued to reject his offers, saying, "I want more." At last the magician demanded, "What do you want?"

The boy answered, "I want a magic finger."

Simms noticed that as she told the story, the boy listened calmly, no longer hysterical. The United Nations official in the taxi, puzzled by the storyteller's choice of narrative, asked, "What good was that story?" But the boy said, "I understood the story. The boy will survive because he will settle for nothing less than his future." The boy did have to return to his nightmarish country, but after many months of work Laura Simms finally brought him out of Sierra Leone to safety.

In our own family, storytelling was an essential part of surviving a very difficult time. Our second son was born as close to death as a baby can be, with an Apgar score of two (seven being considered the standard for a healthy new-born). We used to say his first language was BEEP since he spent his first three weeks learning the mother tongue of intensive care, the *beep beep beep* of monitors tolling the electronic measure of his vital signs.

We entered the world of the NICU (neonatal intensive care unit) one August night in 1991. It can be the most clinical of worlds, where human landmarks are hard to find. Extreme hope and extreme dread rule the ward. You live for the doctors' rounds, the marks made on the charts, the slightest sign of progress. You treat the doctors' every word like the message of an oracle. Yet in the midst of the

NICU's medical miracles, one longs for some kind of old and tested wisdom. The ancient, affirming language of fate and tragedy has been replaced by medical test talk, genetic reports and the omnipresent beep. The doctors may save the babies, some of them, but all of their medicines and tests will not give you the bearings you need to navigate this unpredictable, terrifying experience. That wisdom you have to find for yourself.

Emergencies happen at two speeds: rush and reverie. The fast part started the moment he was born. He was as white as paper. They hustled him to the examination table before his mother had a chance to hold him. He was too frail for holding.

He'd been born with his cord wrapped around a leg, blood draining out of his body faster than it was being replenished. The GP had never seen a cord twisted like that. Our son was waxy-looking, his skin curiously uncreased; his eyes as bruised as if he'd gone ten rounds in a dockside bar; his features hung on the tiny frame of his face with no animating force to pull them into proportion; his ears were abnormally low, his chin small. An alien baby too weak to make a human cry. The pediatrician chose his words carefully as he spoke to me out in the hall. Heart? Asphyxiation? There were "subtle signs" of a mysterious syndrome. Or perhaps not. A transfusion would be done if there was no internal bleeding. Tests were needed. He might not live. If he did live . . . the doctor looked grim. The transfer team was on its way over from the Hospital for Sick Children to Women's College, the hospital where he was born.

As the medical crisis speeded up, I fell into a reverie, the other, self-protective cadence of calamity. You focus on one simple thing at a time and leave all panic and fuss to the others. As the baby lay, perhaps dying, on the examination table in the corner, I went to my wife. Her fast, unanaesthesized labour had exhausted her and there'd been no chance for the elation that should be part of the mother's healing from giving birth. I came to her and cried, "We have to give him his name right away!" I had an urgent desire to name him. A name is a talisman, a sign of stepping away from oblivion and towards the world of the living. We had chosen a name earlier, one we'd inherited from her Quaker and my Jewish ancestry. We whispered it aloud to each other and agreed that it would be his name, no matter what happened next. I stepped back to the nurses, midwife and doctors and told them that the baby they were trying to save had a name. He was Jacob.

The transfer team arrived. They quickly began a transfusion, busying themselves with needles and tubes. I leaned over the rolling crib and put my hands on Jacob's head and belly. The nurses were worried he was too weak to be handled, but I couldn't bear the thought he might leave the world untouched, unrocked. I moved him very gently from side to side, a millimetre each way, and hummed the lullaby I used to sing to his older brother. The nurse, in her wisdom, took a snapshot of him as he lay there, slowly regaining colour, his eyes swollen shut with bruising. When they gave it to me I dimly registered it might be the only picture we'd ever have of him.

We set out from Women's College Hospital to the NICU, and I remember being amazed by the subterranean system of passageways we followed to get to the Hospital for Sick Children.

Later that night, when I returned to my wife's room, we weren't sure what to pray for—a mercifully quick leave-taking or the great luxury of hoping he'd pull through. I said to the doctors, "If he's going to die, give him back to us." They talked about the need for more tests. My own tears finally came when I told my wife that Jacob had danced, heard a song, been touched. I also threw things against the hospital wall. We spent the night hugging each other in the single bed.

And so began our vigil by his high-tech crib.

For three weeks I sat next to him and talked non-stop. Each NICU parent finds a way to survive. I used story-telling. The doctors don't prescribe such things, and the nurses would sometimes look at me oddly, but talking was what came naturally. Apart from the incessant beeping and the occasional alarm, the NICU tends to be a quiet place. In the parents' lounge, a formal and sympathetic silence is observed. You don't ask many questions about each other's children, knowing the answers might be too painful to hear. There's a trend now at the NICU to encourage parents to read aloud, sing lullabies and con-verse with their babies; but at the time I seemed to be the only parent yakking away.

It was a long time before he opened his eyes, and suck-led, and made a bit of noise. It took many days for him to gain strength. One of the doctors told me it was truly puz-zling. All of his tests came back negative. Miraculously, no faculties or organs had been damaged by his horrendous experience. But the life-force hadn't flared in him yet. There was another baby on the ward, massively brain-damaged, but suckling like a trooper. Yet our boy had hardly the strength to take in a few millilitres of the milk his mother expressed for him. I asked Dr. Perlman, one of the NICU heads, if we should prepare for life with a special needs child, and he answered cryptically, "Not yet. Sometimes the things we don't understand are the ones that clear up by themselves." That was the hope we held on to. But meanwhile, where was Jacob?

I imagined our son at an immense distance from earth, a Star Boy balancing out among the farthest and coldest stars, loath to make the final jump into a human body. He'd expected warmth, succour, a pleasant shelter, sweet milk. Instead, there was this frail shell smelling of antiseptic, with formula running down a naso-gastric tube and needles stuck in tender places. Not what a Star Boy would much want to get born into. So I decided—or, more truthfully, felt compelled—to tell him stories, stories about the place he wasn't sure he wanted to land in.

The first story I told him was "The Miller's Tale" from Chaucer's *Canterbury Tales*. This is by far the most useful thing I've ever memorized. Its six hundred lines of Middle English hexameters have stood me very well in many difficult situations. Telling Jacob the poem over and over kept me from going mad with worry. As for him, he heard all about the beautiful and "likerous" young wife Alisoun, and Nicolas, her lusty lover. He heard about the trick Alisoun played on the vain Absolon, and how he, thinking he was kissing her on the lips, encountered something rather different: "Aback he sterte, and thoughte it was amiss, for wel he wiste a womman hath no berde—he felte a thyng al roughe and longe yhered . . ." In the flow of Chaucer's poetry, my infant son heard the music of desire, love, wit and surprise. From *The Canterbury Tales* I progressed to Kipling's *Jungle Book* and *Just-So Stories*. They were already on my list of the ten greatest books ever written in English, and reading them aloud in the hospital confirmed my high opinion of them.

Then I told Jacob about my great-uncle Simon and the time his grandmother saved his life. I'd learned this story when I was just becoming a storyteller, and wanted to know more about our family chronicles. Simon lived in São Paulo, Brazil, and I wrote to him asking for stories. This was the story he sent back.

Simon had been a soldier in the First World War. He and his brother were arrested during the demobilization in Europe. They had tried to get food for their sick and hungry mother and been caught still in uniform. For this crime they were shipped to northern Romania, to a military garrison five hundred miles from Bucharest. They were going to be judged by a military tribune and most likely executed by firing squad. The morning of the trial, as they were being driven to their trial, Simon's brother asked, "Do you ever think of grandmother?" "No," said Simon, "she's been dead for so many years." "It's strange," said his brother. "I dreamed of her last night. She was lying on a couch and looked very tired. I asked her why she was so exhausted, and she said, 'If you knew how far I've come to save you today, you wouldn't ask that question!'"

That morning, to their utter astonishment, the seven military judges declared them innocent and free. Their mother had somehow managed to catch a freight train and persuade the tribunal to save her sons. For the rest of his life Simon often marvelled at how their mother had miraculously rescued them; but he was even more amazed by the thought of where his grandmother's spirit had come from to appear in his brother's dream.

I imagined Jacob slowly being led back from wherever he was by a host of family ancestors and ghosts. Perhaps the great-great-grandmother who helped Simon was still roaming within soul's range of earth, still able to help a frightened Star Boy. I wanted to put all the warmth, desire and beauty of the earth into a continuous stream of story-language. I wanted to guide our Star Boy home. And so I kept talking the way an air traffic controller must talk a frightened novice down when the real pilot dies at the controls. Except that instead of a steady, reassuring flow of navigational data and instrument drill, I was trying to land Jacob with a beacon of stories.

There's a Jewish legend—and I told him this story near the end of his hospital stay—that says we each have a guardian angel. After we're conceived, the angel takes our soul on a world tour. We visit all the places we'll live in, see all the friends we'll make. And though this world is different from the celestial glory we've been accustomed to, it is also, in its way, wonderfully beautiful and desirable. Then, just before we're born, God presses us in the middle of our upper lip. At that moment, we forget everything we have just witnessed on our travels. The legend says we still bear the mark of this touch, on our upper lips, under the nose.

The dimple is strong on our son's lip. To survive such a rough beginning, perhaps an extra bit of angelic forgetfulness was necessary ahead of time. We left the ward after three weeks, the baby still a mystery to the doctors.

Jacob somehow landed. He is eleven now, as I write this in 2003. When he was younger, after breakfast and before school he liked to lie on the couch, wave a massive toy sword in the air, and tell himself long stories about a superhero named Jacob. I listened at the door and thought of the immense distances heroes travel, and the great risks they take on their journeys. I remember how a Star Boy followed the signal of a human voice and chose to come all the way in.

I once heard someone ask Dr. Hugh Morgan Hill— a.k.a. Brother Blue—why he tells stories. He answered, "I tell stories to keep people from committing suicide." When normal talk breaks down, only the language of Story can express the extreme truths, both bitter and joyful, of human experience. "The story," claims an elder in Chinua Achebe's *Anthills of the Savannah*, "is our escort. Without it, we are blind. Does the blind man own his escort? No, neither do we the story; rather it is the story that owns and directs us." Scheherazade's thousand and one stories redeemed the king's sick soul because they made a tapestry large enough to reflect and challenge even Shahriyar's violent despair. Edward the farmer heard something in the absurd folk tale that sparked a long-lost laugh. The doomed child soldier from Sierra Leone caught an echo of his own possible future in the story Laura Simms told. And what did the three-week-old infant hear through his haze of pain and ubiquitous soundscape of beeps? I like to imagine the stories carried enough love and warmth and beauty that the baby's soul, hearing such earth-music, chose not to leave. Perhaps all storytelling is emergency storytelling.

≪ DREAMING A NEW MYTH ≫

With myths, one should not be in a hurry.

ITALO CALVINO, *Six Memos for the Next Millennium*

A STORYTELLING FRIEND ONCE TOLD ME a story about an anthropologist who happened to be in an African village when the first television was introduced. For about two weeks, the people were captivated by its images, sounds and shows. The old man who was the tribe's greatest storyteller stayed by his fire. After a while, people began to drift away from the TV and gather again by the fire. The anthropologist, observing this, asked one of the villagers why they no longer watched TV. "Don't you think the television knows more stories than the old man? He's never left the district and the TV brings in shows from around the world." "Oh yes," replied the villager. "The television knows more stories, but the storyteller knows me."

A Gaelic proverb says that *Every force evolves a form.* The forms of the storytelling renaissance have sprung from a deeply felt hunger for intimacy, for community, for continuity with the past, for a language of Story through which to speak wisdom. We live at a time of great changes, some positive, some so troubling they are almost beyond human capacity to comprehend. With all of our new technologies of instant data transmission, human beings have never felt more disconnected from our neighbours, families, communities, and nature.

I believe that without forgetting our old and long-standing stories and religious beliefs, we must find a new cycle of stories to help us navigate this unknown terrain. At various periods of history, humans have turned to myth to provide a frame of moral and spiritual understanding. Such a moment has come again. It is time to dream a fresh myth.

In *The Lord of The Rings,* Tolkien has a wise old tree-creature recall the way the ancient earth-people gained their extraordinary power: "They always wanted to talk to everything, the old Elves did." Our greatest hope for survival today is to take a lesson from these elven conversational skills. If we only ever hear and repeat our own story, if we fail to open our ears to new and different voices, the consequences will be both dangerous and extreme. We need a myth to teach us how to listen in a new way to the earth, to each other, to our children, to our dreams. The hero of our new myth could be called, simply, *Listener.*

Listener, of course, isn't new at all. In fact, Listener is one of the oldest spirits in the world, and is an essential part of our everyday lives. Listener was present when I sat by our son's crib in the neonatal intensive care unit and recited Chaucer for dear life. Listener was there as the Bolton Camp boys sat around the campfire hearing ghostly tales. Listener is part of every storytelling jam in the world, giving the host the courage to welcome others to the fire. Listener blesses the rare councils where the poor and the powerful hear each other's stories, or when enemies hear a note of truth in each other's voices. Listener's spirit sustains the storyteller's art, from the concert stages of our great festivals to the loving words of every mother or father who puts a child to bed with an improvised yarn. Listener also lives in scientific labs and field studies. My friend Keith Hopper, a scientist who studies insect populations around the world, recalled what his professor George Salt used to tell his students: "Like St. Francis, zoologists must speak with animals. The trick is to speak clearly enough that the animals hear, and to listen carefully enough to make sense of their response—and never to speak so loudly that the only response is fright." All of these things take place within the circle of Listener's powerful blessing. Listener is the mysterious force that allows stories to spark from a storyteller's tongue—human and beyond-human—directly into the soul of the "behearer."

We can find traces of our myth-to-be in the old wonder tales. In these stories, the act of listening is often as heroic as any battle with a dragon. Say you're walking down the road and you hear a voice down by your shoes. "Friend, I'm hungry. Share your bread and I'll share a secret." On the ground, looking up at you, is a skinny mouse. The mouse is talking to you. What do you do next? The once-upon-a-time stories counsel you to stop and listen, no matter how urgent your journey. Rest a while. Share your bread, even if you've little enough as it is. Above all, don't show your surprise that the mouse is talking, or your shock that you understand its words. Those who ride haughtily by, too proud to listen to a dusty mouse, condemn themselves to dreary inconsequence; sometimes they get turned to stone, but mostly their terminal mediocrity is its own punishment. The true hero, so the stories teach, is the one who is open to hearing new voices, no matter how strange their provenance. In wonder tales, wisdom speaks in unexpected voices. The trick is learning to listen. Your open-hearted listening shows that you have the quality to one day contend with dragons and discover firebirds.

It isn't easy to listen like this. We like our talk to come in familiar voices and from familiar places. Socrates, in his dialogue with Phaedrus, tells an ancient myth and Phaedrus scoffs, "It is easy for you, Socrates, to make up tales from Egypt or anywhere else you fancy." Socrates responds, "Oh, but the authorities of the temple of Zeus at Dodona, my friend, said that the first prophetic utterances came from an oak tree. In fact the people of those days . . . were content in their simplicity to listen to trees or rocks, provided these told the truth." We don't go through daily life listening to mice, dreams, oak trees or, as in Harold Courlander's West African story "Talk," yams: "Well, at last you're here. You never weeded me, but now you come around with your digging stick. Go away and leave me alone!" (The farmer runs away screaming when he hears this indignant yam.)

In Jaime de Angulo's *Indian Tales*, an account of California's Pit River people, a shaman gives this advice: if you want to find power, you must be willing to hear about it from strange sources; go walking alone in the mountains; keep your ears open; sing your best medicine song: "The dragonfly came to me / with news from my home. / I lie in the afternoon / looking toward the hills."

Our world today can seem far removed from myth and mythtellers. "Because a people coevolve with their habitat," writes Sean Kane in *Wisdom of the Mythtellers,* "because they walk the paths their ancestors walked, mythtelling assumes that the stories already exist in nature, waiting to be overheard by humans who will listen for them." He is writing about hunting/gathering societies quite remote from where and when I live, in Toronto, Canada, in the early years of the twenty-first century. As I write this book I can hear streetcars clatter by, jets fly overhead, a telephone ringing, a microwave beeping, and a cartoon character bellowing from a television in the living room. It's not easy to hear the voice of myth in a world that has so thoroughly forgotten its ancestors and their paths.

Yet myth does echo in our lives, even when we don't realize it. I was giving a storytelling workshop to camp counsellors at a camp on Lake Couchiching. When I asked them if the camp had a resident ghost, they told me they didn't go in much for scary stories. I asked if there wasn't *some* kind of spirit haunting the woods, and the young counsellors smiled and said yes, come to think of it, there was a traditional camp spirit. Finnigan the Elf was said to live out there in the forest around the camp. Finnigan wasn't a scary monster, but more like a leprechaun. He helped lost children and befriended lonely ones. They liked to tell the story of Finnigan to first-year campers to help them feel at home there.

Camp Couchiching is in Anishnabe territory, land that has been continuously inhabited for many thousands of years. When I heard about Finnigan the Elf, I remembered Basil Johnston's story "The Little Boy in the Tree" (you can find it in *Next Teller: A Book of Canadian Storytelling,* which I edited in 1994). Johnston, a great Anishnabe storyteller and scholar, describes the *maemae-gawaehnse,* "a little being akin to an elf, who dwells in the forest. This being bears a special kinship to children, coming to them to uplift their spirits should they be despondent, or conducting them back home should they wander away into the forest on their own." The *maemaegawaehnse* had never stopped haunting—or more accurately, blessing—the forest on the shore of Lake Couchiching. It had simply taken on a different name. The counsellors were astonished to realize they had re-created a myth that had been told on that land, in those woods, by that lake, since the beginning of time.

I believe that humans have never lost our instinct for myth. As a child, for example, I fell in love with Athena. I also admired one-eyed Odin, gentle Baldur, fiery Thor, mischievous Hermes; but I felt quite passionate about the beautiful, grey-eyed goddess of wisdom. I was fascinated by the idea that these gods and goddesses once walked among us, shifting or imposing our fate, partaking of human emotion on a divine scale. "To those who *think* the myths," writes Robert Bringhurst, describing the Haida mythtellers of the nineteenth century, "the creatures who inhabit them are real and not fictitious." I *thought* the myths, and wanted them to be real; but I also knew to my sorrow that Athena wouldn't ever visit my middle-class Jewish neighbourhood in northwest Detroit. Even so, I enjoyed the idea that she'd once been a real part of things; had once, for example, guided Odysseus, my hero and hers too, home to Ithaka. Faraway as these things were from my 1950s American childhood, I loved the idea that

world-shaking thunder, mind-shaking wisdom, surpassing desire, great craft and divine skill had once been so
closely woven into the warp of human affairs.

Alongside my awe and affection for the old gods, there
was also, of course, *God,* the protective, though sometimes
wrathful, force I knew from my own ancestry. To this One
I made my evening prayers, asking for blessings for my
parents, my grandparents and my dog (a black mutt
named Cerberus, after the three-headed dog that guards
the gates of Hades), and protection from the hydrogen
bombs we were sure were about to fall on Detroit. I was
around eleven when I switched allegiance from Mount
Olympus to a more modern but equally immortal hero
whose chariot was an Aston Martin, whose nectar was a
martini (shaken not stirred), and who had a Zeus-like
predilection for mortal women. Yet even in the world of
007 I never forgot my first love for grey-eyed Athena and
one-eyed Odin.

Now I'd like to dream a new myth for an ancient spirit.
For this myth to become a real part of our lives, many
others must join in the dreaming. Myths, I'm convinced,
are born from shared dreams. The Australian aboriginals
call Creation the Dreamtime, and their myths the
Dreaming. It may be the world is ready for a great new
dreaming. If we put all of our stories of listening together,
Listener's story will emerge.

One of my favourite Hasidic stories is about a time the
Baal Shem Tov and his faithful scribe went on a pilgrimage to the Holy Land. The ship was becalmed, and the
sailors blamed their Jewish passengers, assuming they had
brought bad luck, and threatened to kill them. The worst
part of it was that the Baal Shem Tov had forgotten all of

his mighty prayers, and couldn't call for divine help. His student implored him to try, but he remembered nothing. Finally, the great teacher and storyteller asked his scribe what *he* could recall. Slowly, painfully, he remembered something: the first two letters of the Hebrew alphabet. He began, tentatively, to murmur them aloud: *Aleph, bet.* The Baal Shem Tov repeated the letters, and even these, the simplest elements of language, had such power that they were saved from catastrophe.

The observations, stories and ideas in this book are my "Aleph, bet." They are still only fragments of a myth, the barely audible echoes of Listener's footsteps coming over the horizon of our twenty-first-century lives. "Not we but those who come after," wrote J. R. R. Tolkien, "will make the legends of our time." If that great mythteller is right, then it is our grandchildren who may one day tell the story of Listener's beneficent spirit, and of a time when men and women learned again to listen to each other, to nature, and to the wee mouse on the road.

Listener,
you abide wherever
stories are told
guiding the words home
to the hearts of the behearers—
You are there when a parent tells at a child's bedside,
when a bard performs before the queen,
when a camp counsellor spins ghost-talk by a bright
    fire,
when the elder gives the tribe its history—
You are there when one prisoner whispers
    deliverance to another,
when the scientist records the language of molecules
    and rivers,
deployments of galaxies and quick chemical
    reactions,
when animals listen to the wind or to each other—
You are there when we try to hear Worldmaker's
    First Story
in the myriad voices of creation—
You are there for the longest stories,
and always stay to the very end,
all-nighters, epics and sagas,
weeklong creation myths,
following the winding thread of the tale
til it ends by dawn-light and ember-glow—
You are there for quick stories told en route and
    every day,
anecdotes, fables, proverbs, miniature wisdoms,
the briefest mind-movie,

the flash of a dream—
All stories belong to you, Listener,
and all storytellers find shelter
in the circle of your ancient blessing—
You teach us to kindle the hearthfire,
to fetch the wine, hand out the cookies,
give granny an extra blanket to coax an extra tale,
for you understand that grannies need extra
    blankets
and storytellers need generous listeners—
You are in the old-time stories,
the ones where heroes fare forth to find their
    fortunes
and there on the road
they meet a misshapen beggar,
a hungry mouse,
an ancient crone,
who says, "Share your bread and I will share my
    wisdom"—
the arrogant older princes,
the haughty, impatient princesses
they can't be bothered to listen
and they ride past to their own dreary destinies—
the true heroes stop,
they share their hearing as generously
as they share their bread—
for this is Listener's way:
when things begin to talk, do not ride past or run
    away—
break your journey, rider,
share your meal—
stay and listen,

even if the story comes from unlikely sources,
a weird mouse or unkempt vagabond,
the earth itself or even a dream—
maybe you'll hear an interesting story—
maybe the story is about you—
maybe the story will change everything—
O Listener,
let us dream a new myth for you,
let us imagine that your great and generous spirit
will dwell among us,
teaching us to hear each other,
to hear nature,
to hear even the smallest voices—
I became a storyteller to honour you,
Many have become storytellers in your name—
O Listener,
May we learn your passion for staying until the very
    end,
your kindness when the storyteller begins,
and your love for every story
the world has to tell.

This is a collection of seven stories from my repertoire. They are all based on traditional patterns that I've rewoven with new yarn. The longest of them, "The Storyteller At Fault," is a linked series of stories told within a frame story about a king and a storyteller. It is a loving homage to the Thousand and One Nights, *and echoes its theme of life-and-death storytelling. The shortest story is a new creation myth about how human tongues came to be red. The others, to varying degrees, I've discussed in a previous chapter. I invite you to retell any you like. A Tuscan proverb has it that "A story is no good unless you add your own spice to it." Please feel free to add spice. I offer these ideas, suggestions and stories in the memory of my own good teachers, and knowing that you—as I continue to do—must find your own voice, repertoire and artistic purpose.*

⟨ WHY ALL TONGUES ARE RED ⟩

This story was inspired by the many creation tales I heard from Mrs. Angela Sidney, a Tagish-Tlingit elder who lived in Yukon Territory.

SCORCH WAS GREEDY. He owned all the fire in the world, and he kept it all to himself. He made his fire blaze high in his cave, glaring and staring at the bright flames and the dancing shadows. He had one eye, and it was red.

The world was cold in those days, cold and quiet. It was cold because Scorch guarded his fire well. In the long winter of the early world, nobody but Scorch had the warmth of the fire. And it was quiet, too, because in those days human beings did not have tongues. We used the language of hands and the language of pictures to talk in those days.

A hunter had once ventured near Scorch's cave. He'd seen the fire, felt its warmth, marvelled at its brightness. But the fire ogre had spotted him with his bright vermilion eye, and thrown a burning coal at him. Scorch wounded the hunter, who barely managed to escape. By the time he staggered back to his people, his death was near. Before he died, he used the language of pictures and the language of his hands to tell what he had seen. For fire, he made a pile of sumac twigs, bright red. Then he drew a picture of Scorch, and put a red berry in the middle of his head to show the one glaring eye. He held his hands over the sumac twigs to show that they were warm. He pointed at the drawing and drew his finger across his throat to show high danger. His wife and his daughter and son held him close, but the wound was too deep.

The people had gathered around the hunter and his grieving family. They looked at these strange drawings and shook their heads. They looked at each other. They shrugged their shoulders. Nobody's hands said anything—people were confused and frightened.

The hunter's daughter was heartbroken. She loved her father, and now he was gone. She kept staring at the sumac twigs and wondering what her father had seen deep in the forest. Red was her favourite colour. She'd dyed her moccasins bright red, and she loved cardinals. She was curious about this strange red force her father had drawn. She knew how cold her mother was in the long winter. She knew her little brother shivered from the cold. She decided to see the sumac-coloured thing for herself.

One day her mother went out to pick berries, and the girl was babysitting her little brother. She decided to take a walk in the forest. Usually the little boy napped for a long time, and she figured he'd sleep while she explored. She left him sleeping in their tent and began to walk into the forest looking for clues. She went in the direction her father had pointed before he died.

She walked a long way.

She walked until she forgot what time it was.

Meanwhile, back at their tent, the little boy woke up. He looked around for his sister. She wasn't there. He couldn't call out for her so he climbed out of bed and started to look for her. He saw the trail leading into the forest, and he started to follow it. Like all children back then, he was a good trail-follower. But somewhere deep in the forest he lost her trail.

She had been wandering a long time when all of a sudden she smelled smoke. It was a new smell to her. It was the smoke from Scorch's private fire. She followed it until she came to a clearing in front of a cave. She crouched in the bushes and watched. There at the entrance of the cave was the most beautiful thing she'd ever seen. Orange and scarlet flames leapt up, sparks cracked up into the air, and the smoke rose grey. Then Scorch appeared. He hunched out of the cave and crouched beside the fire. He was huge and ugly and his one red eye flashed suspiciously around the clearing. She wanted to run away, but she couldn't take her eyes away from the fire. Scorch tossed some dry logs on the fire, and it crackled and burned and looked even lovelier.

Just then she heard the sound of footsteps. Her little brother stumbled out of the bushes, directly in front of Scorch's cave. He had been wandering in the forest looking for his big sister. She couldn't call out a warning—she had no tongue to call with—and she watched with horror as the fire ogre reached out from the cave, curled his claws around the little boy and pulled him inside.

The girl didn't know what to do. Her mother might be picking berries nearby, but she couldn't yell for help. If she ran for the village it might be too late to save the little boy. She decided to fight the ogre all by herself.

She reached down and picked up a rock. Then she stamped her foot to draw his attention. When Scorch turned to see what made the noise, the girl used all her strength to hurl the rock straight at his one glaring eye. Scorch saw her, reached into the fire and picked out a glowing coal. He threw it and it raced towards the girl. He threw it with deadly aim. Her mouth was open and the burning coal flew in. It scalded her mouth, landed deep in her throat and took root there. Scorch's ember turned into the world's first tongue, and when it did, she cried out in pain, and that was the first sound human beings ever made with their voices. Babies have been making that sound ever since, as soon as they're born.

The ogre's coal hit her, but her aim was true. The rock she threw knocked out the ogre's one eye. Blinded, he stumbled and pitched forward and landed in his own fire. His body blazed up like dry cedar twigs, sizzling and scorching in the flames, and there was a great explosion.

She ran past the fire into the cave, and found her little brother. He opened his mouth and started talking—for everybody had received their tongues at the same moment the coal stuck in her throat—and said: "I was really really scared but I knew you'd find me because you're my big sister and why did you leave me all by myself and isn't fire beautiful and wasn't that one-eyed monster ugly and now we won't be cold any more and I wish Daddy could have seen you clobber him and he was wrong to keep fire all to himself and there's mama coming through the woods."

Their mother had heard the huge explosion and come running. She hugged her two children and said, "Are you all right?" That's still the first thing mothers—and fathers—say when they find their kids, before getting mad at them for being lost in the first place.

"Yes, mama," said the girl. "We're fine." And she stuck her thumb up to show they were. Even though she could talk now, she still liked to speak with her hands. "And look at the fire, mama. Isn't it lovely? We won't be cold any more. It was wrong for that mean one to keep it all to himself. Now we can share fire with everyone who needs it."

"And can we have a snack when we get home because I'm starving and I think I have the best big sister in the whole world and that bad guy was *really* ugly and I think I'm going to like talking," said the little boy.

Little brothers—and sisters—have been doing a lot of talking ever since.

And so the girl, her mother and her brother shared their fire with everybody in the village, and the tribe, and the whole early world. Since that day human beings have used fire to stay warm, cook soup, bake bread, harden pottery, melt metal, make toast, launch rockets, dry wet socks, burn things down, gather people into storytelling circles and kindle light.

Since the coal landed in the girl's mouth, all human beings have had tongues, and all tongues are as red as the fire they came from. Like fire, our tongues can be used to bring light or tell lies, to sing or to curse, to cry freedom or speak hate. Best of all, we use our good, red tongues to tell stories.

⟨ RICH AND POOR ⟩

*This is a version of a story well known in Eastern Europe.
I don't remember where I first encountered it, but I've
always loved the image of the circle of men around that
mysterious campfire in the snowy woods. For me, it
echoes the scene in the Japanese story "Urashima Taro,"
when the young fisherman enters the magic garden under
the sea and beholds all four seasons taking place at the
same eternal moment.*

Once upon a time
so long ago the "good old days" were still to come,
and noodles weren't instant, food wasn't fast,
there were no split seconds or rush hours,
and people said, "Come sit down," instead of
   "Hurry up, hurry up!"
and nobody carried watches
but they always had enough time,
and prime-time meant story time,
and people listened before they spoke
and remembered what they heard,

and every granny knew a thousand stories
and each story had more levels than a video game—
back in that time . . .

There was once a woman who was very poor. Her husband had died and left her to raise their five children. Times were hard, she couldn't find a job, and the family barely scraped by. At night, if her children were hungry, she'd sing them her favourite lullaby:

> Summer, autumn, winter, spring
> Turning 'round their blessings bring

When she didn't know what else to do, she and the kids would take a long walk in the woods. She taught them to find extra food in the forest, to gather berries and mushrooms and wild honey. And even if they found no food, they'd come back feeling a little happier.

She had a neighbour who was as rich as she was poor. This woman's husband had disappeared, but she always seemed to have lots of money. She had two kids, quite spoiled. Whatever they whined for they got. They'd play with their stuff for a day or two, then get bored and throw it on the garbage pile: toys, clothes, running shoes, bikes. But they never thought of sharing their things with their poor neighbours, and the poor woman and her children were too proud to ask for help.

One day, after her kids had gone to school, the poor woman heard a knock at her door. It was her neighbour. "My maid ran away," she said, "I need someone to clean, cook and bake today." The poor woman was so happy to take the job that she forgot to ask what the pay was going to be. She cleaned the house, made the beds, picked up the children's toys and dirty socks; then went into the kitchen and began to cook and bake. She baked wonderful loaves of bread for the rich woman and her children. Her mouth watered as she worked. When she finished, she came to the rich woman and said, "I have to go home now. I'd like my pay."

The rich woman barely looked up from her magazine. "Right," she said. "You can keep all the dough stuck to your hands from the baking. That's your pay. Now leave."

The poor woman looked at her boss, looked at her doughy hands—then she heard her children coming home from school, so she hurried away to greet them. The rich woman's laughter echoed behind her.

When she went into the kitchen to make supper for her children, she saw there was nothing to eat. The children came in, looked up at the empty cupboards, and looked at their mother.

"Don't worry, kids," she said, "I'm going to cook something special for supper tonight. Bring a soup-pot. Fill it with water. Light the fire." When they had done these things, she put her hands in the water and began to scrape the dough off her fingers. As she did, she was humming:

Summer, autumn, winter, spring
Turning 'round their blessings bring

She put the pot on the fire and waited. The kids ran away to play, but they came back pretty soon because a delicious aroma was coming from the pot. It smelled like chicken soup, minestrone, beef barley, won ton, cream of mushroom, mulligatawny—all at once. She ladled out a bowl for each kid, and took some for herself. It was the best soup they'd ever tasted, and the best thing was that there was enough for seconds, and thirds, and fourths. Their bellies were full when they went to bed that night. The poor woman stayed up for a long time, thinking and giving thanks for those scraps of bread dough. She remembered seeing the fields of golden wheat back in the summer.

In the morning, there was still plenty of soup left in the pot. They ate it that day, and the next, and for a whole week.

The next day the poor woman came across the street and knocked on her neighbour's door.

"What?" she hissed.

"I've come to see if you need me again this week. I'll work hard, and I don't mind the wages."

The rich woman hired her again, muttering something about fools and beggars. But the poor woman was already busy working, cleaning, cooking, baking. At the end of the day her hands were again covered with dough. She came home, made soup, and the family feasted for another week.

This went on week after week, and there was always plenty of soup—soup made from the scraps of dough from the rich woman's kitchen. The poor woman rejoiced to see her children gain weight, and laugh, and play together. Every night she heard them out in the yard giggling and shouting with well-fed glee.

So did her rich neighbour. She heard the poor kids playing and laughing, and it drove her crazy. Meanwhile, in her own fancy house her own children were always yelling, fighting, biting, complaining, whining. It wasn't fair. Why should those poor kids be so happy, and her kids, who got everything they wanted, do nothing but scream for more?

One day she brought a bag of gold to the local wise woman. She explained the problem.

"When did it begin?" asked the wise woman.

"Since she came to work for me."

"What do you pay her?"

"Nothing but the dough stuck to her hands from her baking."

The wise woman explained: "That's your problem. That dough contains your good luck. Every time she leaves your house, she's taking your good luck away with her."

The rich woman thought about this. How did her fortune wind up in a scrap of bread dough? How could her luck get stuck to a worker's hands?

The next time the poor neighbour came over to cook, clean and bake, the rich woman fired her at the end of the day. She made her wash her hands first, then paid her a dollar and told her to get lost. Sadly, the poor woman crossed the street, and for the first time in many weeks she had nothing to offer her hungry children. The dollar went for a loaf of day-old bread, and that was gone in a minute. But there was no soup that night.

She put the kids to sleep and sang them her song, and there were tears in her eyes as she sang:

> Summer, autumn, winter, spring
> Turning 'round their blessings bring.

When they were all asleep, she did what she always liked to do when things were too hard to bear. She put on her jacket, tied a thin scarf around her neck, and went for a walk in the woods. But it was a cold, cold night, and the snow on the ground made for hard walking. Still, she walked deeper and deeper into the icy forest, humming her good song:

Summer . . . autumn . . . winter . . . spring . . .

All of a sudden, in the middle of the forest, in the middle of the night, there she saw an amazing sight, a campfire blazing bright and all around in the firelight were twelve strange men. They were sitting in a circle. There were three teenagers, wearing sandals, shorts and T-shirts. They sat by the fire holding primroses, daffodils and cowslips. Next to them in the circle were three men in their late twenties. They wore straw hats and held sheaves of wheat. Next were three middle-aged men wearing jackets. They were holding bright red apples and bunches of purple grapes. Then there were three old men with long white beards. They weren't holding anything, just looking at the fire.

The oldest of the old men looked up and saw her standing behind a tree. "We have a guest," he said. "Come and join us. It's cold out here tonight!"

She was glad to step into the circle of men, and come close to the fire.

"We heard your good song a long way off," said the old man. "Now tell me, what are you doing out in the forest on such a cold winter's night?"

"I'm poor," she said, "and my children are hungry. Whenever I'm scared and worried I like to walk in the woods."

"Well," said the old man, "we may be able to help you. But first I must ask you a question. What do you think of the twelve months of the year?"

The poor woman smiled. "I love them," she said, "very much. In spring, the first flowers poke up through the ground and the earth begins to turn green. In summer, the fields are full of golden wheat, and the bread made from it will feed many. In autumn, the leaves turn bright colours, and apples ripen, and grapes grow heavy on the vine. And winter is when the earth is covered with a blanket of white snow, and goes to sleep, and gets ready to waken again in the spring. These are some of my favourite things."

The men were smiling as they listened to her answer. One by one they handed up gifts: flowers, wheat, apples, grapes. Then the old man said, "You have spoken well. Please accept our gifts. This, too." And he handed her a small chest. "Just one thing—do not open it until you get all the way home."

She went around the fire and thanked all the men. Then she started home. If the way there had been long and cold, the way back seemed short and joyful. She got home just before dawn, and waited until the children wandered into the room. They stared at the beautiful spring flowers, the bright red apples, the purple grapes, the yellow sheaves of wheat. Then she asked the youngest child to open the chest. Gold shone in it. It was filled with gold.

They feasted that day. Then the woman took some flour, yeast, honey and eggs, and made a loaf of bread. She took it across the road and knocked on the rich woman's door.

"I told you you're fired," snarled her neighbour.

"I'm not looking for work. I brought you a gift."

"What is it?"

"A loaf of bread. I baked it to thank you for everything you did for me."

"Like what?"

"Well, when you fired me, I didn't know how I'd feed my children any more. So I took a long walk in the woods . . ." And she told her neighbour about singing her song, taking her walk, finding the campfire, receiving the gifts. When the rich woman heard about the chest of gold, she slammed the door. Her neighbour left the loaf of bread by the closed door.

That night the rich woman hurried into the forest. She left her children fighting over the remote. Deeper and deeper she trudged and tramped through the icy woods. As she did, she cursed:

> Winter. Spring. Summer. Fall.
> I hate them all!

Finally she saw something far ahead. In the middle of the forest, in the middle of the night, there was a scary sight— a campfire blazing bright, and there in the circle of the firelight, twelve men. There were three teenagers, wearing sandals, shorts and T-shirts; they held primroses, daffodils and cowslips. Next to them in the circle were three men in their late twenties wearing straw hats and holding sheaves of wheat. Then there were three middle-aged men wearing jackets and holding bright red apples and bunches of purple grapes. Then there were three old men with long white beards. They weren't holding anything, just looking at the fire.

The oldest of the old men looked up and said, "We heard your song through the woods. Why have you come here?"

She barged her way into the circle and stood by the fire. "I want gold," she said, "just like you gave my neighbour."

The old man said, "First, answer my question. What do you think of the twelve months of the year?"

"I hate them all!" hissed the rich woman. "Spring makes me sneeze, summer's too dusty, fall has too many dead leaves, and in winter my feet are always cold. I hate all four seasons! Now where's my gold?"

The twelve men didn't offer her their flowers, wheat, apples and grapes. But the oldest man said, "Here's a chest. I give it to you on one condition. Do not open it until you get all the way home."

She grabbed it and turned away without a word of thanks. Away she hurried through the forest clutching her chest. When she was halfway home, she stopped. "If I take this home they'll all want some and there won't be any left for me," she said to herself. "I'll keep it all for myself!" And she threw the chest down and opened the lid. The chest was full of white snow. She was furious. She kicked the chest over, and the snow poured out and began to swirl around her and turned into an icy blizzard. When they sent the search party out the next day, they found her frozen in the middle of the woods.

What happened to her two kids? They moved across the street to live with the neighbour woman, the one who had once been so poor. And because their new brothers and sisters treated them with kindness and respect, they quit being such brats and were happy with their new mother. As for the woman, if anybody came to her door hungry, poor or cold, she always welcomed them in. She would listen to their story, tell them her story, and offer a nice hot bowl of soup and a loaf of fresh bread. Her children grew up to do the same, and they never forgot their mother's favourite lullaby:

> Summer, autumn, winter, spring
> Turning 'round their blessings bring.

This story is a retelling of "The White Snake" by the brothers Grimm. I've always been fascinated by the motif of the hero gaining the power to understand the language of the animals. Great knowledge can be won, but equally great and unpredictable consequences released.

ONCE THERE WAS A KING who knew things nobody else did. People wondered where he got his mysterious wisdom, but if they ever asked him, he would give a little smile and say, "Oh, a little bird whispered it in my ear." And he wasn't lying, as it turned out.

Every night his trusted servant brought the king a covered dish, and then everybody had to leave the room while the king ate.

One night the servant was so curious about what was in the dish that he carried it to his own room, locked the door, and lifted the lid. There on the dish he saw a white snake, cooked and coiled. He reached out, took a little piece, and put it in his mouth. He ate it. Just at that moment, his ears tingled and—

He heard voices new and strange
Chirping out of human range.

The voices were coming from the windowsill. When he looked, he saw there were some sparrows eating seeds. They were talking. "Would you like another seed?" "Oh, no thanks. I'm full." He understood every word they chirped! The white snake had given him the power to understand the language of the animals. Now he knew the secret of the king's great wisdom.

Unfortunately, that very day the queen came running to the king with terrible news. "Somebody stole my most precious ring!" she said. "I left it in my bedroom and now I can't find it."

"How could this be?" cried the king. "The only people who go into your room are you, me and the trusted servant. The trusted servant . . . Guards! Bring me the servant immediately!"

The guards ran out and arrested the young man. They brought him in chains before the king, who said, "I thought I could trust you, and now look what you did! You stole the queen's most precious ring!"

"No," said the servant bravely, "that is not true. I did not steal the ring. I am innocent!" (He didn't mention that he had stolen a taste of the king's secret snake.)

"Because you have been trustworthy until now," said the king, "I will give you twenty-four hours to prove your innocence. If you cannot bring the ring back in that time, your head will be chopped off."

Well, the servant hadn't taken the ring; but he had no idea where to look for it. They undid the handcuffs, and the servant walked out into the palace garden. Just as he passed the pool, his ears tingled and—

He heard voices new and strange
Gabbling out of human range.

There by the palace lily pond were two geese. They were talking. "Oi," said the grey one, "my stomach is killing me!"

"Why?" asked the other.

"I don't know. I must have eaten something I shouldn't have. Something fell off the queen's windowsill and I gobbled it up without looking."

"Ach, you silly goose!" said his companion. "Never eat something you haven't seen before!"

When the servant heard these words, he walked over to the pond and grabbed the grey goose by the neck. He took it to the cook in the royal kitchen and said, "I think this would make a nice feast for the king and queen."

When they killed the goose and took out the guts, there was the queen's ring. The servant cleaned the goose guts off and took it to the king. "You see," he said, "I am no thief. Here's the queen's ring."

The king knew he'd been wrong to accuse his trusted servant of theft, and he said, "To make up for my unjust accusation, ask me for anything you want and I'll give it to you."

The young man didn't hesitate. "I would like only three things," he said. "My freedom, a horse and enough money to travel with."

The king and queen gave him his freedom, and a purse of money, and bade him go into the stables to find himself a horse. As he was walking past the fine stallions and mares, his ears tingled and—

He heard a voice new and strange
Neighing out of human range.

"Choose me!" a mare murmured, looking sideways at him as he walked past. So he did. He led the horse out of the stables, said goodbye to the king and queen, and rode off to seek his fortune.

He got on his horse and rode away
He rode all night and most of the day

Until he came to a road that ran alongside a river. As he rode past some reeds, his ears tingled and—

He heard voices new and strange
Gulping out of human range.

There the young man saw three fish, stranded in the reeds. They were gasping and gulping, and crying for help. "Please, help us!" they called. "We're stuck in these reeds and we cannot get free!"

He listened, sitting in the saddle, until his horse murmured, "Go help them. They'll die if you don't."

So he jumped down and walked over to the fish. He bent down, picked them out of the reeds, and carried them back to the river. As they splashed down into the water, one of them looked back and said, "Thank you. One day we'll help you too." Then they swam happily away.

He got on his horse and rode away
He rode all night and most of the day

until his ears began to tingle and—

He heard voices new and strange
Peeping out of human range.

The sounds were coming from the road beneath his horse's hooves. A line of ants was trying to cross the road, just where he was riding. One stood in front of him and peeped, "Please stop, human rider. Can't you see you're crushing my people?"

The young man looked down at the ant and said, "I'm sorry. I didn't even see your people."

"That's the problem," said the king of the ants, for that's who it was. "You humans never pay attention to the little people of the world. Just because we're so small doesn't mean we're not people!"

The young man sat there staring down at the ants until his horse murmured, "We'll go the long way around. That way we won't hurt any more ants." So he pulled on the reins and they left the road. As they rode away, he heard the king of the ants call out, "Thank you, human! One day we will help you!"

He rode and he rode, until he came to a great tree. There was a raven's nest in the tree, and as he rode by his ears tingled and—

He heard voices new and strange
Cawing out of human range.

Three baby ravens were calling for help. "Get out of the nest," cawed their father. "We're tired of feeding you," screeched the mother. And they tossed the three nestlings out of the nest onto the ground below. "Please help us," said the little ones. "We're too young to find food for ourselves!"

The young man looked down at the baby birds.

His mare murmured, "Feed them."

"But I don't have anything to feed them with," he said. "They eat carrion—dead meat."

"Kill me," said the horse, "and give my body to the baby ravens."

"I can't do that!" cried the young man. "I love you, and you've helped me so much."

"You must," said the horse, "and if you do, perhaps something will happen that is meant to happen."

So, weeping, he took his sword and killed the horse and fed the meat to the baby ravens. "Thank you," they cawed. "We will help you one day, too."

He walked on
A long way or a short way
Only the First Storyteller of the World
Knows how far he walked.

But his heart was full of grief for his horse, and he could no longer understand the languages of the animals.

One day he came to the gates of a great city. A trumpeter blew on a trumpet and made this announcement: "Hear ye, Hear ye! The princess of this city has decided to get married. Whosoever can pass the three impossible tests is eligible to be chosen."

"What happens," asked the young man, "if you try the tests and fail?"

"Something terrible," said the trumpeter.

"May I see the princess before I decide?" asked the young man. And when he beheld the princess, he was amazed at her beauty. Something about her looked familiar, as if they'd met before—her long mane of shining hair, her fine white teeth, the way she moved, her graceful neck. He said, "I'll try the three impossible tests, because the most impossible thing of all would be to live without her."

He'd fallen in love as quickly as a storyteller can say the words "in love."

For the first test, the princess led him up to a cliff overlooking the ocean. She took off a gold ring and held it shining and sparkling in front of him. Then she cocked her arm and pitched the ring away over the cliff. He watched it splash into the waves far below. "Bring back my ring," she said.

The young man tramped down the trail to the beach. He stared at the waves rolling in, cresting and breaking endlessly on the shore. All of a sudden, three fish poked their heads out of the water. One of them held something in its mouth. The fish swam over and dropped it in his hand. It was the ring. "Thank you," he called out, but the fish had already vanished under the waves.

He took the ring and carried it back to the princess. She couldn't believe he'd found it. For the second test, she led him to the palace. There were ten sacks of millet seeds. She opened the sacks and began to scatter the seeds everywhere on the ground, even under the couch in the royal living room. Then she said, "By tomorrow at dawn, pick up every seed and put it all back into the sacks. If there's one left, you die."

He got down on his hands and knees and started to scoop up the millet. It ran through his fingers like sand. Finally he lay down to rest a bit before he met his terrible fate. He woke up just before dawn to feel a tiny pull on his ear. There was the king of the ants, and lined up on the floor, a million of his little people. The ten sacks were full. "Thank you," he whispered, but the ants had already turned and marched away.

The princess was astonished when she beheld the full sacks. Then she said, "Your third test is the most impossible of all. Go to the end of the world and bring back the Apple of Life!"

Even that, he thought, is not as impossible as losing you! But he didn't say it out loud. He just stood there wondering which road might lead him to the end of the world. Just then he heard a cawing in the blue sky above. Three black ravens, full-grown now, were circling above him.

One had something in its beak. It was an apple. The apple fell into the young man's hand. "Thank you," he cried out, but the ravens had already wheeled off through the clouds.

He turned to the princess and handed her the apple. When she held the Apple of Life, she smiled at the young man who had passed her three impossible tests. She cut the apple in half, and gave him half. They ate it together, and found so much joy together that only the First Storyteller of the World could find words to describe it.

After they were married, the young man often gazed at his wife. Was she or wasn't she? The strangest part of the story is that, even though he once knew the language of the animals, sometimes he still found it very hard to understand the language of women. But what he'd learned from the white snake, the sparrows, the geese, the fish, the ants, the ravens, and, of course, the mare—so beautiful, with her flowing mane and gentle voice—was that you have to keep trying. So he did. And whenever his wife saw that he was truly listening, she tossed her magnificent hair and gave a low whinny of delight.

This story grew out of "Wicked John and the Devil," in Richard Chase's Grandfather Tales.

THIS IS A STORY ABOUT A TIME the devil came to Toronto. It happened in Little Italy, where I used to live, in a café called the Café del Diavolo—the Devil's Café. The café wasn't called that because anything bad went on there, but because the owner, a man named Renato, liked to cook his food very *piccante*—spicy. In Italian cooking, you call it cooking something *alla diavola*: as hot as the devil. His most famous dish was *pasta alla Diavola*—which is why the story is called "The Devil's Noodles." I was always trying to get him to tell me his secret recipe, but he never would. He'd lean over the counter, white chef's hat on his head, and whisper, "Hey, Dan, can you keep a secret?"

I'd nod eagerly, hoping to hear the recipe.

"Well, so can I!" he'd laugh, turning back to stir the soup.

Renato was a bit of a *diavolino*, it's true. He chain-smoked, drank too much *vino rosso* (which he called grape juice, kept in an unplugged freezer at the back, and sold without a liquor licence), never paid his taxes, didn't go to church, and told his neighbours exactly what he thought about them. As if that weren't enough, he gambled on the horses every day. In fact, if his horse won that day, the price of your meal would be low. If his horse lost, the price went up. The neighbours used to say he was a little *pazzo*—a little crazy. But for all his sins, the café was like a community centre. Old men came over to drink espresso and talk politics, kids came by after school to get free biscotti. Renato loved children. He and his Filipina wife, Perry, didn't have kids themselves, although they'd wanted to. If you walked into the café with a *bambino*, Renato would come out from behind the counter, chef's hat on and cigarette dangling from his mouth. He'd sweep the baby up in his arms and waltz around the café singing "Volare." He was also kind to old people, always helped out the poor and loved his wife, who was as quiet-spoken as he was voluble.

One day, something happened. If it hadn't happened, how could I tell you about it? I was sitting in the café eating some *pasta alla diavola* and sipping some grape juice when I saw a parade go by on the street outside. There were always little parades on the streets of Little Italy. This one seemed to be in honour of a saint. I saw the kids from the local church march by, and the priest, and a band. Behind them was a big Cadillac filled with soccer players. They were shouting, "Viva Italia!" All of a sudden the crowd pulled back. Right in front of the window where I was sitting, a raggedy old man stumbled onto the sidewalk. His clothes were shabby, his beard unkempt, his hair sticking out every which way from under a broken-down old hat. Not only that, he was in a state of immoderate inebriation. I mean, this old man, he played nine, he'd been drinking too much wine! He was feeling no pain. In fact, he seemed to be enjoying the parade, weaving along and hollering, "Go, angels, go!"

The crowd was getting mad. Some of the bigger teenagers started to taunt the old fellow. "Hey, *vagabondo!* Get out of here! We don't need tramps like you spoiling our parade!" Just as it was starting to get ugly Renato came storming out of the café, white chef's hat on his head, wooden spoon in his hand and fire in his eyes. "How can you treat an old, homeless man like that!" he yelled at the crowd. "Just because he's poor doesn't mean he has no pride!" And he took the old man's arm and led him into the café. Then he put him at the table next to me and began to serve him a meal fit for a king. He brought him devil's noodles, salad, bread, chicken, even grape juice from the freezer. For dessert, he served him one of his famous cappuccinos, covered with thick foam and shavings of chocolate.

The old man began to eat like he hadn't had a meal for many days. The problem was I was sitting next to him, and it was not a pretty sight. He gobbled and guzzled and slurped and burped. The bread crumbs tumbled down his shirt, and the noodles flapped as he chewed them. I lost my appetite and got up. When I went to pay, I said to Renato, "Why did you let him in? He smells bad!"

"Because we have to take care of poor people," he said. "If I didn't help him, who would?"

I paid and left. The rest of this story I did not witness myself. I heard it from Perry, who heard it from Renato, and she says that he says it's true.

Apparently, just a minute or two after I left, Renato had turned away to do the dishes, and when he turned back again, the old man had disappeared. Yet sitting in the same chair, at the same table, was a new old man. This new old man was dressed in a thousand-dollar Italian suit, a Panama hat, beautifully shined shoes. The strangest thing was that he was sipping from the beggarman's cup of cappuccino, holding it as delicately as a king might hold a golden goblet. Renato's jaw hit the ground and his eyes hit the ceiling. "Eh!" he said. "Where's the other old man, the *vagabondo* who was just here? Who are you?"

The new old man rose from the table, made a courtly bow, and said, "I am the *vagabondo*. Allow me to explain. You see, Signor Renato, I am an angel from heaven. Once a year I dress in rags and wander through the world looking for kind people. In the city of Toronto nobody would help me but you."

"It was nothing," said Renato, a little embarrassed.

"It was not nothing," said the angel. "It was a good thing to do. I'm even going to give you a reward for your kindness."

"I don't want anything," said Renato.

"Still, here it is," said the angel. "I'm going to give you three wishes blessed with the power of heaven. You can have anything you want. Choose well."

Renato laughed. "Three wishes from heaven? But . . . to tell you the truth, angel, I don't really need anything. My wife loves me, business is not too bad, my friends come by to keep me company. I don't even want to win every time on the ponies—it wouldn't be fun then. The only thing I've ever wanted with all my heart and soul was a *bambino* of my own. But what can I do? I've got too many grey hairs on top of my head for that. No, how about you give my three wishes to somebody who could really use them." The angel stared at him. "I can't do that," he said. "Wishes from heaven are nontransferrable. You have to use them yourself. There have to be some things you can think of."

"Well, yes . . . but I'm not sure you'll approve," said Renato, with a twinkle in his eye. "Okay, here goes. See those bar stools over there? The kids like to come in after school and spin around on them. Then, when the old guys come by, I tell the kids to get off—and you know what kids are like, they keep spinning and spinning. So here's my first wish. Give me the power to teach the kids a little lesson. If they want to spin, I'll make them spin. I'd like the power to make their bums stick to the stools and spin 'em at a hundred kilometres an hour. That should teach them a lesson."

The angel was not amused. "That's a bad wish," he said. "You've just wasted a wish from heaven on a stupid practical joke!"

"Yep," chuckled Renato, "and I've just thought of my second wish. See this frying pan? I made it myself. I used to be a blacksmith in the old country, and I made my own pots and pans. The trouble is the neighbours borrow it. Then they bring it back rusty. That makes me mad. I'd like the power to make somebody I don't like sit in the frying pan when it's on the stove filled with olive oil. That should teach my neighbours a lesson."

The angel was about to say something, so Renato hurried on. "And here's my third wish. I'm always worried that somebody suspicious might come into the café—the liquor inspector, the tax collector, who knows, maybe the devil himself. I'd like the power to make somebody like that get in my freezer at the back of the café and stay there until I let them out."

"It's true what they say about you," said the angel. "You are truly a *diavolino!* Anyway, before I go back where I came from, I've got a little tip for you. Fifth horse in the fifth race at five o'clock!" And so saying, the angel disappeared.

Renato could barely wait until the afternoon horse race. He took five hundred dollars and headed to the racetrack. He bet the whole amount on the fifth horse running in the fifth race at five o'clock—and it came in fifth! When his wife heard about how much money he'd blown at the racetrack, she was furious. She threw a bowl of tortellini at him and shouted, "May the Devil take you!" Normally she was a gentle, quiet-spoken woman, but this time she was very cross.

Later that night, around midnight, Renato was sweeping up when he heard a knock at the door. When he opened it, there was a little boy standing there. A little boy devil.

"I've come to get you," he said. "My daddy sent me."

"And who's your daddy?" asked Renato.

"He's the *padrone*, the boss," said the little devil.

"Boss of where?" asked Renato.

"You'll find out," the boy devil said, with a wicked smile.

Renato thought fast, and then said, "Hey, I'll be with you in a minute. I just have to finish cleaning the place up. How about you make yourself at home. There's a plate of *biscotti* over on the counter—help yourself."

The boy devil came in and jumped up on a bar stool. He grabbed some *biscotti* and stuffed them in his mouth. Just then, the bar stool began to spin. It went faster and faster, one hundred, two hundred kilometres an hour, and that little devil was looking pretty bad as he whipped around on the stool. "Help!" he yelled. "Make this thing stop! I'm going to toss my *biscotti!*"

He did look pretty green as he spun faster and faster. Renato finally said, "Bar stool, stop! As for you, get out of here and don't ever come back."

The little devil went spinning out the door and down College Street, and Renato stood in the entrance, white chef's hat on his head, wooden spoon in his hand—and he laughed and laughed.

It might have stopped there, but about a week later Renato had a funny gambler's feeling. He took four hundred dollars and bet it on the fourth horse running in the fourth race at four o'clock. The horse came in fourth. This time Perry took the big frying pan and chased him all around the café. She was pretty upset. "Ai! You're wasting all the money we saved to go back to Italy! May the Devil take you!"

Be careful when you say things like that to someone you love. That night, as Renato was cleaning up, he heard a knock at the door. It was midnight. He opened the door and saw a teenager standing there. He had baggy pants, a baseball cap turned backwards, and a few rings and studs and other things in his face. "Yo," he said, "my daddy sent me. And I don't appreciate what you did to my little brother. He's still spinning around doing pirouettes in hell. Let's blow this pop stand."

Renato thought fast. "Hey—I was just going to cook up a midnight snack. Some *pasta alla diavola*. I'll make it extra *piccante*."

Teenagers are always hungry, and the devil said he'd stay. Renato took the cast iron pan, poured in some extra virgin olive oil, chopped up some garlic, onions and hot peppers, and put it on the stove behind the counter. When the oil was smoking hot, he turned to the teenager and said, "Please get in. I'm going to fry some *diavolo alla diavola!* I like my devils well done!"

The teenage devil climbed up and sat down bum-first in the burning oil. He twisted and turned, but the pan kept toasting his buns. "Let me go!" he screamed.

"I didn't hear you use the magic word," said Renato.

"Please!" he shouted.

"This is Canada. What about French?"

"*S'il-vous plaît!*"

"This is Little Italy . . ."

"*Per favore!*"

"Make up a poem," said Renato. "I'm in the mood for some poetry."

What could the teenage devil do? He had to rap a poem.

"Please Mr. Renato,
Listen to me,
Your frying pan's causing me agony,
I beg you make it stop real fast,
Before it permanently burns my—"

"*Basta!*" said Renato. "Enough. Get out of here and don't ever come back."

The devil hoped out of the frying pan and ran down College Street holding his tender tushie.

About a week later, what with heaven, hell, horses and hot peppers running around his head, Renato took a thousand dollars and went to the races. He bet it all on the first horse running in the first race at one o'clock. He was so nervous he couldn't even watch the horses; he just listened to the race over the loudspeakers. His horse came in last.

When his wife heard the news, she was not amused. In fact, she began to yell, "*Il gioco ha il diavolo nel cuore!* Gambling has the Devil in its heart! *Pazzo!* You've just wasted all of our savings! May the Devil take you out of my life!" She slammed the door and stomped upstairs.

He felt awful. How could he have done such a crazy thing? He sat on a bar stool and poured a glass of grape juice from the freezer. Around midnight, there was a knock at the door. Renato opened it. There was a tall man wearing a very fine dark suit and sunglasses. On the sidewalk, parked illegally, was a stretch limo with smoked glass windows.

"Renato," hissed the man in a cold, low voice. "I think you know who I am."

"Si."

"And you know why I've come."

"I can guess."

"I'm not very happy about the way you treated my two little devils, so I've come to do the job myself. I've been waiting to meet the famous noodle-maker for a long time. I think you'll find things down there plenty *piccante*."

"Signor Diavolo," said Renato, thinking fast. "Before you take me away, let's have a toast. I've never met anyone as famous as you before. I've got a nice bottle of Chianti in the freezer at the back."

The Devil wasn't averse to a glass of good Italian wine. He walked to the back of the café and opened the lid of the freezer. Renato shouted, "By the power of heaven, get in the freezer you big gangster!" The Devil jumped in, the lid slammed shut, and Renato began to laugh. He walked over, plugged the freezer in, and turned it from normal to coldest. Then he did what many men would do in a situation like that. He took a box of the finest Italian chocolates and went upstairs. He knocked on the door. Perry yelled, "Get out of here! I never want to talk to you again! You wasted all our money."

"Darling," he said, "*mio amore* . . . I have some chocolate." After a long pause, she said, "Come in."

He went in, apologized for gambling, and she forgave him. Married people have to be very good at forgiving each other!

In the morning he went downstairs. There were muffled screams coming from the freezer. He walked over and said, "Hey, Popsicle! You still in there? I'll let you out if you promise to never bother me again."

"I . . . I . . . I . . . p . . . p . . . promise . . ."

Renato lifted the lid and the Devil climbed out. His teeth were chattering and his sunglasses were all frosted over. He walked stiffly to the door, ice-cubes falling out of his pants. The limo had been towed. The last anyone saw of the Devil, he was heading east on College Street towards City Hall.

The story is almost over. Renato and Perry did save their money again, and moved back to Italy. He became a tour guide near Firenze. One day, not long ago, I got a letter from Perry. She wrote:

Dear Dan,

I have some good news and some bad news. The good news is Renato wrote down his recipe for *pasta alla Diavola*. It's inside this envelope. He wants you to learn how to cook it. The bad news is he's not feeling too well. Too many cigarettes and grape juice. The doctors think he'll make it, but he says he's not too worried either way. Even if he dies, he figures the angels will remember him from that parade. And if he can't get in upstairs, he says the Devil will be too scared to let him into hell. Maybe he'll just give him a big radicchio full of hellfire and tell him to go start a hell of his own somewhere. Anyway, we remember Toronto and we think of you often. Renato says most of that *pazzo* story about the Devil is true.

   Amore,

   Perry

P.S. Renato was wondering—how's your new *bambino*?

If you ever visit Toronto, go to the southeast corner of Beatrice and College, just past the Gatto Nero café. There's a fruit store where Renato's place used to be. The whole area's becoming a little more fashionable than when I lived there, but the old-timers still remember the great cook who was a bit of a *diavolino* and who made the best pasta in town.

≪ THE DEVIL IN DON MILLS ≫

This story is about an encounter with a shady computer salesperson in a suburban shopping mall. It grew from a poem by Baudelaire, based on the Faust legend (from his Fleurs du Mal *to my* Fleurs du Mall!*) and from Mikhail Bulgakov's evocation of Satan in his novel* The Master and Margarita.

LET'S SPEAK OF THE DEVIL. I know we usually don't. Most of you don't even believe in him any more. You think he's just a stale-dated relic from the bad old superstitious days. Even his dread and ancient names sound more like skipping rhymes than invocations of evil: *Apples peaches pears and plums, something wicked this way comes, Beelzebub, Mephisto too, Lucifer will come for you!*

The Devil has become a kind of Unidentified Flying Object of the moral firmament. Sightings are reported regularly on the back pages of supermarket tabloids: "Teens Caught Skinnydipping in Nepean Town Reservoir— Mayor Suspects Satan Worship!" "New Jersey Couple Claims Three-year-old Daughter Possessed by Devil—

Nobody Can Exorcise Her Tantrums." Yep, you can read all about it, along with that terrible story about the alien abduction from the convenience store in Calgary, or Elvis's latest appearance somewhere in the clouds north of Nashville. No wonder you don't believe the Devil's still around.

But I do. I know for a fact he hasn't taken a time-share option in some other galaxy. And it's not because I'm less scientific than the rest of you. I believe in progress, science and enlightenment, just like you. In fact, I never even read my horoscope (that's a characteristic of Virgos, by the way), I haven't seen *The Exorcist*, and I always read *Scientific American* on airplanes, if all the *People* magazines have already been taken. No, I believe in the Devil for one very good reason. I once met him.

It happened in a shopping mall in Don Mills, Ontario. Don Mills is a famous suburb of Toronto. It was Canada's first planned community. Planners planned it all according to plan. They laid it out well: house house house house parkette school church house house house. And in the middle of the suburb, they laid the centrepiece, the jewel of the crown: Don Mills Plaza, which everybody just calls "the Plaza." It's a little-known fact that when they first built the Plaza, it didn't have a roof. It was more like an old-time village marketplace. But after a few cold winters, everybody complained, and they put a roof over the whole thing, and now it's just like the mall near you. But it didn't start out that way. They say Don Mills is nice, if you like living in a planned community. Me, I prefer downtown.

Anyway, one day I was driving by the Plaza and decided to stop in, for no particular reason. Sometimes I just like to drift with the crowd and meander through the mall. I wasn't looking to buy anything. Even if I'd wanted to, I was no longer the master of my Mastercard. I was strolling and window-shopping. School had let out, and the mall was full of sneering, leaning teenagers. Everybody seemed to be hustling, hurrying, lingering, loitering, and I floated along the halls observing my fellow-humans. After a while I looked at my watch and was amazed to see a whole hour had gone by as if it had never been. What happens to time in the suburbs? I was hungry and felt like a glazed dough-nut. I thought I'd walk up to the food court, pick up a day-old doughnut, and head home.

Just then I noticed a shop I'd never seen before. The name was Eden Memory Systems, and the window was full of computers. Two angels held a monitor while a neon sign flashed below them: Let Eden Remember for You! There was a man standing in the doorway, and something about him caught my eye. I've always been a people-watcher. When I was little, my parents were embarrassed to take me to restaurants because I'd stare so much at the other diners. At first, I couldn't figure out what was dif-ferent about him. His clothes could have been bought at any of the chain stores up and down the mall. He looked quite ordinary, though his tan did glow a bit under the hazy fluorescent light. He was tapping his foot to the Muzak and smiling at the passing parade of mallfolk. Then it hit me. Everybody else I'd seen in the Plaza looked impatient or bored—but this man looked happy and serene. He was the only person in Don Mills Plaza who looked as if he belonged there.

He saw me standing there, smiled and walked into the store. I decided to follow him. Normally I'm spooked by salespeople, but somehow I felt safe; I knew he'd be gentle with me.

I stepped inside.

"Welcome to Eden," he said. "May I help you?"

"Yes," I said. "I'm thinking of upgrading my system." That was a lie. I didn't even have a system! To tell you the truth, I'm not very fond of computers. I like machines. I've rebuilt transmissions, used my wife's sewing machine, and even gone after bass with a fish-finder. But computers have always left me cold. It was the man, not his machines, that drew me into the shop.

"What kind of equipment are you selling?" I asked, continuing my bluff. I couldn't believe I was doing this to an innocent salesman. See, I've always thought it was wrong to lie to strangers. They're completely innocent. Sometimes with friends, we have no choice; but who could we trust if we couldn't trust strangers? I had a friend once, or really more of an acquaintance, who told me his hobby was lying to strangers. He'd get on a plane and start making up a story for the person sitting next to him. He'd say he was just coming back from the surfing championship at Waikiki, or that he was a neurosurgeon experimenting with brain transplants, or he was a hard rock miner from Yellowknife. The object of the game was to lie so well that his seatmate didn't believe him when they were going through customs and he told the truth, which was that he was an accountant from Ottawa. I think that's a terrible game! Mind you, I'm not sure he was telling me the truth either. And now here I was doing the same thing, telling a total lie to a complete stranger.

He began to show me around the shop. "This is the Malum One, our entry-level system. We have the Gabriel, which is a laptop, and the Paradise 1000 for heavy-duty business use." He went on and on in a pleasant, low voice, using words that always sound like an invocation in some ancient tongue even though we hear every day: RAM and ROM, hard drives and softwares, processors and microchips, megabytes and websites, modems and monitors and memory. He used that word a lot, and it was the only one I understood. He ended his spiel by saying, "Human memory is, unfortunately, a frail vessel. You lose important files, forget to save data, and let feelings corrupt your hard drives. With Eden Memory Systems, all that has changed. We've just made remembering a whole lot easier, safer and more reliable. You can start with a Malum One and upgrade from there. Come on," he said, still smiling— I think he must have realized I didn't know much about computers—"Are you ready to take your first megabyte?"

To tell you the truth, it was starting to sound pretty good to me. I've often thought remembering is one of the harder things humans have to do. I've got a pretty feeble memory myself: especially for facts and figures, like, Did the French beat the English in the Hundred Years War, or did the English beat the French, and was it a Two-Hundred-Year war? Not to mention the terrible things from our own war, and my mother's stories, and what I did to my first girlfriend, and what my second girlfriend did to me. Remembering has never been easy, at least for me. Anything that could help us remember better was worth the price. In fact, how did we ever get along without the damn things? I reached for my wallet to get my credit card to place my order.

Just then I remembered something. Something about Malum, his entry-level system. *Malum*. Something from

THE DEVIL IN DON MILLS   225

my high school Latin class. *Malum*. We used to say, "Latin is a dead language, as dead as dead can be; first it killed the Romans, and now it's killing me." *Malum*. Something from that dead tongue was sending a strong signal. Malum. Malicious . . . malignant . . . malevolent. Malum. Maladroit . . . malapropos . . . Les Fleurs du Mal. Malls. Malum. All of a sudden, I remembered: *Malum* was Latin for apple!

Then I remembered something else. A story. A very old story about a smooth-talking serpent selling sweet fruit to an unsuspecting customer in a place of great abundance. And here I was, with this computer salesman trying to get me to take a megabyte of his Malum . . . in a mall! I began to think—if I switched to an Eden Memory System I would no longer call things to remembrance from within myself but by means of his electronically powered, binary-coded digital database. This was no modern miracle machine for remembering; it was a diabolically clever method to microsoften human memory into mega-processed mush! Diabolical? Oh, my God! Now I knew who he really was! Possessed by a crazy courage, I pointed my credit card at him and uttered his true and eternal name straight to his face: "Satan!"

Nothing happened. He just stood there smiling. Oi, did I feel like an idiot. I was sure he'd punch my lights out, or call the mall security guard, or have me charged for slander. But just then he gave a little bow, looked up, and said, *"Oui. C'est moi."*

Wouldn't you know he'd be bilingual!

"I'll be damned," I said.

"At your service," he said.

I didn't know what to do. Should I put him under citizen's arrest, or run through Wal-Mart screaming, "The

Devil's in Don Mills!'"? Have you ever gotten on an elevator with a famous rock star or politician, and you have a million questions, but by the time you open your mouth the door opens and they step off? That's what it was like now. I'd never met anyone this famous before, and I was bursting with questions.

"You can't be real!" I said. "Nobody even believes in you any more."

"That's fine," he replied. "I still believe in you. And there are a few of you who still believe. Some weapons designers, assistant ministers of defence, poets, storytellers, dancers . . . Besides, I prefer to operate incognito."

"But why here? Why Don Mills Plaza?"

"It's the perfect global headquarters for my takeover operation. Nobody will ever guess it's me," he said.

I was about to point out that *I* had guessed, but then I remembered the old saying: Discretion is the better part of valour. And besides, don't they say that the Devil's favourite ruse is to pretend he doesn't exist? It occurred to me I'd better check my brakes before driving home. You know the proverb: ashes to ashes, dust to dust, if the Lord don't take me, the Devil must.

"How the hell did you get into electronics? What exactly *are* you selling?" I asked him.

"Same ol' same ol,'" he said. "Business as usual. I'm just peddling what I've always sold. In fact, I'm moving more product than ever. I've found a real market niche. I sell innocence—or the next best thing: forgetfulness. You humans are always trying to crawl back into paradise, back to that nice world of binary-coded right and wrong, truth and falsehood, good and evil, off and on. This world is just too complicated sometimes. I understand this.

That's why I came up with my Eden Memory System. Now you can double-click on data and pretend you're getting wisdom. You can double-click on memory and is it my fault you start forgetting what makes things worth remembering in the first place. You humans are the ones who buy it; I just market the stuff."

It was his smile that made me so mad. I looked the Devil in his cathode-bright eyes and said, "I'll be damned if I help you develop your diabolical dominion of duplicity one double-click at a time! I'll never buy your computer! I'd rather do my own remembering, even if I'm not that good at it!"

Actually, what I said was, "I've got to go now. Thanks for showing me the shop. I don't think I'll get one today." I turned to leave, but before I could cross the threshold I heard him whisper in my ear, "Do you like games?"

Damn him. I *do* like games.

"I've got a great new game in the back room. Nobody's played it yet. Would you like to play it with me?"

I followed him to a door at the back of the shop. We entered a beautifully decorated room. It had thick carpets, real wood panelling, recessed lights. And in the middle was a game. Its name was emblazoned with fiery letters on the side: SOULRAIDER.

"What stakes are we playing for?" I asked the Devil.

"The usual ones," he said.

We stepped up to the game and began to play. It was the most exciting game I've every played. There were mazes and chases, aliens and treasures, a girl warrior in a bikini with laser bazookas, adventures and flashing lights and non-stop beeps, levels and more levels. I was dodging, shooting, attacking, escaping—I was completely lost in the game. Then I noticed that his last video creature had cornered my last video creature. I twisted and turned, I fired my weapon. Kabam! Kaboom! Kaplooie—I missed. He didn't. His creature blew my creature to kingdom come. I turned to him and said, "Just let me play one more level!" But the screen went dark, a little voice sang, "That's all, folks, and the game was over.

He gave me a moment to catch my breath, then he asked, "How did you like it?" He sounded like he really wanted to know, like he was market-testing a new product instead of the oldest game in the world.

"Not bad," I told him. Then I realized what had happened. "Hey, have you just won my eternal soul?"

He nodded.

"How come I feel the same as before?" I demanded.

"Oh, very few of you notice much difference at all," he said.

I looked around and saw that this room wasn't so fancy after all. The carpet was threadbare, the panelling was fake, a couple of bulbs had burned out in the ceiling. The Devil was wearing a cheap aftershave, which I'd smelled on the subway many times before. All of a sudden I really wanted to get back downtown.

Before I left I asked him one more question. "Now that you've won my eternal soul, what are you going to do with it?"

For the first time, he looked puzzled. "Not much," he said, "but then, what did you do with it before you lost it?"

I turned and left. Just at the threshold I looked back. The Devil was still standing next to Soulraider. He looked lonely.

I got in my car and headed over to the Don Valley Parkway and drove downtown. The brakes were fine.

It was a long time before I got back out to the suburbs, but I did drop in to the Plaza just the other day. Eden was gone, but I wasn't surprised to see he'd opened a dozen new stores throughout the mall, and every one of them was selling memory machines. My fortunes had improved a little since my last visit, so I decided to buy myself a computer. I didn't really need one, but what the hell, everybody else was using them. When I got hungry I went up to the food court and bought a nice, fresh glazed doughnut. When I bit it I remembered something. An old story. A story about how the Devil had come here in the first place. The trouble was I couldn't remember all the details. Remembering can be damned hard sometimes. I couldn't recall if he was the hero or the villain of the story. Was he the Prince of Darkness or the Bringer of Light? Purveyor of Slander or Revealer of Hidden Truth? The Master of Evil or the loneliest mall rat in the world? And was he kicked out of heaven or was it like that verse in the song?

> God sent an angel down,
> God sent an angel down,
> God sent an angel down.
> Amen, amen, amen.

≪ MR. GLOBUS AND LAUGHING BOY ≫

This story is an update of "The Devil's Three Golden Hairs of Wisdom," in the brothers Grimm.

PART ONE

MR. GLOBUS WAS RICH. He was very rich. He was very, very, very, very, very rich. He owned the biggest multi-inter-transnational corporation in the world. His company made handheld remote-controlled electronic channel changers. He also made the televisions that had the channels you could change with his handheld remote-controlled electronic channel changers. He also built the malls that had the shops that ran the ads that were shown on the televisions that had the channels you could change with his handheld remote-controlled electronic channel changers. And every one of his malls was filled with the same shops selling the same things and the same fast food outlets selling the same hamburgers. "My name and my fame," he claimed, "came from making everything the same."

He and his wife had everything money could buy, but they had no children. He said he was too busy running the business to be a father, but his wife wanted a baby more than all their fancy things. One day she finally became pregnant. When he heard the news, Mr. Globus ordered his chief manager to design the biggest computer, the biggest forecasting program and the biggest database in the world. He wanted to be able to predict his child's future.

Meanwhile, far from the big city, out where the poorest people lived, beyond the last suburb and past the last mall, at the edge of the forest and not far from Wild River, so far away they only got one channel, there was a family living in a little shack and they were very, very poor. The husband was in a wheelchair. He used to work in one of Mr. Globus's factories, but then he was injured, and then he was laid off. They had twelve children, some their own and some street kids they'd adopted, and now the wife was pregnant with the thirteenth. The old grandmother lived with them, too. There wasn't much laughter during the woman's pregnancy. She would touch her belly and sigh, wondering what would become of a child born to poverty and hunger.

But when the time came for her child to be born, something happened. If it hadn't happened, as my own grandmother used to say, how could I tell you a story about it?

When the baby was born, he laughed. His little face was all scrunched up with grins and chuckles. Instead of crying, he giggled. Instead of bawling, he smiled. The neighbours came over to marvel at this merry child, and they laughed when they heard him cackle with glee. Then

Granny came over. She'd been sitting in her rocking chair watching a black-and-white television, which only got one channel, and she hobbled over to the cradle, picked up the baby and said, "We've got ourselves a Laughing Boy, and that's rare at the best of times. That'll be his name from now on because he'll never lose his laugh, no matter what happens to him. And when he's eighteen, he's going to marry the daughter of the richest man in the world, who was born tonight under these very stars." The whole family jubilated with their newborn Laughing Boy. Granny kissed the baby, shuffled back to her rocking chair and her television, and sang softly to herself: "One channel's all I need, the Book of Lives to read . . ."

Meanwhile, Mrs. Globus gave birth that same night to a baby girl. She was a wriggly, squiggly, bebopping, boogie-woogie baby. Her mother laughed with joy and said, "You're a real Dancin' Girl, you are, and that will be your name!"

When Mr. Globus heard the news, he immediately called the chief manager and yelled, "*Run the program!* I want to know what my daughter's future will be!"

The chief manager keyed in the question: WHAT IS THE DESTINY OF DANCIN' GIRL? He waited and waited, but no answer came. Then the huge computer began to whir and shake, the mouse began to smoke, the screen began to flash and fizz. Just before the hard drive squeaked, he heard a voice begin to speak: "One channel's all I need, the Book of Lives to read . . . Dancin' Girl will never stop dancing. And when she's eighteen she'll marry the poorest boy in the land, a Laughing Boy who was born tonight under these very stars . . ." Then BOOM! The computer blew up.

"What's the answer?" said Globus.

"Boss," said the chief manager. "The system crashed. I think someone hacked into the program!"

"That's impossible! It's the best system money could buy!" yelled Globus. "You'd better tell me something about my daughter's future. Or else!"

"Well," said the chief manager, "there is a little data . . . but I'm not sure you're going to like it. The hacker says your daughter will be dancing her whole life . . . but the bad news is, she'll marry the poorest boy in the land, who was born tonight under these very stars, some kind of a laughing boy."

"You're fired!" yelled Mr. Globus. "That's the stupidest prophecy I've ever heard!" But just to be on the safe side, he decided to search and destroy that little boy. He'd kill that little upstart before he became a start-up.

He went by himself because he didn't trust anyone else on such an important mission. He didn't go out as the richest man in the world. He disguised himself as a travelling salesman, switched his Lamborghini for a Chevy, and started peddling disposable diapers in every city, town and village throughout the land. And everywhere he went he asked for news about babies who were particularly merry. One day he pulled up to a gas station away out where the poorest people lived, at the edge of the forest and not far from Wild River, so far away they only got one channel. "I'm selling plastic diapers," he told the man at the pump. "You know of any babies born recently?"

"Yep," said the man. "But folks around here are too poor for those use-'em-once, throw-'em-away things you've got. We've got to make things last as long's we can. But now that you mention it, there was a baby born not long ago. The people live down that road with about twelve other kids, an old woman, the dad in a wheelchair, and just about the giggliest little baby you'll ever see!"

Mr. Globus drove his Chevy right up to the shack where the poor family lived. He knocked on the door, and a woman opened it. She was holding a baby boy. When the baby saw Mr. Globus standing there, he started to laugh.

"Hello, madam," he said. "I'm a travelling diaper salesman, and I was wondering if you'd like to buy some disposable diapers?"

"Nope." she said, "Can't afford them. Ever since my husband got laid off, we can't afford anything fancy."

"What a handsome little boy you have," said Globus. "May I ask when he was born?"

She told him, and it was the same night as his own baby girl. This was the child he'd been searching for. But how could he get it away from the mother and father?

"Say," he said, "this might just be your lucky day. I've been looking for a baby to advertise my diapers. What do you say to a fee of $100,000 and a lifetime supply of plastic diapers? Just let me borrow that fine-looking baby of yours for an ad campaign. I'll take good care of him, don't worry."

"Nope," said the woman, "no deal."

Her husband wheeled up and shook his head.

But then Granny spoke up. She'd been sitting in her rocking chair drinking a cup of tea and watching a black-and-white television (it only got one channel) and she said, "Take the money and give him the baby. You've got twelve other kids to think about. Besides, he's our Laughing Boy and no harm will come to him. We'll see him again for sure." Then she went back to her show and muttered to herself, "One channel's all I need . . ."

And so the woman handed over her newborn son, Mr. Globus gave her the money and a note guaranteeing a lifetime supply of disposable diapers; she cried, he smiled, the door closed, the deal was done. He had the baby. He tossed Laughing Boy into the back seat and drove straight down to Wild River. He parked the Chevy, took the baby out, and put him down on the riverbank, and picked up a big rock. "You'll never marry my daughter!" he screamed, as he held the rock over the little boy.

Just then the baby giggled. Laughing Boy chuckled and chortled, snickered and gurgled, cackled and cooed, and laughed out loud. Even Mr. Globus couldn't hurt a baby who was having that much fun. "Hmmm," he growled, "I'll just let the river do the job for me." He put the baby in a green plastic garbage bag, tied it shut, and tossed it out into the middle of the river. Mr. Globus watched the bag float downstream. Then he got in the car and drove back to the city, straight to the headquarters of Globus Incorporated. Just to celebrate, he fired 10,000 workers and watched his stock go up 10 percent.

But the bag didn't sink.

It floated downstream and not one drop of water touched the baby inside. The bag bobbed along Wild River, floating deeper and deeper into the forest. There was a fisher standing on the bank, casting her rod. She saw the garbage bag, hooked it with her line, and reeled it in to shore. She lived in a cabin in the forest with a hunter. She called Hunter over and the two women gently carried the bag into their kitchen and opened it. When they beheld the baby in the bag, they gasped with joy.

"A gift!" cried Fisher. "A gift from Wild River."

"Yes," said Hunter. "A gift somebody else threw away. Now we have a child of our own we can raise here in the forest."

The baby started to giggle so the two women named him Laughing Boy.

Time passed as swiftly as a story, and Laughing Boy grew up. He was a fine-looking, bright, brave, kind-hearted, clear-headed young man. He was always helping his mothers around the place, hunting, fishing, baking bread.

Then one day, when he was eighteen years old, something happened. If it hadn't happened, how could I tell you a story about it?

One day Mr. Globus was touring the countryside, looking for class A farmland and old-growth forest to buy and bulldoze and turn into malls. He was at the edge of the forest, not far from Wild River, when a great storm blew up and his Lamborghini got stuck in the mud. He tried to call for help, but his cellphone wouldn't work. He got out of the car and began to walk through the forest looking for shelter. Near the shore of the river he saw the lights of a cabin. He knocked on the door and a woman opened it. Next to her was another woman, and beside her stood a young man. The young man was laughing.

"Come in," the women said, "come out of the rain."

Mr. Globus ate the food they gave him, and sipped the home-made wine they poured for him. He was waiting for them to recognize him, since his picture was on the TV almost every night—but they wouldn't have known that; they had no TV.

"What brings you out here," asked Hunter, "to the back of beyond?"

"I'm looking for land to buy so I can build malls and highways and subdivisions. My name is Globus, and I run the biggest multi-inter-transnational corporation in the world. You've probably heard of me. My name and my fame came from making everything the same. My Lamborghini's stuck in the mud."

"Oh," said Fisher. "I sure hope you don't build any malls near Wild River."

"Depends on how much money I could make," said Mr. Globus. "It's all just real estate to me. Can I use your phone?"

"We don't have one," said Hunter. "But you're welcome to stay here overnight and in the morning our son can show you out to the main road, or help you get your car started."

He decided to stay. Laughing Boy was preparing the dough for the next day's baking, and Mr. Globus couldn't keep his eyes off him. "That young man seems to know his way around the kitchen," he said.

"Yes," said Hunter. "We've raised him pretty well. We're lucky to have him because he's a foundling. Strange as it seems, about eighteen years ago we found him floating down Wild River wrapped up in a green plastic garbage bag. We've raised him as our own child ever since."

"I . . . see," said Globus, staring at the young man.

"We named him Laughing Boy because he has such a nice laugh," said Fisher.

"How . . . charming," muttered Globus.

"Some evil-hearted maniac threw our son into the river," said Hunter, as she cleaned the barrel of her gun. "I hope whoever did it falls into Wild River himself one day, without two loving women to pull him out."

"How . . . dreadful," said Globus, thinking quickly. "I just remembered something very important. I have to get a message down to my chief manager at the headquarters of Globus International. Could your son find a way out of the forest and into the city tonight? If he can, I'll pay him a hundred dollars."

"Sure I can," said Laughing Boy. "I'll take my bike. It's only a few hours if you know the way."

"And you may as well see a bit of the world while you're out," said Hunter. "No need to hurry back."

Mr. Globus took a piece of paper and wrote a letter. "Dear Chief Manager: We have a problem . . ." He sealed it in an envelope, gave Laughing Boy a hundred dollars, and told him to hurry. The young man said goodbye to his moms, fastened his helmet, got on his bike, and rode away. His light shone the way through the trees as he pedalled along. He'd been riding about an hour when the light broke. Then he got a flat. He pushed his bike down the trail, and even Laughing Boy was barely smiling as the forest grew thicker and the night grew darker. He was overjoyed when he saw a light shining in the window of a cabin up ahead. There, in the deepest part of the woods, was a little house he'd never seen before. In the yard were twelve black Harleys. He knocked on the door, and a woman opened it, peering suspiciously out into the night.

"What do you want?" she asked.

"Am I glad to see you!" he said, and laughed out loud. "I'm trying to get down to the city to deliver a letter for Mr. Globus, but now I'm lost and I need a place to stay the night. Can I stay here with you?"

"Not a good idea," she said. "We don't like strangers around here."

"I promise I won't tell," he said. "I live in the forest myself."

Just then an old woman spoke up. She was sitting in a rocking chair in the corner drinking a cup of tea and watching a black-and-white television that only had one channel. "Let him stay," she said, "he has such a nice laugh. . . ."

The woman opened the door and Laughing Boy walked in. There were twelve bikers sitting at a big table guzzling beer. "Who the heck are you!" they yelled. They always watched their language around their granny.

"He's just a poor boy from another part of the forest," said Granny,"and he's our special guest tonight. Y'all better behave—or else! He's a messenger carrying a letter from Mr. Globus. Come to think of it, somebody'd better check to see what's in that letter."

After Laughing Boy went to sleep, they pulled the letter out of his pocket, cracked the seal, and handed it to their mother—the woman who'd opened the door. She read, "Dear Chief Manager: We have a problem. I want you to kill the young man who delivers this letter. Make it look like an accident. Don't wait until I get home. Don't let him meet my daughter. Your boss, Mr. Globus. P.S. Don't let him meet the girl's mother either."

The bikers were not amused. "That crook, that creep, that criminal!" they cried. "This is a death warrant, not a letter!"

But Granny was giggling. "Time to write another letter," she said, "and pipe down, you'll wake him up."

They took a new piece of paper, and the mother got ready to forge Mr. Globus's handwriting. Granny dictated, "Dear Wife, as soon as you read this letter please introduce this handsome, smart, kind-hearted, clear-headed young man to our wonderful daughter. I think they will make each other very, very happy. She has my permission to get married if she likes him. I hope you agree he's a good choice. Your husband, Globie. P.S. Don't wait until I get back." They put it in an envelope, wrote "Mrs. Globus" on it, and put it back in the boy's pocket. When he woke up in the morning, Laughing Boy was surrounded by a roomful of giggling bikers. They fed him his breakfast and showed him the way. They'd fixed his bike, and he rode down the trail. After a few hours, he passed the rush-hour traffic jammed up on the highway, and found his way downtown to the headquarters of Globus International. He took the letter out of his pocket and was surprised to find it wasn't for the chief manager after all; but how was he going to find Mrs. Globus? Just then a girl got off the elevator. She was wearing a jogging suit, and dancing across the floor. She moved so beautifully he laughed with joy. She shimmied up to him and said, "Are you a bicycle courier?"

"Yes," he said. "I'm trying to deliver a letter for Mr. Globus's wife. Do you know her?"

"Yes," she answered, "she's my mother." Then she jumped a little and said, "You have a nice laugh."

"Well, they call me Laughing Boy. And you're a great dancer!"

"I'm Dancin' Girl!" she said. Then she took him up the elevator to her mother's office. "Mama," she said, "this young man has a letter for you from Father."

He handed over the letter. She opened it and read it. Then she looked at Laughing Boy. He was laughing while Dancin' Girl taught him how to waltz, jitterbug and pirouette. "Daughter," she said, "have you ever thought about getting romantically involved with someone?"

"Not really . . ."

"But if you met the right person?"

"Oh, yes . . . if . . ."

"Well, what do you think of the young man who brought the letter?"

"I like him *A LOT!*" she said, and did a foxtrot to the window and back. "I could live with his laugh forever."

"And do you like my daughter?" she asked.

He laughed and said, "I sure do. And my moms would like her, too."

"Well, why don't you two consider getting together? Your father and I would both be very pleased. You can get married when he comes back. Meanwhile, go have some fun. I know how impatient you young people can be."

And so, laughing and dancing, the two young people went off to find a little privacy.

And Mr. Globus finally got his Lamborghini out of the mud.

And deep in the forest, not far from Wild River, an old woman sat in a rocking chair drinking a cup of tea and watching a black-and-white television. She smiled to herself as she sang, "*One channel's all I need, the Book of Lives to read . . .*"

PART TWO

I WISH I COULD TELL YOU that when Mr. Globus saw what had happened, he changed his ways; that he stopped laying off workers, and started giving raises all around;

that he stopped paving over farmland to build malls, and stopped trying to make everything the same. But no, Globus was as greedy and stingy as ever. And he was furious that all of his money and stocks and managers and factories hadn't kept that poor boy from taking his most precious possession.

He wondered how could he get rid of him before the wedding took place.

One day his chief manager—the new one—called him with an idea. "Boss, I know how to make that kid stop laughing. Forever," he said.

"Make it look like an accident," said Globus, "and I'll double your wages."

"Here's the plan. Before he marries your daughter, tell him he has to prove himself by bringing you something you don't already own."

"But I already own everything money can buy!"

"Exactly! He'll never find it, and he'll never come back. Tell him to search for something that can't be bought, will never be sold, is always free yet more precious than gold. He'll never find it because it doesn't exist!"

"Something more precious than gold . . . ! Aha! I get it! There's no such thing," said Mr. Globus. "He'll never come back from his impossible mission!" He sent for Laughing Boy and said, "If you want to marry my daughter, you must prove yourself. I want you to find the thing I don't already own. It's something that can't be bought, will never be sold, is always free yet more precious than gold."

"Where should I look for it?" he asked.

"You young fool," he snarled, "if I knew, I'd go and get it all for myself."

Laughing Boy went to say goodbye to Dancin' Girl. They laughed, they danced, they kissed. And three hours later he left. It was a long kiss.

He got on his bike and rode away; he rode all night and most of the day, until he came to a strange community. It had a high fence all around it, and a big locked gate. Laughing Boy rode up to the gate and saw that everyone inside was very, very old. The whole place was dry and dusty, the leaves on the trees and the flowers by the shuffleboards had all turned yellow. An old man limped over to the gate and spoke to him.

"Why'd you come here, young fellow?" he asked. "Nobody's come for a visit in the longest time. They don't even call. Is it so hard to pick up the phone?"

"I'm looking for something that can't be bought, will never be sold, is always free, yet more precious than gold. Do you have any here?"

"I don't remember," said the old man. "There's a lot I don't remember any more."

"Why is everyone so old in there? Why's it so dry and dusty?" asked Laughing Boy.

"We moved to this gated community to stay young," said the old man. "Every day a rain would fall: the wild, wonderful Rain of Youth. But then the rain stopped, and everything dried up, and we became as parched as the palm trees. We've even forgotten whether we shut the gate ourselves, or if somebody shut us in because they had no time for old people. Now everyone's forgotten us, and nobody comes to visit, and nobody even calls. Is it so hard to pick up the phone?"

"If I can," said Laughing Boy, "I'll find out why the rain stopped."

But the old man had already started to walk away from the fence.

Laughing Boy got on his bike and rode away; he rode all night and most of the day; he rode until he came to a strange city. Everyone was walking around looking at mirrors and then staring at ads. They all looked sad. A woman came over to him and asked, "Don't you think I'm ugly?"

"Why, no," he said, amazed by her question. "You look very beautiful to me."

"But I'm not as beautiful as those ads," she said, pointing to a billboard down the road, and then looking at her mirror. "Where are you going?"

"I'm searching for something that can't be bought, will never be sold, is always free, yet more precious than gold. Do you have any of that around here?"

"I don't think so," she said. "Do you think a diet would help?"

"Why is everyone looking at mirrors?" asked Laughing Boy.

"Because we used to have a well filled with the wonderful, wild Water of Beauty," she said. "When we drank it we felt beautiful. Then one day the well dried up, the fizz and bubbles stopped, and now we feel ugly all the time. We'll never be as pretty as the people in the ads. What do you think of my hair?"

"I think you're lovely as you are." he said. "And if I can I'll find out why your beauty pop stopped. Be careful with those diets—they never work for very long."

He got on his bike and rode away, he rode all night and most of the day, he rode until he came to a river deep in the forest. He knew it was Wild River, although he'd never seen it so wild before. An old man sat in a ferryboat moored to the bank.

"Where are you going, young man?" he asked.

"I'm looking for something that's hard to find. It can't be bought, will never be sold, is always free, yet more precious than gold. Do you know where it is?"

"I don't," said the boatman, "but you might try the dragon on the other side of the river."

"Dragon?" asked Laughing Boy.

"Yes. Across the river they say there's a dragon who knows every truth, half-truth and lie ever told. I'll bet the dragon might know what you're looking for. They also say the dragon has a treasure so great that it'll blind you if you try looking at it."

"Can you take me over?" asked Laughing Boy.

"I could," said the boatman, "but I'm not sure it's a good idea. I've rowed many young men over but I've never rowed any back again. They say the dragon is a fierce, terrible, ugly, man-eating, homicidally maniacal serial killer. They also say if you look at the dragon you'll puke with terror before dying of fright. And they also say—"

Laughing Boy laughed and said, "It sounds like 'they' say a lot of things. I'd like to go now, please." And he laughed again, for no good reason.

"That's good," said the boatman, as he began rowing across the water. "Laugh now, while you still can. And if you do meet the dragon, and survive, could you find out the answer to my riddle? Why must I always row back and forth on the river? Why can I never go free?"

Laughing Boy promised he'd find out. He jumped out on the other side of Wild River and walked away, he walked all night and most of the day, he walked until he came to a little house in the forest, and he knocked on the door.

"Come in," said a voice from inside.

"Thank you," he said, and opened the door. In the house there was an old woman sitting in a rocking chair, drinking a cup of tea, watching a black-and-white television. He was pretty sure he knew how many channels it got. "Hello. How are you today?" he asked her.

"Can't complain," she answered, "but you've come a long way to be nice to an old woman. What are you looking for?"

"A dragon," he said. "I have to find a dragon."

"Why?"

"So I can keep my Dancin' Girl. She and I love each other but her father, Mr. Globus, won't let us get married until I bring him something he doesn't already own, but that's impossible because he's the richest man in the world and he already owns everything money can buy, and while I've been looking for something I'm not even sure exists, I met some people who are in big trouble and I want to help them by finding answers to their three hard riddles, and I heard there's a dragon hereabouts who knows every truth, half-truth and lie ever told, and also has a great treasure, and I'm hoping the dragon can help me find all the things I'm searching for, so I was wondering if you know where I can find that dragon?"

"Yep," said the old woman. "You've come to the right place. I am the dragon. Would you like a cup of tea?"

"You!!!" Laughing Boy laughed. "But I heard you were a fierce, ferocious, mean, ugly, man-eating, homicidally maniacal serial killer! You look like another old woman I met along the way who was very nice to me and who had a rocking chair, a cup of tea and a television just like yours."

"Sounds like my little sister," said the dragon. "Haven't seen her for a while. Be sure to say hi if you see her again."

"But all those things they say about you—"

She pointed out the window to a pile of white bones. "Not everyone knows how to show respect to old women," she said. "So what are you looking for?"

"I need to help those people by finding out why the Rain of Youth stopped falling, and the Well of Beauty dried up, and the boatman must always row back and forth and is never free. And I need to keep my Dancin' Girl by bringing Mr. Globus something that can't be bought, will never be sold, is always free, yet more precious than gold."

"Well," she said, "those are good questions. And because I like your laugh, and you remind me of my sister, and you know how to talk to old women, and most of all because you're trying to help others and not just yourself, I'll tell you the answers. The Rain of Youth stopped falling because those people tried to stay young for too long. They were afraid of growing old so they locked their gates to keep old age out. If they open their gates the wild, wonderful Rain of Youth will fall again. The Well of Beauty dried up because they looked for beauty in ads and mirrors instead of finding it within themselves. They must break their mirrors and throw away their ads for the wild, wonderful Water of Beauty to flow again. And that boatman, he came looking for my treasure, but he wanted to keep it all for himself instead of sharing it with all who need it. He'll row back and forth on Wild River until he gives his oars into the hands of another greedy man. As for the thing you need to bring back to Globus, why, it's called 'wisdom.' Wisdom's the thing can't be bought, will never be sold, is always free, yet more precious than gold. You've already picked some up along the way, because you found yourself some good questions. Wisdom always begins with a question. That's what my old grandma used to say."

"Thank you," said Laughing Boy. "But how do I take wisdom back to Mr. Globus?"

"You can't," she said. "You can't own it or loan it or double-click on it, or trade it or give it. He must go and live it."

For the first time in his life, Laughing Boy began to weep. Now he would never get to marry his Dancin' Girl. The dragon watched him quietly, and when he finally stopped she said, "You can't give him any wisdom, but you might show him one of these." And she lifted the veil from the bowl beside her and took out the biggest diamond in the world. "Give it to your Dancin' Girl, but make sure you show it to Globus first."

Laughing Boy was almost blinded by the brilliantly dazzling jewel. He bent down and kissed the dragon, took the diamond, and by the time he left, he was laughing again.

When he came to the riverbank, the boatman was waiting for him. He rowed across and Laughing Boy jumped out. "If you want to be free," he said, "give your oars into the hands of another greedy man."

Then he rode his bike straight to the town of ads and mirrors. "Break your mirrors," he told the people, "and turn off your ads and your well will be full again." When they did this the well bubbled up with the wild, wonderful Water of Beauty. They tasted it and looked at each

MR. GLOBUS AND LAUGHING BOY 249

other. They saw undyed hair and big bellies and every colour and shape of person—but instead of feeling sad, they rejoiced that there could be so many kinds of beauty in the world. When they wanted to give him a reward, Laughing Boy just laughed.

He rode to the gated community, and told the old people to break the lock. With all their strength, they cracked the lock and the Rain of Youth began to fall, and the earth was refreshed. All the old people came out and danced in the wild, wonderful Rain of Youth. They still had their wrinkles, but now they felt young and full of hope. They threw open the gates and took down the walls, and their children started calling, and they even came to visit. On Sundays they brought the grandchildren. When they thanked him, Laughing Boy just laughed.

He rode straight downtown, to the headquarters of Globus International. When he got there, Laughing Boy went up to the boardroom and stood in front of Mr. Globus. "I found the thing that can't be bought, will never be sold, is always free, yet more precious than gold," he said. "It is wisdom, O father of my best beloved, but you'll have to go find your own. I can't own it or loan it or double-click on it, or trade it or give it. You must go and live it. Oh, and I also found this diamond for my Dancin' Girl."

Globus was almost blinded by the dazzling brilliance of the diamond.

"Where, my dear son-in-law-to-be," he whispered, "did you get that diamond?"

"On the other side of Wild River," said Laughing Boy. Then he laughed and said, "There's a big bowl of them waiting for the right owner."

Mr. Globus didn't even say goodbye to his wife and daughter. He rushed away alone and left the chief manager in charge. He hurried all the way to the bank of Wild River, where the water runs darkest and wildest, and he found the boatman. "Take me across," he shouted. "I want to get it all for myself!"

The boatman put his oars into the hands of Mr. Globus, and ran away.

Back at headquarters, Laughing Boy and Dancin' Girl decided to have a big party to celebrate their wedding. First, though, they let—well, they *made*—the chief manager take early retirement, and they took over the corporation. But they didn't like everything to be the same, so they gave the malls and restaurants and factories to the people who worked in them, and let them decide what to do. After a while, the hamburgers tasted different everywhere you went.

What a party it was! The bikers showed up, and Hunter and Fisher, and his first mother, and her mom, and the whole wild bunch of them got along very, very well.

As for Globus, he began to row back and forth, back and forth, always across the current and never with the river's flow. Unless he finds someone else as greedy as he is, he'll row there forever.

And deep in the forest, across Wild River, a dragon sat in her rocking chair drinking a cup of tea and watching a black-and-white television. (It only gets one channel.) She smiles and sings softly to herself, *"One channel's all I need, the Book of Lives to read . . ."*

THE STORYTELLER AT FAULT

This interconnected series of stories is an homage to the creators of the Thousand and One Nights. *In my version of the Scheherazade story I've updated the settings, motives and characters. But, as in the* Thousand and One Nights, *my storyteller must do some serious emergency storytelling to get out of a very tight situation. It was first published as a book by Ragweed Press in 1992. The Canadian fiddler/composer Oliver Schroer created an original score to accompany the piece, and we have performed it at festivals throughout the world.*

ONCE UPON A TIME *a king went blind. His son set out to find a cure and rode so far he left his father's kingdom far behind. One day a golden feather lay blazing in the prince's way, and when he bent to pick it up he heard his horse speak up and say: "Don't touch that feather, my friend, for it will bring you fearful trouble. This is a feather from the shining wing of the Firebird herself . . ."*

"Save the file! Scribe, save it and print it! Guards, take him away!"

"What's going on, Your Majesty? Where are your guards taking me? What's making that awful sound?"

"That is the sound of your death, Storyteller. My scribe is printing out your stories. All these nights while you were speaking, my scribe was hiding in the shadows with his special machine. It is a machine for memory, Storyteller, and unlike you, it will never forget these stories. As you said the words out loud my scribe keyed them into his machine. Now they are safe and sound and stored in a database. My memory machine will remember your stories forever. Listen well, Storyteller; that is the sound of a thousand nights of word of mouth turning into hard, hard copy."

"Hard indeed, Your Majesty, if it means the teller himself must die. Have mercy on me!"

"Stand up, Storyteller. Take courage from your own stories of courage and heroism. In all of the tales you told me, not one hero or heroine ever begs for their life."

"Those heroes and heroines live in fairy tales that always end happily ever after. I'm a real person, a living man with a wife to love and children to raise. I know that one day I will have to die; but not tonight! I'm not quite ready, Your Majesty. I'm really a bit too young to die . . ."

"Guards!"

"And anyway, why is this night different from all our other nights, when you seemed to enjoy my stories and asked for more? Why must I die tonight for the stories I've told you?"

"Because tonight, Storyteller, you have come to the end of your own memory. Tonight you began to tell me the story of the Firebird. That is the first story my scribe entered into the memory machine, a thousand nights ago. You have no more stories to tell, and so you must die."

"But Your Majesty, the first time I told it to you the hero was a young archer. Tonight he's a prince. I also know another version where it's a young woman with raven-black hair."

"Details, details. I'm sure they all ride forth to find a radiant destiny. It is the same story, even if you change the names of your characters. No, Storyteller, you have come back to your own beginning. Take him away without delay!"

"At least tell me my crime, Your Majesty. What is the true reason for this dreadful judgment?"

"I will tell you the truth, Storyteller. I owe you that much for the gift of your splendid stories. When I first listened to you I was enchanted by your tales of wonder. You used the same words as everyone else, but in your mouth those common words turned to pure gold. Your voice conjured distant lands, fabulous treasures, yes, even the beauty of the Firebird herself. But one day the spell was broken. I grew afraid that your precious stories would be forgotten, would vanish into breath and dust and be lost without a trace. I heard the echo of death in your charming voice. I was so afraid that I commanded my scribe to invent a machine to save your stories from oblivion. He caught your stories with his memory machine and locked them away in chips of glass and gold. Now we have a new, improved way to remember stories. Now they will never unravel, or lose their colours like a carpet left out in the rain. Now they belong completely to me, their greatest and most dedicated listener."

"But now that you have captured the words from my very lips, surely your Highness can spare the life of his humble storyteller."

"No, tonight you must die. You see, Storyteller, as my hoard of stories grew larger, my fear turned into anger. I was outraged that you, of all people, could be so heedless with your own stories. You cast them forth by word of mouth, like flower petals thrown on a fast river, as if you didn't know the name of that river was Time. One day even your mighty memory would loosen its hold, losing a word here, a word there—until finally all would be forgotten."

"I will *never* forget my stories!"

"Yes, Storyteller, one day you would betray your own stories. I condemn you to death not because I hate your art, but because I love your stories all too well. You are at fault for the crime of forgetfulness you would inevitably commit. At least you will die knowing that your stories will outlive you. Guards!"

"Your Majesty . . . there is one more story. It is my secret story, and I have never told it anyone. If I perish tonight my story will die unheard. Would you have the death of a story on your hands as well as the blood of a storyteller?"

"Storyteller, you may tell me one last story. Then you will die."

"You are merciful, Your Majesty. The name of my story is:

THE LAST STORY

Once upon a time there was a father who loved to tell stories to his little boy. Every night he'd go into the boy's room, sit on the bed, and tell him fairy tales. One night the father was about to begin when the little boy turned away. He buried his face in the pillow and pulled the blanket over his head. The father could hear the little boy breathing hard, close to tears.

"What's up?" he asked, but the little boy didn't answer. "How about a story?"

Then the boy burst out crying and said something that surprised his father very much: "No, Daddy, I don't want to hear any more stories."

After a while the tears slowed down and the father put his hand on the boy's shoulder and said, "How come you don't want to hear any more stories?"

The boy was still turned away when he whispered, "I hate fairy tales. They're not true."

Now, this child usually loved fairy tales, the longer the better. The father said, "Not true?"

"Yeah. They always end happily ever after and that's not true. There's no such thing as happily-ever-after . . . It's a big fat lie."

The father sat for a time in the dark room, remembering when he was that age. Then he said, "Remember when you kids found that dead robin a couple of days ago? You dug a hole by the apple tree and buried it in a shoebox. I was watching you from the kitchen window. Is that bird still on your mind?"

The boy nodded into his pillow. "And Grandpa bein' sick," he whispered.

"Yes," said his father. "Birds and grandpas. Well, that's a riddle, all right, maybe the hardest one in the world. A bird's alive one day, flying around, doing loop-de-loops, stealing flower seeds from your mom's garden, making a nest, teaching its young 'uns to fly; then one day it's lying still on the ground, and you wonder where the flying part's gone. Same with grandpas, and all of us. It reminds me of when I used to ask *my grandmother that same, hard riddle. She told me a story when I was little, and I never forgot it. She called it 'the story of Tortoises, Humans and Stones.' I don't I've ever told it to you before."*

"Tell it."

"All right:"

A long time ago, in the beginning of the world, Worldmaker made all the living creatures and all the things of the earth. In those days Worldmaker made all the living creatures so that they could live forever and they never had to die. But there was one condition: they could never have children. One day two tortoises, male and female, came to Worldmaker and said, "There's a problem with the world you made. We want to have baby tortoises."

"But if I let you have baby tortoises, you'll have to start dying. Otherwise there'd be too many of you."

"We're willing to die, if we can have baby tortoises," they said.

So Worldmaker gave them the gift of life, but also the gift of death.

Human beings saw this and a man and woman came to Worldmaker. "We would like to have children," they said.

"Are you willing to die?"

"Oh, yes," they said, "if we can first look on the faces of our children, we are willing to die."

And so it was that all the living creatures came to Worldmaker and they all chose to have children, even though they had to begin dying.

"And that's the story my grandma told me that explains how it is that death came into the world."

"But Daddy, what about the stones?" asked the boy. "You said there were stones in this story."

"Ah, yes, the stones. Well, Grandma said the stones never wanted to have kids, and that's why stones never have to die."

The boy turned over and looked at his father. "How old are you?" he asked.

"I'm as old as my tongue and older than my teeth."

The boy laughed and said, "No, really."

"I'm forty."

"Is that old?"

"Well, it's older than you and younger than your grandfather. Why?"

The little boy didn't answer for a while; then he said, "You can tell me fairy tales again, Daddy. But I still don't want them to end happily ever after. Do you know any other kind of stories?"

"Sure I do. I know lots of stories. My grandma gave me a headful of good stories, and I still remember them. How about I tell you ten for now, one per night, and not one of them will end with the words 'happily ever after'? Tonight's story was the one about the stones. Tomorrow you'll hear another one."

He kissed the little boy, turned out the light, and closed the door.

On the second night the father told the little boy the story of "The Dreamer and the Butterfly."

I heard this from my grandfather. He said it happened to two friends of his during the war.

The two soldiers had been separated from their company during a battle, and they'd spent the day walking through the fields trying to catch up. It was a quiet, sunny day, peaceful after all the shooting. The two men walked into a lovely meadow and decided to eat. They found a creek in the middle of the meadow, dipped their cups in it, and drank the cool, fresh water. They sat in the long grass at the end of the meadow and munched their K-rations. The war seemed far away at that moment. One of the soldiers stretched out to have a short nap, leaving his friend to stand guard.

The soldier who stayed awake was watching his friend's face, and all of a sudden he saw something amazing. The moment his friend fell asleep, his mouth opened and a pale, blue butterfly came out. It rose into the air above the sleeper's head, fluttered here and there as if trying to decide where to fly, and finally began to float across the meadow.

The young man got to his feet and followed the blue butterfly. It flew slowly and close to the ground, and was easy to keep up with. The butterfly approached something white that gleamed in the green grass. The soldier saw that it was a skull—Grandpa never told me what kind—and a crowd of flies and bees swarmed in and out of the eye sockets. The blue butterfly landed on the skull and folded its wings and walked in. The buzzing increased inside the skull until, after a while, the butterfly came out again and resumed its flight.

It flew towards the little stream of water that wound through the meadow. When it reached the stream it flew this and that way, but didn't fly across. The man laid his rifle over the water and the butterfly flew across, as if it were a bridge. On the other side of the stream it flew to a small mound of earth at the far end of the field. It disappeared into the mound. Finally it came out again, flew back across the meadow, over the water, past the skull, and hovered over the face of the sleeping man. His friend watched with astonishment as the butterfly dropped to the sleeper's mouth, folded its delicate blue wings, and disappeared.

At that moment the sleeper awoke. He yawned and stretched and shook his head. He looked at his friend and said, "What a strange dream I just had. If only I could have what I just dreamed about!"

"What did you dream?" asked his friend.

"Well, first I dreamed I was walking and walking, for a very long time. Finally, I came to a great palace made of pure white marble. I entered the gates of the palace and met many lords and ladies dressed in fine clothes. They were singing and talking, and they greeted me warmly. I stayed with them for a while, but then I left. Although they begged me to stay, I continued my journey. I came to a river too wide to get across. After much searching I found a bridge that spanned the river, and I crossed to the other side. Then I travelled for a long time until I came to a huge hill. There was an entrance on the side, and when I walked in I saw that it was an ancient burial mound, such as they used to bury kings and queens in a long time ago. I entered and saw in the middle of the tomb there was a dead king. At his feet was a treasure. I went closer to take the treasure, but just then I wanted to see the face of the king. I was just about to lift the cloth and see who he was, when I woke up. What a strange dream!"

His friend listened very carefully to the dream, and then said, "Follow me." He led the dreamer through the meadow, past the skull, over the stream, and up to the small mound at the far end of the field. "Let's dig this up," he said.

The dreamer was puzzled, but he knelt down and brushed the dirt away. There they found a soldier's helmet. They picked it up and turned it over. Inside, there was a photograph. In the photograph a young woman and a little boy were smiling and waving goodbye.

"How did you know this was here?" the dreamer asked.

"I followed the blue butterfly," said his friend, and told him what had happened. Both men marvelled at this strange experience. They tried, but they never found out whose helmet it had been, or who the woman and child were waving to.

On the third night the father told the little boy the story of "The Green Mist."

A long time ago people believed that everything in the world was alive: the water and the earth and the weather. Everything had its own spirit.

In those days people would go out into their fields in late autumn and sing lullabies to the earth, preparing it for the long sleep of winter. When winter came they bided close to home. They were afraid the spirits of the earth grew restless in the long, cold nights. For protection, they would carry a light all around their homes before turning in for the night. And they'd always be sure to leave a bit of bread and some salt out by the threshold to keep the spirits from going hungry. As winter neared its end, the people would go out into their fields at dawn, turn over a clod of earth, and recite the strange, ancient prayers they had heard from their grandparents. They would pray for the Green Mist to rise up from the ground and signal the beginning of spring.

There was a certain family back then who had endured a long and bitter winter. The worst of their troubles was that the daughter of the family, a lovely, tall teenager, had taken sick and was getting sicker by the day. She had wasted away during the winter and now, near winter's end, she'd barely the strength to lie beside the window and gaze out at the patches of snow. She would lie there all the day long, watching for a flash of cardinal's red, or a show of green buds, or any sign of spring at all.

"Oh, Mother," she'd say, over and over, "if only I could wake the spring with you, the Green Mist might bring my strength back to me, when it brings strength to the flowers and the corn and the apple trees."

And her mother, working, mending, cooking the girl's broth, would look at her daughter lying there and look away, shaking her head.

Spring was late coming that year, and the girl was failing fast. She grew as pale and wan as a snowflake melting in the sun. She knew now that she'd never be able to go out into the fields with the others to dig up the clod of earth and wake the spring.

"At least," she whispered to her mother, "at least take me to the door for the prayer, and I'll put out the bread and the salt."

"Yes, darling," answered her mother, "I promise."

And every morning the people went out to see if the earth had wakened; but winter still lay white and heavy on the land.

One day towards nightfall, as the house filled with shadows, the girl turned away from her window. She watched her mother for a long while, her eyes open and unblinking. Then she said, "If the Green Mist doesn't rise tomorrow I shall never see it again. The ground is calling me, Mother, and the seeds are bursting that will one day bloom over me. Oh, if only I could see the spring wake once more, I swear I'd be happy to live as long as one of the cowslips by the gate—and to die with the first of them at season's end."

"Hush, daughter," whispered the mother, bending to the earth, "hush, my beloved."

But the very next morning the Green Mist did rise, and the land was filled with the fine, soft scent of spring. The snow melted quickly and the buds appeared and the seeds sprouted and the air smelled sweet and new. The mother and father carried the girl to the threshold and she crumbled the bread and salt and cast it forth, into the garden. She murmured the old welcoming prayer and her parents, holding her, said the words with her, slowly and quietly. Then they put the girl back to bed and she slept for a very long time. She dreamed of yellow sunshine and bright wildflowers.

Soon the cowslips bloomed and the girl came back to life. Each day she found more health and vigour, until she was able to leave her sickbed and run out to the garden. Her parents stood at the window and marvelled to see her running in the sunshine. She stopped at the gate and gazed down at the pretty primroses. Then she walked among the flowers and held her head and hands up to the great, golden sun.

And so the days passed. On sunny days she would be in the garden, dancing and joyous; on cloudy days, when the sun was hidden and the flowers stayed furled, she stayed indoors near the fire, shivering and white.

The garden was in full bloom now, and the girl could

not leave her flowers alone. The people were astonished to see the girl lively and beautiful again. They often came around to watch her at her gardening, to look at her graceful, young body bending to tend the flowers, to listen to her songs. Her mother, joyful but worried, would say, "You're out here too much, daughter, too much . . . Is it good to be with the flowers so much?"

"Yes, Mother," she answered, "for they'll be fading soon enough . . . soon enough."

One day a boy from the village stopped at the gate to have a chat. He was talking to the girl's mother and he bent down and picked a cowslip. The girl joined them and saw the flower in his hand. "Where did you pick that flower?" she asked, never taking her eyes from it.

"From beside your own garden gate," said the boy; then, noticing her loveliness, he said, "I picked it for you." He held the flower out to her and she took it from him.

She held the flower in her hand. She looked at it for a long time. Then she looked at the handsome lad, and at her mother. She looked at the garden and the apple trees, and the ripening fields. Then she looked up at the bright, burning sun itself. She gave a high, strange cry, like a frightened animal. Then she shrank away from the light as if it scorched her, and she turned and ran back into the house.

She never rose from her bed again. She held the pretty, pale flower and watched it fade and wither, and she faded with it. By nightfall she was dead—a wilted, broken thing, lying beside the window. Her mother took the flower from the girl's hand and kissed them both, the girl and the cowslip.

The people around there said afterwards that the spirits of the earth had heard the girl's wish. They had let her bloom with the early spring flowers, and die with the first of them.

On the fourth night the father told the little boy the story of "The True Father of the House."

Once there was a traveller who was walking down a lonely road. He didn't know where he could stay the night, and it was getting darker and darker as he walked. Luckily, there was a big farmhouse down the road; and huge it was, looming like a castle out of the darkness. The traveller hastened towards it thinking he'd find room there, and hospitality for the night.

When he came up to the front door, he saw an old man chopping wood. "Good evening, Father," said the traveller. "I'm out on the road tonight and I'm in need of shelter. Have you room in your house for a traveller?"

The old fellow put down his axe and answered, "I'm not the father of this house. You'll have to go inside and ask my father. Go into the kitchen. You'll find him sitting by the fire."

The traveller opened the massive farmhouse door and walked into the kitchen. In the kitchen was a great stone fireplace, and in front of it on his hands and knees was a very old man trying to blow on the embers of the fire. The traveller came near him and said, "Good evening, Father. Can you put me up for the night?"

The old man looked up from the sparks and ashes and replied, "I'm not the father of the house. Go into the parlour and ask my father. He is reading at the table."

When the traveller came to the parlour he saw a very, very old man sitting at a table and reading a book. He barely had the strength to turn a page, and each page that he turned raised a cloud of dust. The traveller spoke up: "Good evening, Father. Can you give me shelter in your house tonight?"

The old man raised his eyes from the ancient volume. "I am not the father of the house," he said. "You had better ask my father. He's sitting on the sofa smoking his pipe."

The traveller noticed a shape bundled up in blankets and sweaters. Two thin hands poked out of the blankets, one holding a pipe and the other a match. The hands shook so that the pipe could not be lit. The traveller walked over and held the match steady. The old man on the sofa lit his pipe. The traveller said, "Good evening, Father. Is it possible for me to stay in your house tonight?"

In a voice as thin as the blue pipesmoke the old man answered, "I am not the father of the house. Go ask my father. He is resting in bed."

The traveller passed into the bedroom of the house. There was a bed, and in the middle of the bed was a small bump. When the traveller bent over he could see that the bump was a very, very old man. He was so old and wizened that only his eyes seemed to have any life in them. They were open and luminous. The traveller looked at those eyes and repeated his request: "Good evening, Father. Can you put me up for the night?"

"I'm not the father of the house," came the reply. "You'd best go ask my father. He's lying in his cradle."

There was a cradle in the bedroom. The traveller stepped over to it and looked inside. A man lay there. He was so old that he was no bigger than a baby. His beard curled around him like a wispy blanket. Except for a wheeze that rattled up from time to time there was no way to tell if he was alive or dead. "Good evening, Father," said the traveller, "and have you room in your house for a lonely traveller this night?"

It took a long time to get an answer and the answer, when it came, took a long time coming. "I," the old man wheezed, "am not"—the voice was a dry as a leaf in autumn—"the father of the house. Go ask my father. He is hanging in the horn upon the wall."

The traveller now saw a great hunting horn hanging upon the wall. Slowly, very slowly he approached it. He peered within and saw something there. It was white as ash and tiny: a human face. The traveller now cried out, "GOOD EVENING, FATHER. CAN YOU PUT ME UP FOR THE NIGHT?"

The voice that came from within the horn was as light as a tomtit chirping. The traveller strained to hear what it said, and what it said was this: "Yes, my child, and you are welcome."

Then a table appeared, laden with delicacies and fine wines; and when the traveller had eaten, in came a bed all covered with soft reindeer-hide blankets. The traveller curled up to sleep, and just before he closed his eyes he thought to himself: it is good to find the true father of the house.

On the fifth night the father told the little boy the story of "The Bird Colour-of-Time."

Long ago, back in the time when kings and lords tried to run things, there lived a certain king, and he had an only daughter. She was next in line to rule the land if her father the king quit or died.

One day the princess fell gravely ill. For a long time she stayed in bed, and nobody knew whether she would live or die. Finally, just as this story begins, the princess became very feverish. All through the night she got hotter and hotter, and then, just at dawn, the fever broke and she began to feel a little better. As the days passed she became stronger, and then one spring day she climbed out of bed and went to see her father. She was still wearing her pyjamas as she walked into the court, past all the lords and ladies and royal guards, and marched right up to the king's great throne. She had a big favour to ask him.

"Father," she said (she never called him daddy or papa), "I was very, very sick. Then I was very, very hot. Now I'm getting better, and it's time for you to give me a gift because I didn't die. The night I stopped being so hot I had a dream. I dreamed I met the fastest bird in the world. Would you find it and bring it to me?"

"What kind of bird was it?" asked the king, a little worried by his daughter's strange request.

"It was a little bird, and it was the colour of time," she said.

Now, the king had heard of bluebirds, blackbirds, goldfinches, yellowhammers, cardinals, hummingbirds and hawks. But he'd never heard of the Bird Colour-of-Time. "What colour is that, exactly? White or black or clear or the colour of rainbows or what?"

"Dunno," said the princess. "It's just its own colour. I only saw the tail-feathers in my dream. But it is the fastest bird in the world! Can you get it for me, Father?"

The king was not amused. He had no idea where to look for such an extraordinary creature. Besides, truth to tell, the king was a little frightened of strange birds. He knew that a man could be tickled to death by even one feather—especially from a bird the colour of time. This king didn't like the idea of dying laughing, or any other way. So he stalled for time. He hemmed and he hawed, he stared at the ceiling, he gazed at his shoes, he pulled his earlobe, he cracked his knuckles, he whistled "God Save the King," he peeked over at the big clock ticking on the palace wall . . . and still his little daughter stood before him, patiently waiting for his reply.

Finally an idea popped into the king's head. A flying contest, he thought; that's how we'll see who's the fastest birdie of them all!

No sooner thought than done. The king organized a grand affair, the World's First Speed Flight Competition for Birds, a truly spectacular sporting event. No expense was spared. Invitations were sent by passenger pigeon (they weren't extinct in those days) to every bird for miles around. Each species was invited to send its speediest flyer.

On the appointed day the racers gathered at the starting line, which was the border of the king's realm. The rooster gave the signal (he and the hen weren't in the race) and with a loud COCKETY CROW! the birds were off and flying. They rose and raced across the sky in a vast cloud of every colour and hue, each one straining to fly higher and faster than the rest, passing overhead with a terrific beating of wings and piping of birdcry.

For a time they were all racing beak to beak; but then, all of a sudden, the mighty Eagle pulled ahead. He soared towards the finish line, leaving the rest far behind. The majestic, the one and only Eagle was a sure bet to win.

The king looked up and thought, "What a fine, what a strong, what a *kingly* bird—*C'est magnifique!*"

The little princess watched the race and shook her head. "That's not the one," she said. "That's not the bird I saw in my dream."

The Eagle glided forward, taking his sweet time, as if he had all the time in the world to cross the finish line.

Then something happened. Just before the Eagle reached the end of the race, a tiny bird that had stowed away in the great bird's neck-feathers shot forward and flitted ahead and across the line—winning the race by the beat of a wing.

The princess leapt to her feet and yelled, "That's the one! That's Bird Colour-of-Time!" But the king was furious. It was outrageous, it was a scandal! That regal bird losing the race to such a disgraceful, cheating little hitchhiker! There was tumult, there was commotion—and in the uproar the winning bird disappeared. Only the little girl saw where it went, and nobody asked her, and she never told.

The magnificent Eagle was so embarrassed by his loss that the feathers on his head turned completely white. They have stayed white to this very day. He flew away to his own country and became a recluse, always roosting in the highest mountains and brooding on his shame. To console him for his defeat, people turned him into a symbol of victory. Now you can find his picture on flags and shields and money and government buildings.

As for the little princess, she was happy. Her dream-bird hadn't stayed around, but she knew it wouldn't. She was healthy again and, as time went on, she grew up. At the proper time, she became a wise and well-loved queen.

Time passed, and stories were told about the Great Flying Contest. But you know the way it is with time and stories. The more stories were told, the less people agreed on what really happened so many years before. Some people claimed that the winning bird was nothing but an ordinary wren, a common, everyday sort of a bird out to have a lark with the proud Eagle. Others said no, it wasn't a wren at all, it *was* a lark. The only thing they all remembered was that *something* had flown by awfully fast; something had won the race at the very last moment.

Whenever she heard her people talk, the queen would smile to herself. She knew perfectly well who had won the race, who wins every race. For there's only one thing that can outrace eagles, only one thing in the world so swift. Sometimes you see it in a fever-dream, sometimes as a season wheels past, sometimes at the edge of an ordinary sky, glanced at and gone. All you ever see are the tail-feathers as it flashes past—that little bird, fastest of all, Colour-of-Time.

On the sixth night the father told the little boy the story of "How Heart Came into the World."

A long time ago, in the beginning of things, Worldmaker made the world. Worldmaker made the earth and stars and water and creatures. Man and Woman were given intelligence but in those days they did not yet possess Heart.

One day Worldmaker called Sun, Moon, Darkness and Rain. "My children, I have almost finished making the world. Soon the time will come for me to leave. I am going to send Heart in my place. Before I leave you, my children,

I would like to know what you plan to do when I have gone. You, my bright Sun, what will you do?"

Sun answered, "Worldmaker, I will become hotter and hotter, and shine upon the Earth with all of my strength!"

Worldmaker spoke to Sun and said, "No, my child. That is not a good idea. You would burn the world with your heat and dazzle it blind with your brightness. No, Sun, here is what you must do. Take turns with Rain. After you warm the Earth, let Rain come and refresh it. That is the proper way to be. And you, Rain, what did you have in mind?"

"Oh, Worldmaker, I want to pour and pour and pour upon the Earth, and cover it with my waters!"

"No, my dear one. If you flood the Earth, all the creatures will be swept away and all that I have made will be destroyed. Instead, take your turn with Sun. You will cool and water the Earth in the proper season, and Sun will warm it again. How about you, Darkness, what are your plans?"

"I want to rule forever!" shouted Darkness.

"Child, this cannot be. If you ruled forever, the creatures of the Earth would not be able to look upon the loveliness I have made for them. No, Darkness, you will rule only when Moon is in its last quarter. Only then will you have your dominion. And as for you, Moon, my sweet, strange child, I will tell you what is to be. The night will be yours to shine in, sometimes full and round, sometimes thin and curved. Up and over you will go through the night sky, cutting tethered dreams free. So it will be forever, my children. But my time has come to leave you, and to leave this world that I have made. I will send Heart in my place."

So saying, Worldmaker disappeared.

Not long afterwards Heart came into the world. Heart was small and red, about the size of my fist. Heart was crying. Heart came to the children of Worldmaker and said, "I am looking for the one who made me. Tell me where I can find the one who made the world."

Sun, Moon, Darkness and Rain replied, "We do not know where Worldmaker has gone. We do not know where you must search."

Heart said, "I long to meet the one who made me, but since Worldmaker has gone away, I will enter into Man and Woman; through them I will continue searching."

So it is, that ever since that time long ago, every child born of Man and Woman has been born with a longing to meet the one who made the world. We call that longing "Heart."

On the seventh night the father told the little boy the story of "The Master of the Tea Ceremony."

Long ago in Japan there was a master of the tea ceremony. The teamaster practised his art in the palace of Lord Tosa.

One day Lord Tosa was invited to visit the Shogun in the city of Yeddo. He brought with him not only his warriors but also the master of the tea ceremony. He wanted the Shogun to enjoy the teamaster's great art.

The custom of the Shogun was that every man who entered his palace should be dressed in the traditional costume of a samurai warrior. When the teamaster arrived with Lord Tosa's entourage he too began to wear the two crossed swords of a samurai, although he had never worn a sword before in his life.

On many occasions in the next few days Lord Tosa asked his teamaster to perform the tea ceremony, and the teamaster became a favourite of the lords and ladies of the Shogun's court. After a few days, the teamaster was given leave to spend a few hours out in the streets of the city. He was delighted to leave the palace and wander about, watching the hustle and bustle. Seeing the children play in the schoolyards reminded him of his own little boy and girl back home, and he smiled.

When it was time for him to return to the palace, the teamaster began to walk back the way he had come. He came to a bridge and began to cross it. Coming towards him on the bridge was a large, mean-looking man. This man was a *ronin,* a free-lance mercenary who roamed the countryside, sometimes serving an honest cause but more usually making trouble for law-abiding citizens. The *ronin* was in an ugly mood. As he passed the little teamaster he jostled him so that he fell to the ground. When the teamaster stood up and tried to walk away, the *ronin* stopped him and said, "How dare you push me and knock me around!"

"Pardon me," said the teamaster politely, "but I believe it was you who knocked against me. I was the one who fell."

"Are you calling me a liar?" the big man shouted. He hadn't failed to notice that the teamaster was short and slight of build. "Come on, take out your sword and let's settle this argument right here and now!"

"Ah, I'm afraid that I cannot oblige you with a fight," said the teamaster. "Let me explain. You see, I'm not really a samurai. I practise the tea ceremony for Lord Tosa. I am wearing these garments and swords because my lord is visiting the Shogun, and I must dress like a warrior to enter the palace. I have never held a sword in my life."

"So you say," sneered the *ronin,* "and what I say is that you are nothing but a coward. If you refuse to give me satisfaction, if you refuse to fight, I will tell the whole town that your Lord Tosa is served by men who have no honour."

The teamaster had no wish to bring dishonour to his lord. He stood before the *ronin,* his mind racing and his heart pounding. All of a sudden he had an idea. He remembered that on his meander through Yeddo he had passed an academy of swordfighting. He thought to himself, "I will return to that academy and learn at least how to hold the sword properly; then when he kills me I will not die in a shameful manner."

He spoke to the *ronin* and said, "I will fight you. Before I do so, grant me two hours to complete a certain errand. I promise to meet you back here on the bridge and settle our dispute with swords."

The mercenary thought that the little man must be going off to get some money so he could offer a bribe instead of a fight. He was happy to grant the delay. "See that you return in two hours," he said, "or all of Yeddo will know of your disgrace."

The teamaster hurried down the street to the door of the swordfighting academy. He explained breathlessly his urgent need to see the swordmaster, and the doorman brought him in. As quickly as he could, the teamaster described his dilemma, concluding, " . . . so you see I have come to learn from you how to hold a sword properly so that when I receive my deathblow, at least I will die with honour."

"I understand," said the swordmaster. Then he smiled.
"What's so funny?" asked the teamaster. "I myself find
nothing amusing in the situation."

"Pardon my smile," said the swordmaster. "Most of my
students come to me to learn how to avoid death, and how
to bring death to their enemies. You are the first man who
has ever come to me to learn the art of dying."

"Do not mock me!" cried the teamaster. "Please teach
me what I need to know."

"Before I teach you my art," said the swordmaster,
"would you be so kind as to show me yours?"

The teamaster knew that this would be his last chance
to practise his art. With a great effort he began to prepare.
He assembled the elements and utensils of the tea ceremony: the tea, the water, the whisk, the clay vessel, the
brazier. Then he prepared himself. When all was ready,
with a peaceful spirit he was able to serve the tea to the
swordmaster.

The swordmaster observed the teamaster carefully
and, after he had sipped from the bowl of tea, he said, "I
see now that you are already a great master. I have nothing further to teach you. You already know everything
necessary for your combat. Let me just make one suggestion. When you return to the bridge for the fight,
approach your enemy as if he is a good friend. Go to him
as if he is your most honoured guest at the tea ceremony.
When you arrive, be sure to greet him politely and thank
him for waiting for you. Take off your jacket, roll it, and
place it on the ground. Place your fan upon it. Roll up
your sleeves. Tie the headband of resolution around your
forehead. Face your opponent. Grasp your sword by the
hilt, draw it, and hold it above your head. Announce your

readiness for his attack. Then close your eyes. When you hear his battle cry, bring your sword down with all your strength. If you do exactly as I say, I assure you that all will be as you desire. Farewell, and have a good death."

The teamaster was puzzled by the strange advice. But there was no more time for a lesson in sword-holding or swordfighting. He thanked the swordmaster and took his leave. He began to walk back to the bridge. As he walked, he tried to prepare himself not for a fight but for a tea ceremony. He felt calm, as if he were going to serve tea for a well-loved friend. He approached the scene of the combat. Step by step he let go of his hope, and step by step he let go of his fear.

By the time he reached the bridge he could see the *ronin* striding about, shouting and brandishing his sword. A crowd had gathered, eager to see blood. The teamaster walked slowly up to the *ronin,* greeted him, and thanked him for waiting. He placed his jacket and fan upon the ground, rolled up his sleeves, and tied the headband of resolution about his head. He took his sword, held it above his head, and said that he was ready to fight. The sword felt amazingly light in his hands. Then he closed his eyes.

He had no tea this time. He had no water, or whisk, or clay vessel, or fire, or brazier. The only thing left to offer was himself.

The teamaster stood there for a long time, but the *ronin's* cry of attack never came. Finally the little man open his eyes. He saw an astonishing sight. The *ronin's* sword lay on the ground in front of him. The mercenary soldier was backing away from him, his eyes full of terror and confusion. He broke into a run and dashed around the corner.

When the *ronin* had looked at the face of the teamaster, standing quietly in front of him, he lost his nerve. He did not know how to fight an enemy who showed neither hope nor fear. He did not know how to attack a man who stood peacefully, eyes closed, sword held without a quiver high above his head, waiting to serve, not tea, but his whole life. The *ronin* had been so scared that he'd thrown his own sword down and made his escape, glad he hadn't been slaughtered by so powerful an enemy.

The teamaster picked up his things and returned to the Shogun's palace. Before leaving Yeddo he visited his friend at the swordfighting academy. He served the swordmaster tea, told him the story, and the swordmaster smiled again.

On the eighth night the father told the little boy the story of "The Silent Prince."

Once there was a king and a queen and they had a son. As he grew older, the little boy became strange and silent. By the time he was a teenager he had altogether quit talking. And so he became known as the Silent Prince.

The prince's parents were desperate with worry. The queen never gave up hope that her son might become normal, but the king was sure his son was terribly damaged. When the prince was almost eighteen years old, the king and queen had an idea. They issued a proclamation that said: "Whoever can make the Silent Prince speak will win a great reward." In fine print at the bottom of the proclamation were the words: "Whoever tries and fails will have his or her head chopped off."

Despite the dire consequences, many brave men came and tried to win the great reward, and many brave men had their brave heads chopped off. Whatever they said to him, whatever they tried, they always failed; the prince could not or would not speak.

Down the road from the palace lived a young woman with her grandmother. One day the girl said to her grandmother, "Granny, I would like to try to make the Silent Prince speak."

"That is not the cleverest thing you have ever said, Granddaughter. Do you not know the punishment for failure?"

"Yes, Granny, I do. But you are a wise old woman. You've spent time in the forest, you know the powers of herbs and flowers, you've read many books, you know many poems by heart. Please teach me what you know, Granny, and perhaps I'll have a chance."

And so the grandmother said to her granddaughter, "Very well. I will teach you my wisdom on one condition. You must listen to me all night and not interrupt once."

The girl agreed and the grandmother began to speak. It wasn't easy, listening for such a long time, but the girl did. In the morning, her grandmother finished speaking. "I have taught you my wisdom," she said, "and the rest is up to you. Good luck, my beloved."

She kissed the girl, and the girl set off towards the palace. When she arrived, she told the guard she wanted to go in. He led her before the king and the queen, and she told them that she'd come to make the Silent Prince speak.

"Here are the rules," said the queen. "You will spend the night with our son in his bedroom—with a witness. In the morning the witness will tell us what he saw."

The girl went into the prince's bedroom and sat down. She didn't say anything at first, and this surprised the prince very much. All of the men who had come to make him speak had done all of the talking. The girl just sat there. The prince looked at her. He thought she was very beautiful. Finally, the girl began to speak, but not to the prince. She turned to the witness and said, "Tomorrow I am going to die. Could you tell me a story to give me courage to face my death?"

"I'm sorry," said the witness, "but I don't know any stories. I'm just a witness."

"Would you at least listen to my story if I told it to you?" she asked.

"Yes, I'll listen," said the witness.

The girl began:

There were three women once and each had a special power. They were about eighteen years old. One of them had a telescope, and when she looked through it she could see anything that was happening anywhere in the world. The second woman had a magic airplane, and she could travel instantly to anywhere in the world. The third woman had lived for many years in the forest and knew about herbs and healing plants. She'd found an apple tree that grew special apples: one bite could cure any sickness. The three women were good friends, and one day they met and began to show each other their gifts and powers. The first one looked through her telescope and said, "My friends, I see a palace on the other side of the world, and in it a young man is dying." The second one said, "Get on board my airplane and we'll go there right now." All three travelled instantly to that palace. The third woman, the herbswoman, went to the young man's bed and offered him a bite from her magic apple. The young prince was instantly cured. He leapt from his sickbed and saw three beautiful

*young women in his bedroom. He thought to himself, "I'm
healthy now, and I'm single. I'd like to ask one of them to
marry me."*

And here the girl stopped her story and said to the witness, "I have a question for you. Each one of the women
did something to make the sick prince well. Which one did
the most? Which one should he ask to marry him?"

The witness answered, "I don't know. I'm not very
good at riddles."

But the prince had been listening very carefully and he
opened his mouth and said, "I have an idea."

"I'm very pleased to hear you say that," said the girl.
"What is your idea?"

"I think he should ask the young woman with the
apple. The one who used her airplane lost nothing by
using it; the one who used her telescope lost nothing
by using it. But the woman who gave up a bite of her apple
will never get that bite back again. She is the only one who
gave up something for the sake of the sick prince."

"A wise answer, O prince," said the girl. "May you also
one day find someone who is willing to give something up
for you."

In the morning the king and queen came in and asked
the witness what had happened during the night. He was
very pleased to be able to tell them that the Silent Prince had
finally broken his silence. The queen was over the moon
with joy. "Thank God," she cried, "I knew he could speak!"

But the king didn't believe it. "Why," he said, "should
my son start speaking now, just because a beautiful young
woman spent the night in his room? I insist on a second
night with two witnesses!"

So that night the girl was in the room with the prince and two witnesses. Again she sat for a long time and did not say a word. Finally she turned to the two witnesses and said, "My friends, tomorrow I will die. Will you tell me a story to give me courage to face my death?"

"We're not storytellers," they said, "we're just witnesses."

"Would you at least listen to my story if I told it to you?" she asked.

They agreed to listen and the girl began:

There was a young girl who lived in a village, and she was a witch. She was very much in love with a young man, but she never told him she was a witch. She was afraid he would leave her if he found out the truth. One night the young man was walking alone in the woods, and up ahead he saw a witch. He picked up a large stone and threw it at her. She turned to escape, but the stone caught her on the back of the leg. The next day when the boy went to visit his girlfriend he noticed she was limping. When she turned around he saw that there was a wound on the back of her leg, in the same place he'd thrown his stone. He said, "So it's you . . . you're the witch!" And she admitted everything: "Yes, I am the witch."

The girl stopped her story and said to the two witnesses, "I have a question for you. Now that the boyfriend knows the truth about his lover, what should he do?"

"We don't know," they said, "we're not very good at riddles."

The prince had been listening very closely to the story, and he opened his mouth and said, "I have an idea."

"I am very pleased to hear you say that," the girl replied. "What is your idea?"

"I think he should marry her, and they should keep her secret together."

"A wise answer," said the girl, "and an unusual one for a man. Many men would have said—she is a witch; drive her away; burn her. But you understand that when people love each other, not only do they give up their secrets, they learn new ones as well. May you also find someone who will give up a secret for you."

In the morning the king and queen came in and asked the two witnesses what had happened, and both of them said, "Your Majesties, last night your son spoke!" Again the queen was overjoyed; but the king still didn't believe it. "I insist on one more test," he said, "with three witnesses."

And so the same thing happened for a third night. The girl, the prince and the three witnesses sat together quietly for a long time. Finally the girl turned to the witnesses and said, "Please, my friends, tomorrow I may face my death. Tell me a story to give me courage to face my death."

"We have no stories," they all said.

"Would you listen to my story if I told it to you?"

They agreed to listen and the girl began:

Once there was a man who dreamed of firebirds. One day when he was in the woods there was a great flash of golden light. He hid behind a tree and closed his eyes. When he dared to look he beheld a beautiful woman taking off a suit of golden feathers and stepping into a pool to bathe. He gazed at her loveliness. Then he reached out and stole her golden feathers and hid them away. When the woman came out of the pool she searched for them but could not find them. The man came out of his hiding place and said,

"Come with me and I will give you shelter." The woman knew that she could not fly away and so she followed the man through the woods to his house. He had a good house, and he was gentle, and she stayed with him. One day she gave birth to a child, a little boy. She loved her son very much. The boy was about five years old when he came running to his mother, one day when his father was away. "Mama," he cried, "I was playing in the woods and I found something pretty! Come and see!" The woman went with her little boy. They came to a tree, and there in a hollow place she found her golden feathers, blazing with their golden light. She picked them up and went back to the house with her son. She sang him lullabies and put him to sleep. With one hand she stroked the little boy's hair, and with the other she held her golden feathers.

And here the girl stopped her story and said, "I have a question for you. Now that the woman can fly again, what should she do?"

The three witnesses shook their heads. "We don't know," they said, "that is the hardest riddle of all."

But the prince had been listening very carefully and he opened his mouth and said, "I have an idea."

"I am pleased to hear you say that," the girl said. "What is your idea?"

"I think that it is not up to me to judge the woman of your story, nor can I judge the man. Your story is both bitter and sweet at the same time. If I were the man in your story, and could see the firebird in her true form, I think that I too would do anything to keep her with me. And if I, like the woman, had once come from the sky, I think that I would never lose my desire to return to it."

"A wise answer, O prince," said the girl. "Some stories are not meant to be judged, but only to be heard and remembered. The woman kissed her son, stepped outside, put on her golden feathers and flew away. When the man returned, the woman was gone."

"And what happened to her little boy?"

"Some people say that when he woke up and found his mother was gone, he cried so much that he lost his voice and became silent. And other people say that when he awoke he found a golden feather shining on his pillow, and this feather brought him luck and joy and courage and love for the rest of his life."

In the morning the king and queen came in and the three witnesses all agreed: "Last night," they said, "your son spoke!" The queen was jubilant and the king also believed them. They turned to the girl and said, "You have done what no man was able to do. What would you like as your great reward?"

For the first time, the girl was silent. All this time she had not been thinking about her reward, but only about her stories. The prince rose and walked towards her. He took her by the hand and lifted her up and looked her in the eyes. "Choose me," he said.

And the girl said, "I have an idea. I'll take him!"

So it was that they were married. It was a grand celebration. In the seat of honour was the girl's grandmother. She was holding a big bouquet of wild herbs and flowers that she'd picked that day in the woods. As the girl walked by, the grandmother handed her the flowers and said, "You see, you should always listen to your granny!"

On the ninth night the father told his son the story of "Ali the Persian's Bag."

Long, long ago there lived in the city of Baghdad a mighty Caliph named Haroun al-Rashid. He loved to walk through the streets of his own city in disguise, peering in through garden gates, eavesdropping at secret windows, listening to the stories his people told. But he had trouble sleeping at night. One night as he tossed and turned he called his vizier Jafar and said, "Jafar, my heart is heavy. Find some way to lift my spirits."

"I hear and obey without delay," said Jafar. "I happen to have a friend known as Ali the Persian. He is a renowned storyteller, and if anything can lift a troubled heart it's a good story. I will bring him to you."

When Ali the Persian came before the Caliph he bowed and said, "Your Majesty, would you like to hear a story about something I heard, or something I saw with my own two eyes?"

"Tell me the truth," said the Caliph.

"I will try," answered Ali. "I will tell you of something that happened to me the other day. I was standing in my shop in the marketplace when I noticed a man from Kurdistan come in. He looked at this and he looked at that, and finally when he thought I wasn't looking, he picked a bag off the shelf and walked out without paying for it. I followed him into the street, seized him by the sleeve, and began shouting, 'Shoplifter, shoplifter! Give me back that bag!'

"'Never!' he cried. 'This bag is mine. Yesterday someone stole it from me, and today I found it in your shop!'

"We began to quarrel and a crowd gathered around us. They took us to the courtroom of the local *cadi*, the district judge, who looked at us both and said, 'What is the cause of this dispute?'

"'This bag is mine,' I said, 'and this fellow stole it!'

"'No, no,' said the Kurd, 'the bag is mine and I found it in the man's shop.'

"The judge said, 'For me to come to a proper judgement, you will each have to tell me what the bag contains.'

"'I can tell you what it contains,' said the Kurd, 'because it is my bag. It has:

a silver jar of eye-shadow

two make-up brushes

a candlestick

two lemonade glasses with gilded rims

a waterpot with two ladles

a small carpet with two matching cushions

plus:

a pregnant cat

a jar of rice

two sacks of wheat

a bedroom suite

a female bear

a racing camel

a canopy

a kitchen with two doors

and a company of Kurds—

and they have all concurred that the bag is mine!'

"When I heard this nonsense I said to the judge, 'Your Honour, do not let your judgement be blurred by the absurd words of this false Kurd you've just heard! The bag is mine and I can tell you what's inside. It has:

a house in ruins
a school for adolescent delinquents
a dog kennel
four chess players
tents and tentpoles
the city of Basra
the city of Baghdad
the ancient palace of Shaddad ibn-Aad
a smithy's forge
a shepherd's crook
a fishing net
five handsome boys
twelve delightful girls
and one thousand leaders of caravans—
and every single one of them will tell you that this bag
is mine!'

"The Kurd burst into tears. He said, 'Most honourable
magistrate, do not let your mind be misled by the malice
of this mendacious Middle Eastern merchant! The bag is
mine and only mine and it contains:

one stone fort with fourteen towers
thirty-two alchemical powers
four more men playing chess
a mare and a stallion and a newborn foal
a lance
a rabbit
a roaring lion
three kings from the east
two courtesans and a comedian
a rabbi with two cantors
a priest with two deacons
a mullah with two servants

a captain with two sailors
an honest man with two liars
and a judge with two witnesses
and both of them will swear and testify that the bag is
mine!'

"When I heard this nonsense my fury rose to my nostrils (and believe me, Commander of the Faithful, it hurts to have your fury right up your nose), and I cried out, 'O Judge, the bag is mine and it has in it:

lotions and potions
philtres and enchantments
miracles and wonders
shades and phantoms
a garden with figs and apples
grapes and vines
whispers and cries
murmurs and sighs
nibbles and giggles
two lovers rising from their bed
a loud blast from behind
two quiet poofies
plus:
rahatlokoum
and *babaghanoush*
and *imambaldi*
and green eggs and ham
and *baklava*
and toasted pita
and double-cheese pizza
and a parade with drums and banners
flags and flutes
singers and dancers

and a man playing the clarinet
and a plank
and a nail
and one thousand silver coins
and the city of Kufah
and the city of Gaza
and the old children's library behind the plaza
and it also contains
all of the land that stretches
from Cairo to Jerusalem to Damascus to the Middle
Kingdom to Isfahan
In addition to which, my bag contains:
a foolish shopkeeper
a noble Kurd
a sleepless Caliph
a brave girl
a wise granny
a silent prince
a warrior who fights without swords
plus, the sun and the moon and darkness and rain
and a human heart born crying
and seven old men
and a curious traveller
and a sick princess
and a dreambird Colour-of-Time
and a primrose
and a green mist
and two soldiers
and a blue butterfly
and tortoises, stones and human beings
and a little boy who ponders deep riddles
and a father who loves him

and an angry king
and an anxious storyteller
and happy listeners
and the greatest fiddler in the world
and loud clapping
and more loud clapping
and also
a coffin
a shroud
and a razor for the beard of the *cadi*
if he does not agree the bag belongs to me!'

"The judge looked puzzled as he listened to our amazing lists. The he said, 'Either the two of you are making fun of the law and its representative, or this bag is as deep as the Abyss and as all-encompassing as the Day of Judgement itself. I see that I shall have to open the bag and see for myself what it contains.' And he opened the bag and looked inside."

And the father said to his little boy, "What do you think was in the bag?"

And at that point the Storyteller fell silent. The king grew impatient. "Don't stop there," her said. "Go on!"

"I'm sorry, Your Majesty, that is the end of my story."

"That is not a good place to stop your story, Storyteller! You haven't told me what the father told the little boy Ali the Persian told the Caliph Haroun al-Rashid the judge found inside the bag! You've left everything in suspense."

"I cannot tell you the rest, Your Majesty, because I do not know how this story ends. You see, I am the father in my story and my own son is the little boy. I was telling him that story of Ali the Persian tonight when your guard came to summon me to your presence. I had just asked my son the question, 'What do you think the bag contains?' when I was interrupted and had to leave without hearing his answer. I was going to make his answer the ending of my story. If I had known I would never see my little boy again, I would have given the story my own ending—but what person knows the hour of their own death? Not even kings, not even storytellers . . ."

"If you die tonight you will never hear your son's answer."

"Well, perhaps he will become a storyteller himself one day, and tell his answer to a new listener."

"Storyteller . . . Storyteller, you will not die tonight. You will go home and hear your son's answer. Let your return be the tenth story you promised him, and let it have a happy ending. You have shown me tonight what had been hidden from me. There is a risk in life and a risk in stories. The teller and the tale are one and cannot be separated, for each shelters the other. I see now that only Worldmaker knows the last word in our story, not kings . . . or storytellers."

"You are merciful, Your Majesty."

"By the way, what *did* the judge find inside the bag?"

"What do you think, O King?"

"Oh . . . probably just a few olive pits, a dried crust of bread, an orange rind . . . and a good story."

"You are right! That's exactly what the bag contained. And when Ali the Persian and the Kurd heard this, they both laughed and said the bag wasn't theirs after all. And when the Caliph Haroun al-Rashid heard the story the pain was lifted from his heart, and he laughed and laughed and laughed."

I WAS ONCE TELLING STORIES to a group of seven-year-olds, and when the program was almost over one little boy hollered exultantly, *"Never finish!"* Perhaps this is the whispered, peek-a-boo truth of stories: life ends and stories, too; but stories end in their own good time and with as much "working around" as the teller can fashion, and even in the silence afterwards they are able to keep speaking to us. Stories let us hear the footsteps of our own transformation coming towards us on the pathway of everyday life. We learn from our stories how to dream, tell and remember beyond our own ending, and this may be as close as we can get to never finishing.

THIS APPENDIX is an informal tour of a storyteller's working library rather than a comprehensive bibliography. Instead of a systematic survey, I invite you on a brief ramble through a library that is a work-in-progress, assembled with more love than scholarship.

There are gaps on the tour, and glaring ones at that. I've mostly left on the shelf the classic authors of storytelling literature—Perrault, the brothers Grimm, Andersen, Kipling, Joseph Jacobs. They are good and essential, but there are already many guides to lead you to them. And I won't be walking you through the growing field of story-telling "how to" books, the psychology shelf (although I have read and enjoy Jung, Bettelheim, Bly and Pinkola Estes) or the vast number of audio recordings. As for Internet resources, aside from suggesting a few websites that connect you to storytelling in North America and around the world, I leave this kind of Web-based research to your own double-clicking ingenuity.

I'll begin with some of the books I keep returning to for ideas and inspiration. Walter Benjamin, an essayist and philosopher, wrote a wonderful piece called "The Storyteller." Using the Russian writer Leskov as his example, Benjamin explores the nature of oral storytelling, as an art and as part of everyday life. If you are interested in the relationship between orality and literacy, you will find the oldest and best evocation of this eternal puzzle in Plato's *Phaedrus*. Socrates was truly a great storyteller, and in this dialogue he tells a myth that illuminates the moral consequences of telling and writing as modes of human expression. Chinua Achebe's *Anthills of the Savannah* offers the best example of African oratory I've ever read. It is thrilling to see how Achebe's elder weaves traditional stories and proverbs into the troop-rallying speech in the middle of the book. Italo Calvino's *Invisible Cities* is one of my favourite books. In it, Marco Polo tells Kublai Khan a series of yarns about imaginary places. This great modern fabulist also collected and wrote *Italian Folktales,* one of the greatest collections of traditional oral literature compiled in the twentieth century.

I think the three books that have most influenced me are Geoffrey Chaucer's *Canterbury Tales,* Giovanni Boccaccio's *Decameron,* and *Thousand and One Nights.* I am continually astonished by the way these authors and, in the case of the *Thousand and One Nights*, editors, drew on their lively and sophisticated oral cultures to create such literary masterpieces. I go back to these three medieval sources constantly for inspiration, story ideas and a sense of why oral stories matter.

I came to storytelling via Homer's epics, the *Iliad* and the *Odyssey.* There are many superb translations available, though the Robert Fitzgerald translations have always seemed to me to be particularly fine. Although they came from a literary more than an oral tradition, the Icelandic sagas are wonderful ways to learn about long, interwoven narratives. In these complex, moving stories, the heroes and heroines pursue their difficult destinies across a harsh northern landscape. Other classics of long narrative include the Arthurian stories of the Grail, the *Mahabharata*, the Welsh *Mabinogion*, the *Nibelungen* saga, and *Gilgamesh*, one of the oldest recorded stories in human history. Although I don't tell stories from these cycles, I go back to them for a sense of their sheer grandeur and imaginative range. They have also proven a rich source for contemporary storytellers, and I have heard performances of all of them in concert settings. I love to listen to long stories.

There aren't many books about storytelling as a way of life, but I have five great favourites. In *The Crack in the Teacup: The Life of an Old Woman Steeped in Stories,* Joan Bodger writes about how stories and myths made a frame for her life. French storyteller Bruno de la Salle describes his experiences as a contemporary bard in *Le Conteur amoureux.* The centrality of stories in the lives of three Yukon elders is explored and celebrated in the anthropologist Julie Cruikshank's *Life Lived Like a Story.* Brother Blue's extraordinary life as a storyteller and animator of North American storytelling is celebrated in *Ahhhh! A Tribute to Brother Blue and Ruth Edmonds Hill.* And of course Ruth Sawyer's book *The Way of the Storyteller* continues to be a good companion.

I have a shelf in my library with books I turn to for their wisdom about why oral literature matters. Alice Kane's *Songs and Sayings of an Ulster Childhood* (edited by Edith Fowke) evokes an upbringing filled with poetry, family lore, music, proverbs. When you encounter her great collection of wonder tales, *The Dreamer Awakes* (edited by Sean Kane), you sense how her story-rich Ulster childhood prepared her for a life as a storyteller. Also in *The Dreamer*

Awakes, Canadian poet Robert Bringhurst's introduction is a superb reflection on the nature of wonder tales and their importance as a contemporary art form. Ted Chamberlin's *If This Is Your Land, Where Are Your Stories?* is a fascinating book about the power of stories as a source of personal and cultural identity. Sean Kane's *Wisdom of the Mythtellers* is a thoughtful exploration of myth.

If you're interested in international folk tales and fairy tales, Pantheon Books publishes a series called Fairytale & Folklore Library. It is a comprehensive introduction to the oral literature of a number of countries, and includes classics like the brothers Grimm and Afanas'ev's *Russian Fairy Tales*, as well as Arabic, Chinese, African, African-American, Japanese and Swedish collections. In this series you can find treasures like Howard Norman's *Northern Tales,* Jane Yolen's *Favorite Folktales from Around the World,* and the incomparable *Italian Folktales,* by Italo Calvino.

Other anthologies that I keep returning to include *The Ch'i-Lin Purse: A Collection of Ancient Chinese Stories,* by Linda Fang; Diane Wolkstein's *The Magic Orange Tree and Other Haitian Folktales;* Richard Chase's *Grandfather Tales* and *The Jack Tales; Talk That Talk: An Anthology of African American Storytelling,* edited by Linda Goss, Marion Barnes and Henry Louis Gates Jr.; any of Harold Courlander's many collections: e.g., The *Fire on the Mountain and Other Stories from Ethiopia and Eritrea, The Cow-tail Switch and Other West African Stories; East of the Sun, West of the Moon,* by Asbjornsen and Moe, translated by George Dasent; all books by the Scottish Traveller Duncan Williamson, including *Broonie, Silkie, and Fairies* and *A Thorn in the King's Foot: Folktales of the Scottish*

Travelling People. I also have a Hodja Nasrudin shelf, with several collections of wise-foolish stories.

My own love for Jewish stories has been enriched by many authors and editors. They include Martin Buber, Dov Noy (founder of the Israel Folktale Archive), Penninah Schram, Howard Schwartz, Steve Zeitlin and Diane Wolkstein. Yaffa Eliach's *Hasidic Tales of the Holocaust* is one of the greatest books I've ever read.

There are several reference books you will undoubtedly find yourself visiting during your storytelling travels: *A Dictionary of British Folk-tales,* by Katherine Briggs; Margaret Read MacDonald's *The Storyteller's Sourcebook; The World of Storytelling: A Practical Guide to the Origins, Development, and Applications of Storytelling,* by Anne Pellowski; Caroline Feller Bauer's *New Handbook for Storytellers; Tales, Rumors, and Gossip: Exploring Contemporary Folk Literature in Grades 7–12,* by Gail de Vos; Stith Thompson's *The Folktale,* which looks at folk literature in terms of universal motifs and patterns; and, for a sense of how we first learn to speak the language of Story, Iona and Peter Opie's superb *The Lore and Language of Schoolchildren.*

One of the great things about storytelling today is that one can discover the world of Native North American oral literature through the writings of those who are part of it. A generation or two ago, access to published aboriginal stories was often via European writers, anthropologists and editors. Now, many Native storytellers have brought their art into the written domain. Books I particularly treasure include several by Basil Johnston exploring his Anishnabe heritage, *Earth Elder Stories* by the Saulteaux elder Alexander Wolfe and *My Stories Are My Wealth,* by the Yukon elder Angela Sidney. Joseph Bruchac is a well-known anthologist of Native American stories, and has also compiled a wonderful book titled *Lasting Echoes: An Oral History of Native American People*. *Write It on Your Heart: The Epic World of an Okanagan Storyteller*, by Harry Robinson (compiled and edited by Wendy Wickwire) brings the Okanagan tradition to life through the perspective of a gifted storyteller. Thomas King, a Native Canadian novelist, has done some very fine retellings of Coyote stories. I also recommend Jaime de Angulo's *Indian Tales*, an astonishing retelling of Coyote stories and medicine songs from California's Pit River people. Robert Bringhurst has done a three-volume translation of Haida oral literature. The first book, *A Story As Sharp As a Knife*, is a profound exploration of myth and the lives of those who tell them. In his passion for what he calls the "classical literature" of North America, Bringhurst reminds me of the cross-cultural thrill Chaucer must have felt when he read and began to translate Boccaccio.

There are many books that record Canada's oral traditions. The Cape Breton storyteller Joe Neil MacNeil's *Tales Until Dawn* (edited by John Shaw) is a fine collection of traditional Gaelic stories. Germain Lemieux has compiled an extraordinary series titled *Les vieux m'ont conté*, bringing together the repertoires of Franco-Ontarian traditional tellers. The series is up to thirty volumes. Helen Creighton and Edith Fowke were contemporary folklorists who collected and published essential story and song collections. I will also dare to include an anthology I edited called *Tales for an Unknown City*, drawing on Toronto's One Thousand and One Friday Nights of Storytelling. The book reflects the multicultural nature of the city where this storytelling event takes place. For tall tales, I must recommend Ted Stone's *Hailstorms and Hoopsnakes,* which evokes perfectly the setting where such stories flourish. Québec has given birth to an extraordinary storytelling movement, and the Planète rebelle publishing house has created a series of books and CDs based on the repertoires of many leading Québécois tellers.

In the United States, August House has played a similarly important role in publishing the repertoires of American storytellers. They have brought into print stories by such tellers as Donald Davis, J. J. Reneaux, Jackie Torrence, Heather Forest and Michael Parent.

There is a strong interest today in how storytelling can serve as a healing art. Two books have recently been published that open a window into this aspect of storytelling. *The Healing Heart: Communities* and *The Healing Heart: Families,* edited by Allison Cox and David Albert, have an impressive selection of stories, essays and personal accounts. They also feature excellent bibliographies organized into topics like "Violence prevention/peace initiatives" and "environmental tales." For a very moving account of using stories in a healing context, see Michelle Tocher's *How to Ride a Dragon: Women with Breast Cancer Tell Their Stories.* I also recommend an anthology titled *Spinning Tales, Weaving Hope,* edited by Ed Brody, Jay Goldspinner, Katie Green, Rona Leventhal and John Porcino. It is a collection of stories that have social justice themes.

There are hundreds of good collections of stories for very young children, and these should be well represented in your local library. I will, however, recommend Celia Lottridge's *Ten Small Tales* as the perfect anthology for anyone who tells stories to children under five. Every story in the book works beautifully with this audience.

For storytellers working in educational settings, there are a number of good books I can recommend. Bob Barton's *Telling Stories Your Way: Storytelling and Reading Aloud in the Classroom* is a fine introduction to this field. *Tales As Tools: The Power of Story in the Classroom,* edited by Mary Weaver, is a compendium of essays and exercises by many North American storytellers. Also useful: *Children Tell Stories: A Teaching Guide,* by Martha Hamilton and Mitch Weiss; *And None of It Was Nonsense,* by Betty Rosen; *Mother Goose Goes to School,* by Bob Barton and David Booth.

Family oral history is a growing field. Many storytellers today develop family lore into performance pieces; others explore it as a way to enrich their understanding of traditional stories. *Telling Tales: Storytelling in the Family,* by Gail de Vos, Merle Harris and Celia Lottridge is a good introduction to this topic. For those who want to actively document their family heritage, Vera Frankenbluth's *Keeping Family Stories Alive: A Creative Guide to Taping Your Family Life & Lore* is an excellent resource. Elizabeth Stone's *Black Sheep and Kissing Cousins: How Our Family Stories Shape Us* has been an inspiring book for many storytellers.

Then there are the hard-to-classify treasures. For a fresh look at how contemporary storytellers work with traditional material, I recommend Kay Stone's *Burning Brightly: New Light on Old Tales Told Today.* If you like grand theories, David Bynum's *The Daemon in the Wood* is a very original book that looks at some of the universal patterns of oral narrative. It will give you a whole new sense of what trees signify in your stories. Albert Lord's *The Singer of Tales,* a study of the bardic tradition, was an early inspiration for me.

To end this tour, let me mention several good magazines and organizations that can serve as guides to the storytelling movement. In Canada and the U.S. you can subscribe to *Appleseed Quarterly: The Canadian Journal of Storytelling* by writing to the Storytellers School of Toronto (www.storytellingtoronto.org) and to *Storytelling Magazine* through the National Storytelling Network (www.storynet.org). I would also recommend *Tale Trader*, a storytelling newspaper published in Louisville, Kentucky. *La Grande Oreille* is an excellent magazine published in France. As well as these journals and magazines, many storytelling associations and guilds publish very fine newsletters. If you are seeking information about storytelling internationally, Margaret Read MacDonald edited a superb edition of *Storytelling Magazine* (volume 14, issue 2) with the theme of Global Connections. Storytellers from around the world describe more than twenty-three storytelling movements and provide contact information. Many of these movements have associated websites, publish directories of professional storytellers, and offer a variety of services and resources. In Canada, you can join Storytellers of Canada/Conteurs du Canada (www.sc-cc.com). In the U.S., you can reach the National Storytelling Network at www.storynet.org. Similar organizations exist in England, Scotland, France, Australia and many other countries, supporting the contemporary storytelling renaissance.

As you fare forth to find your own storytelling resources, it's important to remember that in the world of storytelling, the spoken word comes before the written word. The greatest assemblage of books cannot replace or displace the experience of listening to elders. The best website ever created cannot substitute for a quiet evening spent hearing a master storyteller spin tales from a well-chosen repertoire. The word of mouth is what draws us to this art, not the word of page or word of screen. Which reminds me of a Hodja story (*everything* reminds me of a Hodja story!). I'll tell it to you when we meet.

⪡ ANNOTATED BIBLIOGRAPHY ⪢

Achebe, Chinua. *Anthills of the Savannah*. New York, 1997.

Afanas'ev, Aleksandr. *Russian Fairy Tales*. Translated by Norbert Guterman. Commentary by Roman Jakobson. New York, 1945.

Balfour, M. C. "Legends of the Lincolnshire Cars." In *Folk-Lore II*. September, 1891. I based my version of "The Green Mist" on Mrs. Balfour's Lincolnshire legend. I took the liberty of bringing the story into the language of my own time and place, although I enjoyed sounding out the thick Lincolnshire dialect in which it was originally told and recorded. Both Alan Garner and Kevin Crossley-Holland have used this tale in collections of, respectively, goblin stories and English stories.

Barton, Bob. *Telling Stories Your Way: Storytelling and Reading Aloud in the Classroom*. Markham, 2000.

Bauer, Caroline Feller. *New Handbook for Storytellers: With Stories, Poems, Magic, and More*. 1998.

Beier, Ulli. *The Origin of Life and Death*. London, 1966. My story about how death came into the world in *The Storyteller At Fault* is retold from Beier's "Tortoises, Men and Stones."

Benjamin, Walter. "The Storyteller." In *Illuminations*. Edited and with an introduction by Hannah Arendt. Translated by Harry Zohn. New York, 1969. One of the greatest essays ever written on the art and nature of storytelling.

Bérubé, Jocelyn. *Nil en ville* (recorded album). Montreal, 1976. "The Bird Colour-of-Time" is freely translated and adapted, with permission, from Bérubé's "L'Oiseau couleur du temps."

Birch, Carol and Melissa A. Heckler, eds. *Who Says?: Essays on Pivotal Issues in Contemporary Storytelling*. Little Rock, 1996.

Boccaccio, Giovanni. *The Decameron*. Translated with an introduction by G. H. McWilliam. Middlesex, 1972.

Bodger, Joan. *The Crack in the Teacup: The Life of an Old Woman Steeped in Stories*. Toronto, 2000. A great storyteller's memoir.

Briggs, Katherine. *A Dictionary of British Folk-Tales in the English Language*. London, 1970. This is a splendid, two-volume collection of stories, within a comprehensive, scholarly frame.

Bringhurst, Robert. *Being in Being: The Collected Words of a Master Haida Mythteller SKAAY of the Qquuna Qiighawaay*. Translated by Robert Bringhurst. Vancouver, 2001.
———. *Nine Visits to the Mythworld—GHANDL of the Qayahl Llaanas*. Translated by Robert Bringhurst. Vancouver, 2000.

———. *A Story As Sharp As a Knife: The Classical Haida Mythtellers and Their World.* Vancouver, 1999. I don't know of any other contemporary poet who has delved so deeply and thoughtfully into the world of myth.

Bruchac, Joseph. *Lasting Echoes: An Oral History of Native American People.* New York, 1997.

Brody, Ed, Jay Goldspinner, Katie Green, Rona Leventhal and John Porcino. *Spinning Tales, Weaving Hope: Stories, Storytelling and Activities for Peace, Justice and the Environment.* Gabriola Island, 2002.

Bruner, Charlotte. "Fadhma and Marguerite Amrouche of the Kabyle Mountains." In *The Word-Singers,* edited by Norman Simms. Hamilton, 1984.

Buber, Martin. *The Legend of the Baal-Shem.* Translated by Maurice Friedman. New York, 1969.
———. *Tales of the Hasidim: Later Masters.* Translated by Olga Marx. New York, 1948.

Bynum, David. *The Daemon in the Wood: A Study of Oral Narrative Patterns.* Cambridge, 1978.

Calame-Griaule, Geneviève. *Le Renouveau du Conte: The Revival of Storytelling.* Paris, 1991. An interesting snapshot of the storytelling movement around the world, based on an international colloque that took place in Paris in 1989.

Calvino, Italo. *Invisible Cities.* Translated by William Weaver. London, 1974.

———. *Italian Folktales*. Translated by George Martin. New York, 1980.

———. *Six Memos for the Next Millennium*. Translated by Patrick Creagh. Cambridge, 1988.

Celan, Paul. *Poems of Paul Celan*. Translated by Michael Hamburger. New York, 1988.

Chamberlin, J. Edward. *If This Is Your Land, Where Are Your Stories?: Finding Common Ground*. Toronto, 2003. A fascinating study of how stories define "them" and "us."

Chase, Richard. *Grandfather Tales*. Boston, 1948. A classic collection of stories from North Carolina, Virginia and Kentucky. His "Wicked John and the Devil" is the seed of my story, "The Devil's Noodles."

Chaucer, Geoffrey. *The Canterbury Tales*. In *Chaucer's Major Poetry*, edited by Albert C. Baugh. New York, 1963.

Colum, Padraic. "Storytelling New and Old." In *Horn Book*, 1983.

———. *The King of Ireland's Son*. 1978. One of the finest frame-stories ever written, and a great favourite of Alice Kane.

Courlander, Harold. *The Cow-Tail Switch and Other West African Stories*. New York, 1947.

———. *The King's Drum and Other African Stories*. New York, 1962.

Cox, Allison M. and David H. Albert. *The Healing Heart: Communities* and *The Healing Heart: Families.* Gabriola Island, 2003. Two important additions to the literature on storytelling and healing.

Cruikshank, Julie. *Life Lived Like a Story: Life Stories of Three Yukon Elders, with Angela Sidney, Kitty Smith, & Annie Ned.* Vancouver, 1990. A very powerful exploration of how myth and oral history are interwoven with the life-experiences of three Native Canadian women.

Dasent, George Webbe. *Popular Tales from the Norse.* Edinburgh, 1859.
———. *Tales from the Fjeld.* London, 1874. These two books contain Dasent's great translations of the Scandinavian stories collected by Peter Christian Asbjornsen and Jorgen Moe. I based my story, "The True Father of the House," on a Norwegian story in the second collection.

DeAngulo, Jaime. *Indian Tales.* Foreword by Carl Carmer. New York, 1953.

De la Salle, Bruno. *Le conteur amoureux.* Paris, 1995. A wonderful account of a French storyteller's career and repertoire.

De Vos, Gail. *Storytelling for Young Adults: Techniques and Treasury.* Englewood, 1991.
———. *Tales, Rumors and Gossip: Exploring Contemporary Folk Literature in Grades 7–12.* Englewood, 1996.
———. *Telling Tales: Storytelling in the Family.* With Merle Harris and Celia Barker Lottridge. Edmonton, 2003.

Downing, Charles. *Tales of the Hodja*. London, 1964.
———. *Armenian Folktales and Fables*. Oxford, 1972.

Eliach, Yaffa. *Hasidic Tales of the Holocaust*. Oxford, 1982.

Ellis, John M. *One Fairy Story Too Many: The Brothers Grimm and Their Tales*. Chicago, 1983.

Falassi, Alessandro. *Folklore by the Fireside: Text and Context of the Tuscan Veglia*. Austin, 1980.

Fang, Linda. *The Ch'i-Lin Purse: A Collection of Ancient Chinese Stories*. New York, 1995. A brilliant collection of Chinese tales.

Fauliot, Pascal. *Les contes des arts martiaux*. Paris, 1981. "The Master of the Tea Ceremony" is my free translation, with permission, from Fauliot's book of Zen-like tales.

Finnigan, Joan. *Laughing All The Way Home*. Toronto, 1984.
———. *Legacies, Legends & Lies*. Kingston, 1987. Finnigan is an oral historian of Canada's fabled Ottawa Valley.

Garner, Alan. *The Stone Book Quartet*. London, 1976.
———. *Strandloper*. London, 1996. Besides his many collections of folk tales and his famous fantasy novels, in these two books Garner makes astonishing connections between everyday experience, deeply rooted local history and myth.

Goss, Linda, et al., eds. *Talk That Talk: An Anthology of African American Storytelling*. 1989.

Grimm, Jacob and Wilhelm. *The Complete Grimm's Fairy Tales.* Translated by Margaret Hunt. New York, 1972.

Haddawy, Husein. *The Arabian Nights.* New York, 1990. His translation is based on a text edited by Muhsin Mahdi.

Havelock, Eric. *Preface to Plato.* Cambridge, 1963. A study of Homeric Greece.

Holst, Spencer. *The Language of Cats.* New York, 1971.
———. *Spencer Holst Stories.* New York, 1976. Two great collections of modern fables by someone Allen Ginsberg once described as a "stand-up tragic." A friend introduced me to Holst's writing at the very beginning of my storytelling career, and I've been hooked ever since.

Homer. *The Iliad.* Translated by Robert Fitzgerald. New York, 1974.
———. *The Odyssey.* Translated by Robert Fitzgerald. New York, 1963.

Housman, Laurence. *Arabian Nights.* New York, 1981.

Johnston, Basil. *The Manitous: The Spiritual World of the Ojibway.* Toronto, 1995. One of several authoritative explorations of Ojibway myth by a respected elder.

Kane, Alice. *The Dreamer Awakes.* Edited by Sean Kane. Introduction by Robert Bringhurst. A superb collection of stories from the repertoire of one of Canada's finest storytellers. Bringhurst's introduction shows that the art of the wonder tale lies on a continuum with the world's most powerful myths.

———. *Songs and Sayings of an Ulster Childhood.* Edited by Edith Fowke. Toronto, 1983.

Kane, Sean. *Wisdom of the Mythtellers.* Peterborough, 1994. A fascinating exploration of myth as a living presence in the lives of those who tell and remember them.

Kipling, Rudyard. *The Jungle Book.* London, 1983.

Lee, Dennis. *Alligator Pie.* Toronto, 2001.

Lemieux, Germain. *Les vieux m'ont conté.* Montreal, 1973. Under the direction of folklorist Germain Lemieux, this is an amazing series of books, currently up to thirty volumes, each chronicling the repertoire of traditional Franco-Ontarian storytellers.

Leslau, Charlotte and Wolf. *African Myths and Folktales.* White Plains, 1963. "How Heart Came Into the World" is adapted, with permission, from the Leslaus' "The Creation of the World."

Lord, Albert B. *The Singer of Tales.* Edited by Stephen Mitchell and Gregory Nagy. Cambridge, 2000. A groundbreaking work on Homeric and contemporary epic traditions.

Lottridge, Celia Barker. *Ten Small Tales.* Toronto, 1993. A great book of stories for the very young.

MacDonald, Margaret Read. *The Storyteller's Sourcebook: A Subject, Title and Motif-Index to Children's Folklore Collections.* Farmington Hills, 1982.

———, and Brian Sturm. *The Storyteller's Sourcebook (2002 Supplement): A Subject, Title and Motif-Index to Children's Folklore Collections, 1983–1999.* Farmington Hills, 2001.

MacNeil, Joe Neil. *Tales Until Dawn: The World of a Cape Breton Gaelic Story-Teller.* Translated and edited by John Shaw. Montreal, 1988.

Mardrus, J. C. *The Book of the Thousand Nights and One Night.* Translated into English from the Mardrus French translation by Powys Mathers. London, 1937. I based my story "Ali the Persian's Bag" on a version found in Mardrus, as well as on the John Payne, Edward Lane and Richard Burton translations.

McCaughrean, Geraldine. *One Thousand and One Arabian Nights.* Oxford, 1982. Beware of her use of cream cheese instead of oil when Morgiana kills the thieves.

Morrow, Glenn, et al., eds. *Ahhhh! A Tribute to Brother Blue & Ruth Edmonds Hill.* Cambridge, 2003.

Mudrick, Marvin. *Books Aren't Life but Then What Is?* New York, 1979.
———. *Mudrick Transcribed: Classes and Talks.* Edited by Lance Kaplan. Santa Barbara, 1989.
———. *Nobody Here but Us Chickens.* New York, 1981. Professor Mudrick was the greatest Chaucer teacher who ever lived. It was his inventive and high-spirited introduction to medieval literature that launched me into storytelling. These books show him in action.

Niemi, Loren, and Elizabeth Ellis. *Inviting the Wolf In: Thinking About Difficult Stories.* Little Rock, 2002. An interesting reflection on stories that can be difficult for both teller and audience.

Opie, Iona and Peter. *The Lore and Language of Schoolchildren.* London, 1959.

Paley, Vivian Gussin. *The Boy Who Would Be a Helicopter.* Cambridge, 1990.

Pellowski, Anne. *The World of Storytelling: A Practical Guide to the Origins, Development, and Applications of Storytelling.* New York, 1977. A fine source of information about storytelling as a traditional and contemporary art.

Phelps, Ethel. *The Maid of the North: Feminist Folk Tales from around the World.* New York, 1981.

Plato. *Phaedrus.* In *Collected Dialogues.* Translated by R. Hackforth. Edited by Edith Hamilton and Huntington Cairns. Princeton, 1961.

Rehnman, Mats, and Jenny Hostetter. *The Voice of the Story.* Stockholm, 2002.

Rilke, Rainer Maria. *The Selected Poetry of Rainer Maria Rilke.* Translated by Stephen Mitchell. New York, 1989.

Robinson, Harry. *Write It on Your Heart: The Epic World of an Okanagan Storyteller.* Compiled and edited by Wendy Wickwire. Vancouver, 1989.

Rosen, Betty. *And None of It Was Nonsense: The Power of Storytelling in School.* New York, 1988.

Rosenbluth, Vera. *Keeping Family Stories Alive: A Creative Guide to Taping Your Family Life & Lore.* Vancouver, 1990.

Salinger, J. D. *Nine Stories.* Boston, 1948.

Sawyer, Ruth. *The Way of the Storyteller.* New York, 1942. A classic account of the life and art of one of the pioneers of the storytelling renaissance.

Schami, Rafik. *Damascus Nights.* Translated by Philip Boehm. New York, 1993.

Schram, Penninah. *Jewish Stories One Generation Tells Another.* New York, 1987. A wonderful collection of Jewish tales.

Schwartz, Howard. *Elijah's Violin and Other Jewish Fairy Tales.* New York, 1985. My story "The Silent Prince" was inspired by a story titled "The Mute Princess" from Schwartz's collection. My story shares with his the motif of a silent character who is told riddles and thus drawn into speech. "The Silent Prince" includes three dilemma tales. The first one is adapted from "Who Cured the Princess?," a story recorded by Moshe Kaplan as heard from a Polish rabbi (Israel Folktale Archives 464); collected in *Folktales of Israel,* edited by Dov Noy (Chicago, 1963). The second story was sent to me by children's librarian Carol McDougal, who heard it from a Portuguese girl recently arrived in Toronto from her village in the Azores. The third dilemma story uses the well-known motif of the seal-wife, and mixes it with stories I have heard from Cree and Iroquois friends about the beings they call Thunderbirds. In the western wonder tale tradition, it seems to me these thunder-beings are close cousins to the Firebird.

Simpson, Jacqueline. *Icelandic Folktales and Legends*. London, 1972. My story "The Dreamer and the Butterfly" is based on a story traditional in many northern countries. Versions can be found in Scandinavian, Icelandic and English collections. I particularly enjoy Simpson's story, "The Dreamer and the Treasure."

Stone, Elizabeth, et al., eds. *Black Sheep and Kissing Cousins: How Our Family Stories Shape Us*. 1989.

Stone, Kay. *Burning Brightly: New Light on Old Stories Told Today*. Peterborough, 1998. A very interesting study of how six contemporary storytellers worked with traditional stories.

Stone, Ted. *The One That Got Away*. Saskatoon, 1990. A wonderful teller of tall tales (also see his *Hailstorms and Hoopsnakes*).

Tocher, Michelle. *How to Ride a Dragon: Women with Breast Cancer Tell Their Stories*. Toronto, 2001. An important book for those who practise storytelling as a healing art.

Tolkien, J. R. R. *The Lord of the Rings*. London, 1954.

Weaver, Mary, ed. *Tales As Tools: The Power of Story in the Classroom*. Jonesborough, 1994.

Widdowson, John. *Little Jack and Other Newfoundland Folktales.* St. John's, 2003. A collection of stories from one of the strongest oral traditional cultures in Canada.

Williamson, Duncan. *The Broonie, Silkies and Fairies.* New York, 1985.
———. *A Thorn in the King's Foot: Stories of the Scottish Travelling People.* With Linda Williamson. Middlesex, 1987.

Wolfe, Alexander. *Earth Elder Stories.* Saskatoon, 1988.

Wolkstein, Diane. *The Magic Orange Tree and Other Haitian Folktales.* New York, 1980. A landmark collection containing not only wonderful stories but also fine portraits of the tellers and their environments.

Yashinsky, Dan. *Tales for an Unknown City.* Montreal, 1990. An anthology of stories collected from 1,001 Friday Nights of Storytelling.

Yolen, Jane. *Tales of Wonder.* New York, 1983.

Young, Ella. *The Wondersmith and His Son: A Tale from the Golden Childhood of the World.* London, 1927. Along with Young's *Celtic Wonder-Tales* (reissued in 1996), these were two of Alice Kane's favorite collections. She based several concerts on stories from these books.

Zeitlin, Steve. *Because God Loves Stories: An Anthology of Jewish Storytelling.* New York, 1997. A fine collection of stories, essays and anecdotes from tellers' lives.

≪ PERMISSIONS ≫

Grateful acknowledgment is made to the following sources for permission to reprint from previously published material. Every effort has been made to contact the copyright holders; in the event of an inadvertent omission or error, please notify the publisher.

Quotes from Chinua Achebe, *Anthills of the Savannah* (Doubleday), copyright 1987 by Chinua Achebe, by permission of Random House, Inc.

Adaptation of "Tortoises, Men, and Stones" from Ulli Beier, *The Origin of Life and Death*, by permission of Heinemann Publishers (Oxford) Ltd.

Translation of "L'Oiseau couleur du temps", by Jocelyn Bérubé, on his record album *Nil en ville* (Montreal, 1976) by permission of Jocelyn Bérubé. Published here as "The Bird Colour-of-Time."

Quotes from Martin Buber, *The Legend of the Baal-Shem* (Princeton University Press), copyright Princeton University Press, by permission of Princeton University Press.

Quotes from Martin Buber, *Tales of the Hasidim: Later Masters* (Schocken Books), by permission of Random House, Inc.

Quotes from Paul Celan, *Poems of Paul Celan*, translated by Michael Hamburger, by permission of Persea Books.

Adaptation of "The Feast" from Harold Courlander, *The King's Drum and Other African Stories*, copyright 1962, 1990, by Harold Courlander, used by permission of The Emma Courlander Trust.

Quotes from Julie Cruikshank, *Life Lived Like a Story: Life Stories of Three Yukon Native Elders* (University of Nebraska), by permission of University of Nebraska.

Translation of "Le maitre de thé et le ronin" from Pascal Fauliot, *Les contes des arts martiaux*, (Paris: 1981), by permission of Pascal Fauliot. Published here as "The Master of the Tea Ceremony."

Quotes from Alice Kane, *The Dreamer Awakes* (Broadview), ed. Sean Kane, introduction by Robert Bringhurst, by permission of Broadview Press.

Adaptation of "The Creation of the World" from Charlotte and Wolf Leslau, eds., *African Myths and Folktales*, by permission of Peter Pauper Press. Published here as "How Heart Came into the World."

Quotes from Joe Neil MacNeil, *Tales Until Dawn*, ed. John Shaw (McGill-Queen's University Press), by permission of McGill-Queen's University Press.

Quotes from Alexander Wolfe, *Earth Elder Stories* (Fifth House), by permission of Fitzhenry and Whiteside.

DAN YASHINSKY was born in Detroit and came to Canada after attending university in California. He is the editor of four collections of tales, including *Tales for an Unknown City*, which won the Toronto Book Award. Dan has been a working storyteller for almost thirty years. He founded the Toronto Festival of Storytelling in 1979, which continues to grow and delight audiences of all ages. He was also one of the founders of the Storytellers School of Toronto and began the 1,001 Friday Nights of Storytelling in 1978, a weekly institution in Toronto that continues to this day, in spite of having passed the 1,001st night long ago. He has listened to and told stories across Canada and around the world. In 1999, he hosted *The Talking Stick*, a national radio show on CBC. He was the recipient of the 1999 Jane Jacobs Prize for his work with storytelling and community.